The Fannie Farmer Large Print Cookbook

Edited by Marion Cunningham
and Jeri Laber

Large Print Edition edited by
Amy and Peter Pastan

G.K.HALL &CO.
Boston, Massachusetts
1985

Published by G.K. Hall & Co.
A publishing subsidiary of ITT

Published in Large Print by arrangement with Alfred A. Knopf, Inc.

G.K. Hall Large Print Book Series.

Set in 16 pt Times Roman.

Library of Congress Cataloging in Publication Data

Farmer, Fannie Merritt, 1857–1915.
  The Fannie Farmer large print cookbook.

  (G.K. Hall large print book series)
  A selection of 520 recipes from the Fannie Farmer cookbook, 12th ed.
  Includes index.
  1. Cookery. 2. Large type books. I. Cunningham, Marion. II. Laber, Jeri. III. Pastan, Amy. IV. Pastan, Peter. V. Title.
  [TX715.F23425 1985]   641.5   84-27909
  ISBN 0-8161-3726-9
  ISBN 0-8161-3817-6 (pbk)

Contents

Contents

Preface to the Large Print Edition

Since 1896, the *Fannie Farmer Cookbook* has been an indispensable source of proven recipes and timely ideas in the art and craft of cooking. This edition makes available to the Large Print reader a broad range of recipes from the twelfth edition of Mrs. Farmer's classic volume, edited by Marion Cunningham and Jeri Laber.

In compiling the *Fannie Farmer Large Print Cookbook,* we selected the five hundred twenty recipes that we felt both preserved the tone of the original and presented a wide variety of ideas for menus. Old favorites, such as Boston Brown Bread and Apple Pandowdy, are included, as well as dishes that represent current trends in food preparation. We would like to thank Virginia Reiser for her invaluable help with this task.

It is our hope that this Large Print edition will inspire the accomplished cook and encourage the novice. Whether you enjoy these dishes by your-self or with family and friends, we're sure that these recipes will entice you back to the kitchen again and again.

Amy and Peter Pastan
Washington, D.C., 1985

NOTE: Metric equivalents for many of the ingredient amounts in this cookbook are given in parentheses following the English-system figures.

Appetizers & Hors D'Oeuvre

Guacamole (2 cups)

Don't purée the avocados; an authentic guacamole contains small chunks of avocado. Serve with tortilla chips.

2 large ripe avocados
5 tablespoons minced onion
4 canned, peeled green chili peppers, chopped fine
1 clove garlic, minced
3 tablespoons lemon juice or vinegar
¼ teaspoon freshly ground pepper
Salt to taste

Peel and seed the avocados. Mash one avocado in a bowl, and finely chop the other. Mix the two with remaining ingredients. Cover and refrigerate for several hours before serving.

Eggplant Caviar   (2 cups)

Serve with crackers or corn crisps.

1 medium eggplant
2 scallions, minced
2 tablespoons minced parsley
½ teaspoon freshly ground pepper
3 tablespoons vinegar
4 tablespoons olive oil
Salt

Preheat the oven to 350°F (180°C). Bake the eggplant for 1 hour. When it is cool enough to handle, peel and chop coarsely. Blend the scallions, parsley, pepper, vinegar, and olive oil in the blender or food processor. Put the mixture in a bowl and add the coarsely chopped eggplant and salt to taste. Serve chilled or at room temperature.

Yogurt Dip   (2 cups)

2 cups (½ L) plain yogurt
1 clove garlic, minced
½ cucumber, seeded and chopped fine
½ teaspoon dried mint, crumbled, or 1 teaspoon
   fresh, chopped

Mix all the ingredients and chill thoroughly to let the flavors develop.

Green Dip (2½ cups)

1 cup (¼ L) parsley
5 scallions, chopped
1¼ cups (3 dL) mayonnaise
1 cup (¼ L) sour cream
1 tablespoon chopped fresh dill, or 1¼ teaspoons
    dried, crumbled
¼ teaspoon Tabasco
1 teaspoon curry powder
Salt

Liquefy the parsley, scallions, and ½ cup of the
mayonnaise in a blender or food processor. Add
the remaining ¾ cup mayonnaise, the sour cream,
dill, Tabasco, curry powder, and salt to taste, and
chill.

Sour-Cream Dip (2½ cups)

Garden-fresh with raw vegetables in summer.

2 cups (½ L) sour cream
¼ cup (½ dL) mayonnaise
2 tablespoons chopped fresh dill, or 1 tablespoon
    dried, crumbled
1 tablespoon grated onion
1 tablespoon chopped chives
1 tablespoon chopped parsley
Salt
Freshly ground pepper

Mix the sour cream, mayonnaise, dill, onion, chives, and parsley. Season to taste with salt and pepper, and chill.

Clam Dip   (2½ cups)

8 ounces (225 g) cream cheese, softened
½ cup (1 dL) sour cream
6½-ounce (180-g) can minced clams
1 tablespoon Worcestershire sauce
1 teaspoon grated onion

Mix all the ingredients, and chill.

Ham Spread   (1 cup)

A good way to use up leftover bits from a baked ham.

1 cup (¼ L) chopped cooked ham
1 tablespoon grated onion
2 teaspoons prepared mustard
1 tablespoon chutney
2 tablespoons mayonnaise

Cut the ham into small pieces and purée in a blender or food processor. Add the rest of the ingredients, put into a crock, and chill.

Corned Beef Spread. Substitute *1 cup chopped cooked corned beef* for the ham.

4

Salmon Spread   (2 cups)

7¾-ounce (225-g) can salmon
¾ cup (1¾ dL) sweet butter
1 tablespoon anchovy paste
2 teaspoons lemon juice
1 teaspoon Worcestershire sauce

Mix all ingredients, put into a crock, and chill.

Cucumber Sandwiches
(8 small sandwiches)

These used to be called tea sandwiches, but there's no reason why they shouldn't appear with cocktails as well.

4 thin slices fresh white bread
4 tablespoons butter, softened
1 large cucumber
Salt
2 tablespoons mayonnaise
¼ teaspoon dried tarragon, crumbled
Freshly ground pepper

Cut the crusts from the bread and spread slices with butter. Peel and seed the cucumber, chop coarsely, and sprinkle with salt. Let stand in a colander for 10 minutes. Pat dry, mix with the mayonnaise and tarragon, season to taste, and spread on the bread. Cover with the second slices, cut into quarters, and arrange on a plate.

Watercress Sandwiches. Substitute ⅓ *cup chopped*

watercress for the cucumber, and omit the salting and draining.

Aromatic Vegetables (about 4 cups)

Vegetables cut in bite sizes and cooked in a broth of olive oil and Middle Eastern seasonings are unusual and delightfully refreshing with drinks. The vegetables should be firm enough so they can be speared with toothpicks. Each must be cooked separately, but sometimes it is nice to serve several kinds arranged colorfully on a platter.

1 pound (450 g) mushrooms, small onions, or zucchini, in 1-inch pieces, or cauliflower in small flowerets, or 1 package frozen artichoke hearts
⅓ cup (¾ dL) olive oil
2 tablespoons lemon juice
¼ teaspoon coriander seed
¼ teaspoon fennel seed
Pinch of celery seed
2–6 scallions, in ½-inch pieces, using some green, or 5–6 shallots, peeled and sliced
Salt
8–10 peppercorns, lightly crushed
2 tablespoons chopped parsley

Place the mushrooms (quartered if large; halved if medium; left whole if small), or onions, or zucchini, or cauliflower flowerets, or artichoke hearts (thawed), in a heavy saucepan and cover with the remaining ingredients, except the parsley. Add in-

6

dicated amount of water, salt liberally, and boil for the number of minutes recommended:

Mushrooms: ¼ cup water. Boil 5 minutes, uncovered, over medium-high heat, shaking pan frequently.

Onions: ¾ cup water and 2 tablespoons red wine vinegar (instead of lemon juice). Cook, covered, over medium-high heat 10 minutes, then remove cover and cook down 2 minutes, letting onions darken slightly.

Zucchini: ⅓ cup water. Cook, covered, 4 minutes, shaking the pan once or twice.

Cauliflower: ½ cup water. Cook, covered, 5 minutes, shaking pan once or twice.

Artichoke Hearts: ½ cup water. Boil rapidly, covered, 6 minutes, shaking once or twice.

Toss each vegetable with parsley, taste and correct seasoning. Chill several hours in its sauce. Bring to room temperature before serving so the oil is not congealed.

Cheese Ball (2 cups)

8 ounces (225 g) cream cheese, softened
1 ounce (30 g) blue cheese, softened
¼ pound (125 g) sharp Cheddar cheese, grated
1 clove garlic, minced
Dash of Tabasco
¼ cup (½ dL) finely chopped almonds, toasted
¼ cup (½ dL) finely chopped parsley

Combine the cream cheese, blue cheese, and Cheddar cheese in a bowl. Add the garlic and Tabasco and blend until well mixed. Chill 2–3 hours. Form into a ball. Roll the ball in the almonds and then in the parsley, patting the coating in firmly. Chill; remove from the refrigerator 30 minutes before serving.

Chicken and Pork Pâté
(one 2-quart casserole)

A pâté is not unlike a meat loaf—and really not that much more difficult to prepare. But because pâtés are served cold as a tasty appetizer (and one slice goes a long way), they must be full of flavor, rich, and moist. Almost one-third of the mixture should consist of good pork fat because it is the fat that keeps the meat moist during the cooking. After the pâté has been baked, it should be weighted so that some of the fat runs out and the loaf is compressed, thus giving you dense slices that hold together when cut. This particular pâté uses a ground meat base of chicken, pork, and pork fat interlarded with strips of marinated chicken breast, which gives the finished slice a lovely marbled look. The most economical approach would be to buy a whole chicken, 3½–4 pounds, and bone it yourself using the dark meat in the ground mixture known as the forcemeat (and reserving all the meaty bones and carcass for a soup); but for those who don't have the time, buy instead the easily available chicken parts as recommended below. Pâtés are good served with thinly sliced sour pickles, mustard, and French or dark rye bread.

1 whole chicken breast, skinned and boned
¼ cup (½ dL) brandy
1¾–2 pounds (800–900 g) chicken thighs
1¾ pounds (800 g) pork, with some fat on
1 pound (450 g) solid pork fat
3 eggs
½ cup (1 dL) Madeira
2 teaspoons salt
½ cup (1 dL) minced shallots
½ teaspoon ground allspice
¼ teaspoon ground cloves
Freshly ground pepper
¼ teaspoon ground thyme
¾ pound (340 g) bacon

Cut the chicken breast ·lengthwise into ½-inch strips. Toss them with the brandy and let marinate while preparing the other ingredients. Remove the skin and cut away the meat from the chicken thighs (if using a whole chicken, use all the meat you can cut off the bones, after you have put the breast meat to marinate); you should have about 1 pound dark chicken. Grind this along with the pork and the pork fat either by running through the food processor or putting through a meat grinder twice. Add the eggs, Madeira, salt, shallots, allspice, cloves, a generous amount of pepper, and thyme. Beat the mixture until smooth and well blended. If you want to taste to check the seasonings, fry a small amount of this forcemeat and taste when cooked through; it should be highly seasoned, so adjust seasonings if necessary, remembering that flavors are dulled when chilled. Preheat the oven to 325°F (165°C). Bring a large pot of water to a boil and drop the strips of bacon in; let them cook 2–3 minutes, just enough to reduce their saltiness, then drain, rinse, and pat dry. Line a 2-quart casserole with the bacon, as illustrated, leaving overhanging

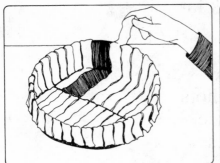
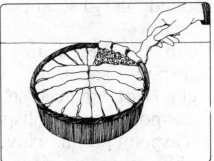

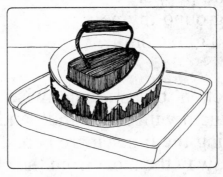

pieces to cover the top. Pat in a layer of the force-meat, then lay strips of chicken breast over in a neat line, about ½ inch apart. Add another layer of forcemeat, then chicken strips, ending with a final layer of forcemeat. Pull the bacon strips over to cover the top of the meat, trimming off excess to avoid a double layer anywhere. Cover with foil and with a snug-fitting lid. Place the casserole in a pan of hot water that comes halfway up the sides. Bake for 1–1¼ hours, or until the fat runs clear. Remove from the oven, uncover, and weight down with a plate that just fits inside the casserole, on which you place heavy cans, or any solid object like an old iron. Let cool completely. Refrigerate, prefer-ably 24 hours, then serve cool, but not ice cold.

Chicken Liver Pâté (3 cups)

¼ pound (125 g) butter
1 onion, minced
1 pound (450 g) chicken livers
4 tablespoons brandy
1 teaspoon dry mustard
¼ teaspoon mace
¼ teaspoon powdered cloves
½ teaspoon freshly ground pepper
Pinch of cayenne pepper
Salt to taste

Melt the butter in a skillet. Add the onions and sauté until soft. Stir in the livers and cook 2–3 minutes over medium-high heat, stirring, until they are just cooked but still rosy inside. Purée the onions and livers in a food processor or blender, or put through a food mill. Over medium heat, pour the brandy into the skillet and scrape up the bits from the bottom of the pan. Add to the liver mixture along with remaining ingredients, and blend until smooth. Pack into a mold and refrigerate until chilled and set. Serve unmolded with thin toast or crackers.

Country Terrine (about 10 cups)

A terrine is the dish in which a meat loaf or pâté is baked. One usually serves the pâté in its terrine so it should be attractive enough to come to the table.

11

1½ pounds (675 g) ground pork, approximately ⅓
   fat
1 pound (450 g) ground veal
1 pound (450 g) fresh spinach, blanched, drained,
   and chopped
1 large onion, chopped fine
2 cloves garlic, minced
2 eggs, beaten
1 teaspoon thyme, crumbled
1 teaspoon dried basil, crumbled
¼ teaspoon nutmeg
¼ teaspoon mace
¼ teaspoon allspice
1½ teaspoons salt
1 teaspoon freshly ground pepper
10 slices bacon

Preheat the oven to 325°F (165°C). Put a shallow
baking dish in the oven with 1 inch of hot water.
Grease a 2½-quart terrine. Combine all ingredients
except bacon. Use your hands to mix and blend
well. Fry a spoonful of the mixture until no longer
pink; taste and correct the seasoning. Lay 6 or 7
bacon strips crosswise over the bottom and sides
of the terrine. Pack the meat mixture into the lined
dish; fold the loose ends of bacon over the top and
cover any blank spaces with the extra bacon strips.
Cover the dish with foil, place in the pan of water,
and bake 1 hour. The meat is done when the juices
are clear. Remove from the oven, cover with a
plate, and weight down with a heavy can to remove
the fat and press out air pockets. Cool, drain off
the fat, and refrigerate.

Meatballs Rémoulade   (50 meatballs)

These are meatballs that can be made ahead and don't have to be reheated; they are served at room temperature.

1 pound (450 g) ground beef
Salt
½ teaspoon freshly ground pepper
4 tablespoons minced onion
3 tablespoons shortening
4 tablespoons prepared horseradish
½ cup (1 dL) tarragon vinegar
2 tablespoons catsup
¼ teaspoon cayenne pepper
1 cup (¼ L) vegetable oil
½ cup (1 dL) finely chopped scallions
½ cup (1 dL) minced celery
2 tablespoons minced parsley

Using your hands, mix the beef, about ½ teaspoon salt, pepper, and onion. Shape into 50 small meatballs about the size of marbles. Melt the shortening in a large skillet and fry the meatballs over medium heat, browning them on all sides. Put them in a shallow dish. Whisk together the horseradish, vinegar, catsup, cayenne, oil, scallions, celery, and parsley until well blended. Add salt to taste. Pour the sauce over the meatballs and let stand at room temperature for at least 1 hour before serving.

Skewered Chicken Livers, Bacon, and Water Chestnuts   (30 skewers)

Before you begin, soak thirty small wooden skewers in water. This will prevent their catching fire later.

1 pound (450 g) chicken livers
1 can water chestnuts, drained
10–15 slices bacon

Preheat the broiler. Cut each liver in three or four pieces. Drain the water chestnuts and cut in half. Cut each bacon slice in four pieces, and wrap a piece around each water chestnut half. On each skewer, thread a piece of liver and a piece of bacon-wrapped water chestnut. Repeat so that each skewer has at least two pieces of liver. Place the threaded skewers on a broiler rack 4 inches below the broiler element and cook 3 minutes each side or until the bacon is lightly browned.

Crab Puffs   (48 puffs)

Miniature crab soufflés: luscious, hot, and puffy.

¾ cup (1¾ dL) mayonnaise
1 cup (¼ L) flaked cooked crabmeat
1 tablespoon finely chopped scallions
⅛ teaspoon cayenne pepper
2½ tablespoons lemon juice
Salt
2 egg whites
48 1½-inch (4-cm) rounds of bread

14

Preheat the broiler. Combine the mayonnaise, crabmeat, scallions, cayenne, lemon juice, and salt to taste. Beat the egg whites until stiff and gently fold in the crab mixture. Spoon a mound of mixture on each of the bread rounds. Place on cookie sheets and put under the broiler until lightly browned. Serve immediately.

Shrimp Puffs. Substitute *1 cup finely chopped cooked shrimp* for the crabmeat.

Cheese Straws   (36 straws)

¼ pound (115 g) butter
2 cups (285 g) flour
¼ teaspoon cayenne pepper
1 pound (450 g) sharp Cheddar cheese, grated
Salt to taste

Preheat the oven to 400°F (205°C). Cream the butter until light; add the flour, cayenne, cheese, and salt. Knead until dough forms a ball, then roll out on a floured board or pastry cloth. Cut into strips 5 inches long and ⅜ inch wide. Place on a greased cookie sheet and bake 6 minutes, until golden.

Cheese Puffs   (48 puffs)

To freeze these unbaked, allow an extra 3–5 minutes of baking time.

2 cups (½ L) grated sharp cheese
¼ pound (115 g) butter
1 cup (140 g) flour
Salt to taste
48 pimiento-stuffed green olives

Preheat oven to 400°F (205°C). Put the cheese and butter in a mixing bowl or food processor, and blend until smooth. Add the flour and salt and mix well. Roll out to ¼-inch thickness. Cut the dough into 2-inch squares and wrap a square around each olive, sealing the seams. Place on a cookie sheet and bake 15 minutes. Check after the first 10 minutes to see puffs don't burn.

Nachos

5-ounce (140-g) bag tortilla chips
1 pound (450 g) Monterey Jack or Cheddar
   cheese, grated
⅓ cup (¾ dL) chopped canned peeled green
   chilies
½ cup (1 dL) chopped onion

Preheat the oven to 400°F (205°C). Lay the tortilla chips on a cookie sheet. Toss together the cheese, chilies, and onion, and sprinkle over the tortilla chips. Bake for about 5 minutes, until the cheese has melted. Serve hot.

Barbecued Chicken Wings   (24 pieces)

12 chicken wings
½ cup (1 dL) honey
2 tablespoons Worcestershire sauce
⅓ cup (¾ dL) soy sauce
Juice of 2 lemons
1 clove garlic, minced

Preheat the oven to 325°F (165°C). Remove the wing tips and break each wing into two pieces. Place in a shallow baking dish. Mix the remaining ingredients and pour over the wings. Bake for 1 hour and serve in the baking dish.

Oysters in Bacon   (24 pieces)

Oysters and bacon are a traditional pair.

24 oysters, shucked and patted dry
12 strips of bacon, cut in half

Preheat the oven to 425°F (220°C). Wrap each oyster in a piece of bacon. Arrange the wrapped oysters, with bacon ends down, on a rack in a shallow pan. Bake only until the bacon is slightly browned. Drain on paper towels.

Soups

Beef Stock (about 12 cups)

Beef stock made from bones alone will be rich in gelatin but will lack flavor unless some lean meat is included. One of the best cuts to use for stock is beef shank because it provides the shin bone with its marrow plus a solid piece of shank meat surrounding it. Have the shank cut up into 2-inch pieces. If you can't get that cut, use whatever bones are available (have them cracked if they are solid pieces like knuckle) and add an equal amount of lean stewing beef. Browning the meat, bones, and vegetables at the beginning will add color and flavor to the finished stock. If you want to be more provident and use the meat for a meal of sliced boiled beef, or in hash or a filling, remove it from the stockpot after 2½ hours, returning the bones to finish cooking.

2 tablespoons shortening, cooking oil, or marrow
4–5 pounds (1¾–2¼ kg) beef shank or 2½ lbs (1¼ kg) beef bones and 2½ lbs (1¼ kg) stew meat
3 carrots, sliced
3 onions, sliced
3 stalks celery, sliced
1 teaspoon dried thyme
1 bay leaf

18

2 sprigs parsley
6 crushed peppercorns
Salt

Preheat oven to 450°F (230°C). Heat the shortening, oil, or marrow in a large roasting pan, add the pieces of shank (or the bones and stewing beef, cut into chunks) and brown them in the oven, stirring, turning, moving them about frequently. After about 10 minutes, add the carrots, onions, and celery to the roasting pan and let them brown, taking care that they do not scorch. When everything has browned, transfer it all to a stockpot or large cooking pot. Pour off the fat in the roasting pan, add a cup or so of boiling water, and scrape up all the browned bits in the pan, then pour into the stockpot. Add the thyme, bay leaf, parsley, and peppercorns, and cover with 4 quarts cold water. Bring the water slowly to a boil, then reduce the heat and simmer very gently, partially covered, for at least 4 or 5 hours, skimming off any scum that rises to the surface during the first 30 minutes or so. Strain and cool, uncovered.

Beef Bouillon. Beef bouillon is a strong Beef Stock, reduced slightly if necessary to intensify the flavor, and seasoned to taste with *salt* and *freshly ground pepper*. It may be clarified and served as a consommé. Sprinkle each serving of bouillon with *finely chopped parsley, chives, or celery.*

Beef Bouillon with Noodles. Add *¼–½ cup cooked egg noodles* or *broken-up vermicelli* for each 2 cups Beef Bouillon.

Beef Bouillon with Marrow Balls (16 marrow balls). Using a wooden spoon, a blender, or a food processor, blend to a smooth paste *2 tablespoons marrow* (from marrow bones), *4 tablespoons fine cracker crumbs, 1 egg, 1 teaspoon finely chopped parsley, ¼ teaspoon salt, ⅛ teaspoon nutmeg.* Shape into ½-inch balls and chill in the refrigerator until ready to use. Drop into simmering 1 quart Beef Bouillon and cook for 5 minutes, then turn each ball with a spoon and cook for another 5 minutes. Taste one to see if it is cooked through.

Chicken Stock   (about 7 cups, 1¾ L)

Simmering 4 to 5 hours enriches a stock, but longer than that isn't necessary. A very rich stock is good as a broth or in sauces, less necessary when used as the base for vegetable soups with many ingredients or for light soups with delicately flavored ingredients that should not be overwhelmed by the taste of the stock.

2 pounds (900 g) chicken backs, wings, necks, bones
1 onion, cut in half
2 carrots, cut in thirds
3 stalks celery with leaves, cut in half
1 bay leaf
6 crushed peppercorns
1 teaspoon dried thyme
Salt

Wash the chicken parts and put them in a large soup pot. Add 8 cups cold water and remaining ingredients, except salt. Bring to a boil, reduce heat, and simmer, skimming off the scum during the first 30 minutes. Simmer, partially covered, for 4 or 5 hours, longer if possible. Salt carefully to taste. Strain and cool quickly, uncovered.

Chicken Stock Made by Cooking a Chicken (7–8 cups). Chicken stock can be made from the water in which a chicken is cooked, and you will have both stock and cooked chicken as the end result. To keep the chicken from being tough, stop cooking it when it is tender and use just the bones and skin to complete the stock.

Instead of the backs, wings, and necks used for regular Chicken Stock, substitute a *4-pound fowl or 4 pounds chicken parts*. Use the same amount of water, vegetables, and seasonings as in Chicken Stock, but set aside any white meat (if you are using chicken parts), adding it after everything else has simmered for about 20 minutes. Cook, covered, until the white meat is tender. Turn off the heat and remove all the chicken from the pot. When the chicken is cool enough to handle, separate the meat from the skin and bones and return the skin and bones to the pot. Continue to simmer, 4 or 5 hours in all. Strain and cool the stock, uncovered. Use the cooked chicken in soups, salads, sandwiches, crêpe fillings, or other dishes calling for cooked chicken.

Chicken Soup. Chicken soup is homemade Chicken Stock (above), seasoned to taste with *salt, pepper,* and a sprig or two of fresh *parsley* or *dill.*

Chicken Rice Soup. Add ¼ cup *cooked rice* for each 2 cups of well-seasoned Chicken Soup. Or add 1½ tablespoons *uncooked rice* for each 2 cups and cook in the soup until done.

Chicken Noodle Soup. Add ¼–½ cup *cooked egg noodles* or *broken-up vermicelli* for each 2 cups of Chicken Soup.

Cream of Chicken Soup. Slowly add ½ *cup warmed cream* for each 2 cups of Chicken Soup. Sprinkle with some *chopped parsley* and some *diced, cooked chicken.*

Turkey Soup (7–8 cups)

Serve turkey soup as a clear broth, or add some cooked noodles, rice, or barley. It can also be used as a base in many vegetable soups.

1 turkey carcass
1 onion, sliced
1 carrot, sliced
2 stalks celery, cut up
6 crushed peppercorns
Salt

Break the turkey carcass into pieces and put them in a soup pot with any small pieces of turkey meat that you can spare. Add 8 cups water, onion, carrot, celery, and peppercorns. Bring to a boil, lower the heat, cover partially, and simmer for 3 or 4 hours. Strain the broth and cool it quickly, uncovered. Chill it and remove the fat when it solidifies, or scoop any fat off the surface with a spoon. Add salt to taste before serving.

Fish Stock or Court Bouillon
(about 7 cups)

Use only white fish to make fish stock. If you use dark, oily fish like mackerel or if you cook a fish stock more than about 30 minutes, the stock will be too strong. Always save liquid in which fish has been cooked (it may be frozen) and add it to the fish stock. Clam Broth diluted half in half with water may be used instead of fish stock in many recipes.

1½–2 pounds (675–900 g) fish skeleton, with heads if available
1 carrot, sliced
1 onion, sliced
2 stalks celery, sliced
2 cloves
½ bay leaf
6 crushed peppercorns
2 cups (½ L) dry white wine (optional)
Salt

Wash the fish trimmings. Combine them with the other ingredients except salt and 8 cups cold water (or 6 cups water and the wine) in a soup pot and simmer, uncovered, for about 30 minutes, skimming any scum from the surface. Season carefully to taste with salt. Strain and cool, uncovered.

Cream of Asparagus Soup   (4 cups)

An appealing-looking soup with a pleasing asparagus taste.

23

1 pound (450 g) fresh asparagus, or 1 package
  frozen
1½ cups (3½ dL) Chicken Stock (p. 00) or canned
  broth
2 tablespoons chopped onion
1 cup (¼ L) milk or cream
Salt
Freshly ground pepper

If using fresh asparagus, wash stalks and cut off the
coarse ends. Cook the asparagus in 2 cups boiling
water until tender. Drain, reserving 1 cup of the
water. Cut off the asparagus tips, chop them, and
reserve. Put the chicken stock, onion, and reserved
water in a pan and bring to a boil. Add the asparagus and simmer for 5 minutes. Put through a
strainer or vegetable mill or purée in a food processor or an electric blender. Return to the pot and
add the milk or cream and salt and pepper to taste.
Reheat and adjust the seasonings. Before serving,
sprinkle with chopped asparagus tips.

Thick Cream of Asparagus Soup. Before adding the
milk, melt *2 tablespoons butter* in a large pot, stir
in *2 tablespoons flour,* and cook for a few minutes
until smooth. Slowly add the milk or cream and salt
and pepper. Then add the asparagus purée and reheat until thickened.

Cheese Soup (4 cups)

This is a very nice change from meat and vegetable soups. The paprika adds good color.

24

1 tablespoon butter
1 tablespoon finely chopped onion
1 tablespoon flour
1 cup (¼ L) well-seasoned Beef Stock (p. 18) or bouillon
2 cups (½ L) milk
¾ cup (1¾ dL) grated Cheddar cheese
2 teaspoons paprika

Melt the butter in a pot, add the onion, and cook slowly until limp. Stir in the flour and continue to cook for 3 minutes, stirring. Slowly add the seasoned stock and milk, and heat to the boiling point, stirring frequently. Stir in the cheese and paprika and whisk until the cheese has melted and the soup is very hot.

Pumpkin Soup (7 cups)

2 medium onions, chopped
2 tablespoons butter
1 tablespoon flour
3 cups (¾ L) chicken broth
3 cups (¾ L) pumpkin purée
Salt to taste
Freshly ground pepper
½ cup (1 dL) cream, whipped
Dusting nutmeg
3 tablespoons toasted pumpkin seed (optional)

Sauté the onions with the butter in the bottom of a heavy, large saucepan over low heat until soft. Sprinkle in the flour; stir and cook 2 or 3 minutes. Gradually add the chicken broth, whisking thoroughly, then the pumpkin purée, and cook gently about 15 minutes. Salt and pepper to taste. Pour into warm bowls and top with a dollop of whipped cream, a dusting of nutmeg, and, if you like, a scattering of toasted pumpkin seeds.

Puréed Pumpkin

Cut the pumpkin into large chunks and arrange on a steamer tray. Check after 30 minutes of vigorous steaming—it will take anywhere from 30 to 45 minutes. Remove when the interior is soft and scrape the pulp away from the skin. Either whip with a hand or electric beater or purée in a food processor.

Creole Soup (4 cups)

A sharp and lively soup.

2 tablespoons bacon fat
2 tablespoons finely chopped green pepper
2 tablespoons finely chopped onion
2 tablespoons flour
1 cup (¼ L) chopped tomatoes
3 cups (¾ L) Beef Stock (p. 18) or bouillon
⅛ teaspoon freshly ground pepper
1 tablespoon prepared horseradish
½ teaspoon vinegar
Salt to taste

Heat the bacon fat in a pot, add the green pepper and onion, and cook slowly for 5 minutes. Stir in the flour and cook for 2 or 3 minutes, then stir in the tomatoes and stock or bouillon. Simmer for 15 minutes. Strain and add remaining ingredients. Serve hot.

Cream of Carrot Soup (7 cups)

4 tablespoons butter
1 onion, chopped
4 carrots, sliced
1 stalk celery with leaves, chopped
2 medium potatoes, peeled and diced
2 sprigs parsley
5 cups (1¼ L) Chicken Stock (p. 20) or canned broth
1 cup (¼ L) heavy cream
Salt
Freshly ground pepper

Melt the butter in a large pot, add the onion, carrots, and celery, and cook for 10–15 minutes, stirring from time to time. Add the potatoes and parsley and stir until coated. Stir in the stock and cook, partially covered, until the potatoes are tender, about 20 minutes. Put through a strainer or vegetable mill or purée in a blender or food processor. Return to the pot, stir in the cream, add salt and pepper to taste, and reheat without boiling. Serve hot or cold.

Cream of Watercress Soup (6 cups)

Cream of Watercress soup is also good cold, as are the Spinach and Sorrel variations. Simply chill thoroughly, add ½ cup more cream, and adjust the salt. Wash the watercress, if necessary (you can always tell if it is gritty by tasting it), by submerging it in several changes of cold water. Pat it barely dry, wrap it in dampened paper towels, and keep in the refrigerator crisper until ready to use.

2 bunches watercress, coarsely chopped
4 cups (1 L) Chicken Stock (p. 20) or canned broth
4 tablespoons butter
2 tablespoons flour
1 tablespoon lemon juice
1 cup (¼ L) cream
Salt
Freshly ground pepper

Put the watercress and the chicken stock in a pot and simmer for 10 minutes. Purée in a blender or food processor. Melt the butter in a large pot, stir in the flour, and cook slowly, stirring, for several minutes. Stir in a little of the purée and then add the rest. Bring the soup to the boiling point, stirring constantly. Stir in the lemon juice, cream, and salt and pepper to taste.

Cream of Spinach Soup (6 cups, 1½ L). Substitute ¾ *pound spinach* for the watercress.

Cream of Sorrel Soup (6 cups). Substitute ¾ *pound sorrel* for the watercress and omit the lemon juice.

28

Cream of Mushroom Soup (3 cups)

4 tablespoons butter
¼ cup (½ dL) finely chopped onion
½ pound (225 g) mushrooms, finely chopped
1 tablespoon flour
2 cups (½ L) Chicken Stock (p. 20) or canned
 broth
½ cup (1 dL) cream
Salt
Freshly ground pepper

Melt the butter in a pot and add the onion and mushrooms. Cook over low heat for 15 minutes, stirring occasionally. Sprinkle with the flour and cook for a few minutes more. Slowly add the stock, and heat, stirring, until it reaches the boiling point. Reduce heat and simmer for 20 minutes. Stir in the cream, add salt and pepper to taste, and reheat before serving.

Cold Mushroom Soup. Use an additional ¼ cup cream and chill. Adjust salt. Serve in cold soup-bowls with *chives* sprinkled on top.

Chicken Gumbo Soup (6 cups)

Diced cooked chicken, if you happen to have some, is a pleasant addition to this and other chicken-based soups.

2 tablespoons butter
1 onion, finely chopped

29

4 cups (1 L) Chicken Stock (p. 20) or canned
    broth
½ green pepper, chopped fine
1 cup (¼ L) sliced okra, fresh or frozen
1½ cups (3½ dL) canned tomatoes, undrained
¾ cup (1¾ dL) cooked rice
Salt
Freshly ground pepper

Melt the butter in a large pot, add the onion, and
cook, stirring, for about 5 minutes or until golden.
Stir in the stock, green pepper, okra, and tomatoes.
Bring to a boil, then simmer for about 30 minutes.
Add the rice, season with salt and pepper to taste,
and reheat before serving.

Vegetable Soup   (6 cups)

Other vegetables—tomatoes, shredded cabbage,
green beans, corn—may be added to this soup,
if you wish.

4 tablespoons butter
2 carrots, diced
2 stalks celery with leaves, diced
½ onion, chopped
1 small turnip, peeled and diced
1 medium potato, peeled and diced
2 cups (½ L) Beef Stock (p. 18) or bouillon
1 tablespoon butter
1 tablespoon finely chopped parsley
Salt
Freshly ground pepper

Melt the butter in a soup pot, then add the carrots, celery, onion, turnip, and potato. Cook over low heat, stirring, for about 10 minutes. Add the stock and 2 cups water, partially cover, and simmer for about 30 minutes or until the vegetables are tender. Before serving, add butter, parsley, and salt and pepper to taste.

Cold Cucumber or Avocado Soup (4 cups)

These soups are very refreshing on a summer evening. They'll have a more interesting texture if you don't overblend them, and hold back enough cucumber to add a slice or two to each soup bowl or enough avocado to dice so you can add about two tablespoonsful to each serving.

2 peeled and seeded cucumbers or avocados
2 tablespoons lemon juice
1 cup (¼ L) chicken broth
1 cup (¼ L) heavy cream
Salt to taste
4 tablespoons minced chives or scallion greens

If you have a blender or food processor, simply chop the cucumbers or avocados in rough pieces, leaving out enough for the garnish, and whirl with all the other ingredients in the machine until just blended. Otherwise, grate the cucumbers or avocados and blend with the other ingredients by hand. Add salt and chill. Serve in bowls with their garnish, and chives and/or herbs scattered on top.

Vichyssoise   (6 cups)

This splendid chilled soup was devised on American soil by a French chef, Louis Diat. It is also good served hot.

4 tablespoons butter
1 onion, chopped
4 leeks, white part only, finely sliced
2 stalks celery, chopped
2 medium potatoes, peeled and sliced
2 sprigs parsley
4 cups (1 L) Chicken Stock (p. 20) or canned broth
1 cup (¼ L) heavy cream
1 tablespoon finely chopped chives
Salt
Freshly ground pepper

Melt the butter in a large pot, add the onion, leeks, and celery, and cook over low heat, stirring often, for 10–15 minutes or until limp but not brown. Stir in the potatoes, parsley, and stock. Cook, partially covered, until the potatoes are tender, about 20 minutes. Put through a strainer or vegetable mill or purée in a blender or food processor. Pour into a bowl, stir in the cream and chives, and chill in the refrigerator. Add more salt and pepper to taste before serving.

Mulligatawny Soup   (8 cups)

This soup from India found its way into American cookery long before the Civil War. A recipe for it appeared in the original *Fannie Farmer Cook Book* of 1896.

4 tablespoons butter
1 small onion, diced
1 carrot, diced
1 stalk celery with leaves, diced
1 green pepper, diced
1 apple, peeled and diced
1 cup (¼ L) diced raw chicken (about 1 pound)
⅓ cup (50 g) flour
1–2 teaspoons curry powder
¼ teaspoon nutmeg
5 cups (1¼ L) Chicken Stock (p. 20) or canned
   broth
2 cloves, crushed
2 sprigs parsley, chopped
1 cup (¼ L) canned or chopped tomatoes
2 cups (½ L) hot cooked rice
Salt
Freshly ground pepper

Melt the butter in a large soup pot. Add the onion, carrot, celery, green pepper, apple, and chicken, and cook slowly, stirring frequently, for about 15 minutes. Mix the flour with 1 teaspoon curry powder and the nutmeg, add it to the pot, and cook over low heat for about 5 minutes, stirring from time to time. Stir in the stock, then add the cloves, parsley, and tomatoes. Partially cover and simmer for about 1 hour. Add salt and pepper to taste and more curry powder if you wish. Pass the rice separately or spoon some into each bowl as you serve the soup.

Black Bean Soup (8–10 cups)

Black bean soup has a distinct personality. Robust and nourishing, it can be a complete meal in itself.

2 cups (½ L) dried black beans
1 onion, sliced
2 stalks celery, chopped
1 ham bone
1½ cups (3½ dL) cooked ham chunks
1½ teaspoons dry mustard
2 tablespoons lemon juice
Salt to taste
Freshly ground pepper

Soak the beans, if necessary, overnight in water to cover (or see p. 192). Drain the beans and add enough cold water to the soaking liquid to make 2 quarts. Put the beans and water in a soup pot and add the onion, celery, and ham bone. Bring to a boil, then lower the heat and simmer, partially covered, for 3–4 hours or until the beans are soft, adding more water to replace any that evaporates. Remove the ham bone. Purée in a blender or food processor, or beat by hand. Add the cooked ham and reheat, seasoning with mustard, lemon juice, salt, and a generous amount of pepper.

Black Bean Soup with Sherry. Omit the lemon juice and add *sherry to taste* during the final seasoning.

Black Bean Soup with Rice. Top each serving with a tablespoonful of *hot cooked rice* and a sprinkling of *chopped onion*.

Black Bean Soup with Lemon and Egg. Top with a thin slice of *lemon* and a slice or two of *hard-cooked egg*.

Bean and Vegetable Soup (9 cups)

Great Northern beans or pea beans are good choices for this soup.

1 cup (¼ L) dried white beans
2-inch cube salt pork, diced small
2 cloves garlic, minced
1 onion, chopped
1 leek, sliced thin
2 carrots, sliced thin
1 cup (¼ L) diced zucchini or summer squash
4 fresh tomatoes, peeled and chopped, or 2 cups (½ L) canned tomatoes
1½ cups (3½ dL) coarsely chopped cabbage
Salt
Freshly ground pepper
Freshly grated Parmesan cheese

Soak the beans overnight in water to cover or use quick method, p. 192. Add enough water to the soaking liquid to make 6 cups. Set aside. Cook the salt pork in a small skillet over very low heat until it gives up its fat. Strain the fat and put 2 table-spoonfuls in a large soup pot; set aside the crisp scraps. Heat the fat and add the garlic, onion, leek, carrots, and squash. Cook over low heat, adding a little more fat or vegetable oil if necessary, for about 15 minutes. Stir in the tomatoes and the soaked beans and reserved liquid. Partially cover and simmer for about 1 hour, until the beans and the vegetables are tender. Add the cabbage and cook 15 minutes more. Add the pork scraps and salt and pepper to taste, and reheat before serving. Pass the Parmesan cheese separately.

Cream of Tomato Soup (6 cups)

Some consider it old-fashioned to add baking soda to cream of tomato soup, but it does seem to improve the taste.

4 cups (1 L) milk or light cream
½ cup (1 dL) dry bread crumbs
½ onion, stuck with 6 cloves
Parsley sprig
½ bay leaf
2 teaspoons sugar
2 cups (½ L) chopped fresh or canned tomatoes
¼ teaspoon baking soda
4 tablespoons butter
Salt
Freshly ground pepper

Put the milk or cream in a pot and add the bread crumbs, onion with cloves, parsley, bay leaf, and sugar. Simmer gently over medium heat for about 5 minutes. Remove from heat and discard the onion with cloves and the bay leaf. Add the tomatoes and baking soda and simmer gently for about 15 minutes. Put through a strainer or vegetable mill or purée in a food processor or blender. Return to pot, add the butter and salt and pepper to taste, and reheat, stirring until the butter melts and the soup is very hot.

Leek and Potato Soup (8 cups)

Leeks tend to be gritty and need careful cleaning: cut off the roots and the coarse green tops, cut lengthwise through the remaining green tops starting within an inch of the white bottom, gently separate the stiff leaves, and rinse well under cold, running water.

3 tablespoons butter
4 leeks, sliced very thin
3 stalks celery, sliced very thin
2 medium potatoes, peeled and diced
3 cups (¾ L) milk
Salt
Freshly ground pepper

Melt the butter in a large pot and add the leeks and celery. Cook for about 10 minutes over moderate heat, stirring often. Stir in 1 cup water, cover, and cook 10 minutes more. Add the potatoes and 2 more cups water, cover, and cook 10 minutes. Stir in the milk, cover, and cook until the potatoes are just tender, about 10 minutes more. Add salt and pepper to taste.

Corn Chowder (10 cups)

You can use commercially frozen corn in this soup, but fresh summer corn is better. Cut the kernels from leftover ears of corn, cooked or uncooked. You can freeze them, if necessary, until you're ready to make this chowder.

2-inch cube salt pork, diced small
1 onion, finely chopped
4 medium potatoes, peeled and diced
2 cups (½ L) corn kernels
3 (¾ L) milk
3 tablespoons butter
Salt
Freshly ground pepper

Cook the salt pork slowly in a deep pan until the fat has melted and the pieces are brown. Pour off all but 2 tablespoons of the fat, add the onion, and cook for 5 minutes. Add the potatoes and 3 cups water, cover, and cook until the potatoes are just tender. Add the corn and milk and cook 5 minutes more. Before serving, add the butter and salt and pepper to taste, and reheat.

Onion Soup   (4 cups)

Allow about 45 minutes to cook the onions. Very slow cooking will give them a deep golden color and release their full flavor.

3 tablespoons butter
4 cups (1 L) thinly sliced onions
½ teaspoon sugar
1 tablespoon flour
Salt
Freshly ground pepper
4 slices dried or toasted French bread
½ cup (1 dL) freshly grated Parmesan cheese

Melt the butter in a large pot, add the onions, and cook them very slowly over low heat, stirring often. Stir in the sugar and flour and cook for 3 minutes. Add 4 cups water and simmer, partially covered, for 30 minutes. Add salt and pepper to taste. Serve with a slice of French bread in each bowl. Pass the Parmesan cheese separately.

Onion Soup with Melted Parmesan Cheese. Before serving, sprinkle each filled bowl generously with grated Parmesan cheese and set the bowls in a 400°F (205°C) oven until the cheese is melted and brown.

Scotch Broth   (8 cups)

Inexpensive cuts of lamb will give this soup the best flavor. Be patient and try to trim off as much of the fat as possible.

3 pounds (1⅓ kg) lamb breast or neck
½ cup (1 dL) barley
2 tablespoons butter
2 carrots, finely diced
2 stalks celery, finely diced
1 small white turnip, peeled and diced
1 medium onion, finely diced
Salt
Freshly ground pepper

Remove most of the fat from the meat and cut meat into small pieces. Put it in a pot with 8 cups cold water. Bring to a boil and stir in the barley. Simmer, partially covered, for 1½ hours or until the meat and barley are tender, adding more water if any evaporates. Remove the meat from the bones. Cool the soup and skim off the fat. Melt the butter in a skillet and add the carrots, celery, turnip, and onion. Cook over low heat, stirring often, for 10 minutes. Add to the soup. Season with salt and pepper to taste, and cook for another 10 minutes or until the vegetables are tender. Serve piping hot.

Split Pea Soup (10–12 cups)

Whoever owned the 1912 edition of the *Fannie Farmer Cook Book* in which we found this recipe had written neatly alongside it: "Good." And she was right.

1½ cups (3½ dL) dried split peas
Ham bone (optional)
2-inch cube salt pork
1 onion, chopped
3 tablespoons butter
2 tablespoons flour
2 cups (½ L) milk
Salt
Freshly ground pepper

Soak the peas overnight in water to cover or use quick method (see p. 192). Add enough water to the soaking liquid to make 2½ quarts. Put the peas and liquid in a large soup pot and the ham bone, if you are using it, and the salt pork and onion. Bring to a boil, reduce heat, and simmer, partially covered, for 1½–2 hours or until the peas are soft. Discard the salt pork. Put through a strainer or vegetable mill or purée the soup in a blender or food processor. Melt the butter in a small saucepan, stir in the flour, and cook over low heat for a few minutes. Add the milk, stirring constantly, and cook until smooth and thickened. Stir this sauce into the soup and add salt and pepper to taste.

Yogurt Soups (4 cups)

These are much lighter than the usual cold soups with a cream base and the yogurt gives a pleasant tangy taste. They're easy to make in a blender or food processor.

2 peeled and seeded cucumbers or avocados or 2 cups (½ L) cooked beets
3 cups (¾ L) yogurt
2 scallions or 1 tablespoon chopped onion
Salt

Garnish

8 thin slices cucumber and 1 tablespoon dill (for the cucumber)
4 slices lime (for the avocado)
4 tablespoons shredded beets, raw or cooked
Additional dollop yogurt or sour cream (optional)

Spin the cucumbers, avocados, or beets in a blender or food processor with the yogurt and scallions or onion until just smooth. Salt to taste and chill. Serve in chilled bowls with the suggested garnishes.

Old-fashioned Fish Chowder
(10 cups)

Use the head and bones from the filleted fish to make a rich fish stock for this chowder. If you can, let the chowder mellow in the refrigerator for a day before you eat it. Serve it with common crackers.

2-inch cube salt pork, diced small
2 onions, thinly sliced
3 medium potatoes, peeled and diced
4 cups (1 L) Fish Stock (p. 23) or clam broth or juice
2 pounds (900 g) fillet of cod, haddock, or any firm white fish
2 cups (½ L) cream or milk
2 tablespoons butter
Salt
Freshly ground pepper

Cook the salt pork very slowly in a small skillet until the fat has melted and the scraps are brown. Strain, setting aside the crisp scraps, and put 2 tablespoons of the fat in a soup pot. Heat the fat, add the onions, and cook over low heat until golden. Stir in the potatoes and toss until well coated. Add the fish stock or clam liquid. Cut the fish in chunks, add it to the pot, and simmer, partially covered, for about 15 minutes, or until the fish is cooked through and the potatoes are tender. Stir in the cream or milk and heat slowly, without boiling. Add the pork scraps. Just before serving, stir in the butter, add salt and pepper to taste, and heat until butter melts.

Connecticut Fish Chowder (11 cups, 2¾ L). Omit the cream and substitute *4 cups canned tomatoes, undrained*. If you wish, you may add ½ *teaspoon dried marjoram or thyme* along with the tomatoes.

Lobster Bisque (8 cups)

A splendid soup with an excellent bouquet of flavors. Have the lobster killed and split at the market, if you can then cook it promptly.

2 cups (½ L) Beef Stock (p. 18) or bouillon
¼ cup (½ dL) rice
3 tablespoons butter
1 carrot, sliced
1 onion, chopped
¼ bay leaf
½ teaspoon dried thyme
1½ pounds (675 g) lobster, killed and split
1 cup (¼ L) dry white wine
4 cups (1 L) Chicken Stock (p. 20) or canned broth
1 tablespoon tomato paste
Lobster liver, if any
Lobster coral, if any
1 cup (¼ L) cream
Salt
Freshly ground pepper

Put the beef stock and rice in a saucepan, cover, and cook over moderate heat until the rice is done, about 15 minutes. Set aside. Melt 2 tablespoons of the butter in a large pot, add the carrot and onion, and cook slowly for 5 minutes. Add the bay leaf, thyme, and lobster, cover, and cook until the lobster shells are red, about 10 minutes. Add the wine and chicken stock, and simmer, partially covered, for another 15 minutes. Remove the lobster and strain the broth. Add the undrained cooked rice to the broth. Remove the lobster meat from the shell and cut it into bite-size pieces. Add it to the broth. Melt the remaining tablespoon of butter in a small pan and stir in the tomato paste and any lobster liver or coral. Cook until smooth, then add to the soup. Stir in the cream, add salt and pepper to taste, and heat to serving temperature without allowing the soup to boil.

Clam and Tomato Bisque   (3 cups)

1 cup (¼ L) clam broth
1 cup (¼ L) peeled and stewed tomatoes or
  chopped canned tomatoes
1 cup (¼ L) milk or cream
Pinch of nutmeg
1 stalk celery, coarsely chopped
Parsley sprig
Small piece of bay leaf
3 tablespoons finely chopped onion
Salt

Simmer the clam broth and tomatoes together for 10–15 minutes. Stir in the milk or cream, nutmeg, celery, parsley, bay leaf, and onion. Heat slowly, without boiling. Strain and reheat, adding salt to taste before serving.

Mildred's Oyster Stew (6 cups)

Very fresh butter, milk, and cream will give this stew a pure, wonderful flavor.

2 cups (½ L) milk
2 cups (½ L) light cream
2 cups (½ L) shucked or canned oysters and their juice
Salt
3 tablespoons butter

Heat the milk and cream in a pot; do not boil. Add the oysters and any oyster juice and simmer for 5 minutes. Season to taste with salt. Add the butter, heat until it melts, and serve very hot.

New England Clam Chowder
(9 cups)

Raw, shucked clams and their undiluted juices are best for chowder; brief cooking in the chowder will keep the juice full of flavor and the clams very tender. Since it takes some skill and practice to shuck them easily, see if you can have this done for you at the fish store. Or steam the clams in a little water until they open, and use them and the broth for the chowder. Clams are also available in cans and clam juice in bottles; these products will produce an acceptable chowder.

3-4 cups (¾–1 L) shucked or steamed chowder clams, with their juice or broth
1½-inch cube salt pork, diced small

1 onion, finely chopped
2 tablespoons flour
3 medium potatoes, peeled and diced
3 cups (¾ L) milk
3 tablespoons butter
Salt
Freshly ground pepper

Measure the clam juice or broth from the shucked or steamed clams and add water, if necessary, to make 2½ cups. Cut the clams in small pieces and set aside. Cook the salt pork slowly in a small skillet until the fat has melted and the scraps are brown. Strain, set aside the scraps, and put 2 tablespoons of the fat in a large pot. Heat the fat, add the onion, and cook slowly until golden. Sprinkle the flour over the onion and cook, stirring, for 3 minutes. Add the potatoes and clam juice or broth. Cover and simmer 10 minutes. Add the clams and simmer 10 minutes more, or until the clams are cooked and the potatoes are tender. Add the milk, butter, and salt and pepper to taste, and heat until the butter has melted. Serve with a few crisp pork bits in each bowl.

Manhattan Clam Chowder (6 cups)

To prepare clams for chowder, see preceding recipe for New England Clam Chowder.

2 cups (½ L) shucked or steamed chowder clams, with their juice or broth
1½-inch cube salt pork, diced small

1 onion, finely chopped
1 medium potato, peeled and diced
2 cups (½ L) stewed peeled tomatoes or chopped
   canned tomatoes
¼ teaspoon thyme
Salt
Freshly ground pepper

Measure the clam juice or broth from the shucked or steamed clams and add water, if necessary, to make 2½ cups. Cut the clams in small pieces and set aside. Cook the salt pork slowly in a small skillet until the fat melts and the scraps are brown. Strain, set aside the scraps, and put 2 tablespoons of the fat in a large pot. Heat the fat, add the onion, and cook until limp. Stir in the potatoes and clam juice. Cover and simmer 10 minutes. Add the tomatoes and simmer 10 minutes more. Stir in the clams and thyme, and cook for another 5–10 minutes, until the clams and the potatoes are done. Add salt and pepper to taste. Serve with a few crisp pork bits in each bowl.

Cioppino (serves six)

From Fisherman's Wharf, San Francisco: half Italian, all-American. This is really more of a stew than a soup and is usually served as a main course.

2 large onions, chopped
3 carrots, chopped
3 cloves garlic, mashed

½ cup (1 dL) olive oil
1 cup (¼ L) chopped parsley
4 cups tomato sauce
1½ teaspoons thyme, crumbled
1 tablespoon basil, crumbled
3 pounds (1⅓ kg) clams in shell, scrubbed
2 pounds (900 g) white fish fillets
2 crabs, cooked and cracked
¼ cup (½ dL) dry white wine
Pinch of cayenne pepper
Salt

In a large kettle, sauté the onions, carrots, and garlic in olive oil until the onions are soft. Add the parsley, tomato sauce, 2 cups water, thyme, and basil. Partially cover and simmer 45 minutes. If the soup gets too thick, add a little water. Add the clams and simmer 10 minutes. Add the white fish and crab, and simmer 5 minutes. Stir in the wine, cayenne pepper, and salt to taste, and simmer 10 minutes more. Ladle some of each variety of fish and shellfish into each bowl with a generous helping of broth.

Fish & Shellfish

Broiled Bluefish (serves two)

A dark-fleshed fish with a distinctive flavor, young bluefish is delicate and makes superb eating when simply broiled.

1 lemon
1½ -pound (675-g) bluefish, split and boned
2 teaspoons butter
Salt
Sprinkling of fresh herbs

Preheat the broiler. Squeeze half the lemon over the fish and let it sit while the broiler heats. Smear a little butter on the broiler rack. Place the fish, skin side down, on the rack, sprinkle with salt, and dot with remaining butter. Broil close to the broiling element about 6 minutes. Do not turn. Serve with a sprinkling of herbs and the remaining half of the lemon, cut in wedges.

Bluefish Baked with Aromatic Vegetables (serves four)

A particularly good way to cook larger bluefish fillets. They are also tasty when baked like mackerel over potatoes with bacon, tomatoes, and peppers (p. 53).

4 tablespoons butter
1 onion, chopped
1 carrot, chopped
1 stalk celery, chopped
¼ pound (115 g) mushrooms, chopped
2 tablespoons chopped parsley
¼ cup (½ dL) dry white wine
3–4-pound (1⅓–1¾-kg) bluefish, split and boned
Salt
⅛ teaspoon paprika

Preheat the oven to 425°F (220°C). Heat the butter in a flameproof baking dish large enough to accommodate the fish. Add the onion, carrot, celery, mushrooms, and parsley, and cook, stirring often, for about 5 minutes. Add the wine and cook 3–4 minutes more. Remove half the vegetables, lay the fish on top. Cover with the remaining vegetables, and sprinkle with salt and paprika. Cover loosely with foil, and bake 20 minutes.

Pan-fried Catfish (serves three)

A firm-flesh fish popular all over the southern United States, catfish is sold whole or in fillets. It can be fried, baked, or broiled. Pan fry whole catfish according to the recipe for Pan-fried Porgy (p. 56).

1½ pounds (675 g) catfish fillets
⅓ cup (¾ dL) flour

1½ teaspoons salt
½ teaspoon freshly ground pepper
2 eggs, slightly beaten
1 cup (¼ L) cornmeal
Oil for frying
Lemon wedges

Rinse the fish under cold water and pat dry with paper towels. Mix the flour with salt and pepper, and spread it on a piece of wax paper. Put the eggs in a shallow bowl and the cornmeal on another piece of wax paper. Lightly dust each fillet in the seasoned flour and shake off the excess. Dip the fillet into the egg. Hold over the bowl to let excess egg drip off. Dip into the cornmeal. Warm a platter in a 250°F (120°C) oven. In a large skillet, heat ¼ inch of oil. Put your hand over the oil in the skillet, and when you can feel a good amount of heat rising, put in the fish and brown on each side. This should take 1½–2 minutes on each side. Don't crowd the skillet; do only a few at a time. Remove to a paper towel to drain, transfer to the warmed platter, and continue frying the fillets. Serve with lemon wedges.

Foil-steamed Cod Steaks (serves four)

Heavy foil, securely sealed around a piece of fish, serves much the same purpose as steaming: it locks in the juices so that the flavors are beautifully preserved. This process works on an outdoor grill as well, and is a clean and easy method of cooking. The package is brought right to the table, and the taste of a bland fish like cod, tilefish, halibut, or flounder is greatly enhanced.

6 tablespoons butter
Four ½-pound (225-g) cod steaks
Salt
Freshly ground pepper
Juice of 1 lemon
2 tablespoons chopped parsley, chives and fresh basil, tarragon, chervil, or dill (or 1 teaspoon dried)
Lemon wedges

Preheat the oven to 425°F (220°C). Liberally butter four pieces of aluminum foil large enough to enclose the fish steaks generously. Sprinkle the fish with salt, pepper, lemon juice, and herbs. Dot with remaining butter and wrap the foil around the fish, folding the edges to seal well. Place on a baking sheet and bake 15 minutes for fillets, 20 minutes for steaks 1 inch thick or more. Serve with lemon wedges.

Foil-steamed Cod with Mushrooms. Instead of using lemon juice, sprinkle a *few drops of white wine* over each piece of fish and spread with *1 tablespoon Mushroom Duxelles* (p. 165).

Foil-steamed Cod with Aromatic Vegetables. Sauté *1 carrot, chopped, 1 stalk celery, chopped,* and *1 onion, chopped,* in *2 tablespoons butter* for 5 minutes, then spread over the pieces of fish along with the lemon juice and herbs.

Halibut Creole (serves four)

In this recipe, as in many others, cod and halibut may be used interchangeably.

1¾–2 pounds (800–900 g) halibut steaks
Salt
Freshly ground pepper
3 large tomatoes, peeled, seeded, and chopped
½ cup (1 dL) finely chopped green pepper
½ cup (1 dL) finely chopped onion
6 tablespoons butter
3 tablespoons lemon juice
⅛ teaspoon Tabasco

Preheat the oven to 400°F (205°C). Butter a shallow baking dish large enough to hold the fish in one layer, and place the fish in it. Season with salt and pepper to taste and spread the tomatoes, green pepper, and onion over the top. Melt the butter with the lemon juice and Tabasco and drizzle it over the fish and vegetables. Bake about 25 minutes, basting with pan juices every 10 minutes.

Baked Mackerel Hungarian
(serves six)

6 medium potatoes
2½ pounds (1¼ kg) large mackerel fillets
1 green pepper, sliced
2 tomatoes, sliced
¼ pound (115 g) bacon, in 1-inch slices
1 teaspoon paprika
1 cup (¼ L) sour cream, at room temperature

Preheat the oven to 400°F (205°C). Peel and cut the potatoes into ¼-inch slices. Boil them in salted water for 5 minutes; drain and scatter over the bottom of a large buttered baking dish. Make slashes in the mackerel about ¾ inch apart and insert in each one a slice of green pepper, tomato, and bacon. Place the fish over the potatoes, sprinkle with paprika, and bake for 20 minutes. Spread with sour cream and bake 5 minutes more.

Ocean Perch Fillets, Filled and Baked (serves four)

Ocean perch is the most common of the frozen fish fillets in our supermarkets. This easy cooking method lends tastiness to the rather bland, lean fish cut from a variety of large ocean fish: to be distinguished, incidentally, from small fresh lake perch, which should be cooked the way you would trout (p. 65). For this recipe you may substitute any other fillet, such as halibut, flounder, or sole.

1¾–2 pounds (800–900 g) ocean perch or other fillets
Salt
Freshly ground pepper
2 tablespoons butter, melted
2 tablespoons lemon juice or dry vermouth
2 tablespoons heavy cream

½ cup (1 dL) Bread Stuffing (p. 163), or
⅓ cup (¾ dL) Mushroom Duxelles (p. 165), or
½ cup (1 dL) finely chopped cooked seafood

Preheat the oven to 425°F (220°C). Butter a shallow casserole large enough to hold half the fillets in one layer. Lay down half the fish, and sprinkle with salt and pepper. Brush with half the butter and sprinkle with the lemon juice or vermouth. Spread with one of the fillings, and cover with the remaining fillets. Season again with salt, pepper, and remaining butter, and pour on the cream. Cover loosely with foil and bake 20–30 minutes, depending on the thickness of the fillets.

Whole Roasted Pompano (serves two)

Serve these superb silvery fish from the Gulf of Mexico by roasting them simply, one to a person.

2 whole pompano, about ¾ pound (340 g) each
1 tablespoon oil
Salt
Freshly ground pepper
Lemon wedges

Preheat the oven to 400°F (205°C). Rub the fish with oil. Season lightly inside and out with salt and pepper. Bake in a shallow pan 25–30 minutes or until you see the skin bubbling slightly and swelling from the flesh—the sign that it is done. Serve with lemon wedges.

Pan-fried Porgy (serves four)

A popular game fish in Atlantic waters, porgy is usually sold whole.

4 porgies, ½–¾ pound (225–340 g) each
½ cup (1 dL) cornmeal
½ teaspoon salt
Freshly ground pepper
4 tablespoons oil
1 clove garlic, minced (optional)
½ teaspoon marjoram or basil
1 lemon
1 tablespoon butter

Wash the porgies and pat dry. Season the cornmeal with salt and pepper, and dredge the fish. Heat the oil in a large skillet, and brown the fish quickly on both sides. Turn the heat to medium, add the garlic (if desired) and herbs, and cook 10–15 minutes. Remove to a warm platter. Squeeze half a lemon into the pan with the butter, scrape up the browned bits, and pour the juices over the fish. Cut the other half of the lemon into slices and garnish the fish with them.

Red Snapper, Stuffed and Baked (serves four)

One of our finest fish from the Gulf Coast, so handsome on the platter when served whole with its glistening silver and pinkish red skin.

6 tablespoons butter
¼ pound (115 g) mushrooms, finely chopped
4 scallions, chopped
1 stalk celery, chopped
½ cup (1 dL) bread crumbs
½ teaspoon rosemary
½ teaspoon salt
Freshly ground pepper
1 whole red snapper, about 2½ pounds (1¼ kg)
2–3 tablespoons dry white wine

Preheat the oven to 400°F (205°C). Melt 5 tablespoons of the butter, add the mushrooms, scallions, and celery, and sauté about 10 minutes. Mix in the bread crumbs, rosemary, salt, and pepper to taste. Fill the cavity of the fish with the stuffing and skewer or sew up the opening. Brush the fish with some of the remaining butter and bake for 30 minutes, basting with what's left of the butter and a little wine twice during the cooking.

Red Snapper Fillets, Florida Style (serves four)

1½ pounds (675 g) red snapper fillets
Salt

Freshly ground pepper
A few gratings of nutmeg
1½ teaspoons grated orange rind
1 teaspoon grated grapefruit rind, or a
   combination of lemon and lime

Preheat the oven to 400°F (205°C). Put the fillets in a lightly buttered baking dish. Sprinkle them lightly with salt and pepper and nutmeg and distribute the grated rinds on top. Cover with foil and bake 15 minutes.

Poached Salmon   (serves eight to ten)

Salmon is one of the most flavorful fish. It weighs between 5 and 10 pounds when whole; larger salmon are generally cut into steaks or sections. The meat is pink, tender, and firm, the flavor mild and delicious. It lends itself to poaching whole, baking split, or broiling (planked or not, as you wish). It is equally delicious cold, and makes a splendid buffet dish.

6-pound (2¾-kg) whole dressed salmon
2 cups (½ L) dry white wine
1½ tablespoons salt
4 carrots, sliced
3 onions, sliced thin
4 bay leaves, in pieces
12 sprigs parsley
1 teaspoon freshly ground pepper
1 recipe Hollandaise Sauce (p. 157)

Rinse the salmon under cold running water. In a fish poacher or a large roasting pan with a lid and rack to hold the fish, combine 4 quarts water with the wine, salt, carrots, onions, bay leaves, parsley, and pepper. Bring to a boil and simmer 15 minutes. If you want to make sure that the salmon remains in one piece, wrap it in a cheese cloth sling before placing it in the broth; it will be easy to lift out later. Lay the fish on the rack; if there is not enough broth to cover it, add some more water. Put on the lid and simmer 25–30 minutes or until meat loses its deep pink color around the backbone. A thermometer will register 140°F (60°C) when the fish is done. Remove the pan from the heat and let the fish remain in the broth until you are ready to serve it, up to 45 minutes. Serve with hollandaise.

Cold Poached Salmon. Follow the recipe for Poached Salmon, but remove the fish from the broth and refrigerate until it is cool. Place on a platter and decorate with *tomato wedges, cucumber slices, black olives,* and *watercress.* Serve with *Mayonnaise* (p. 282) or *Green Mayonnaise* (p. 282).

Broiled Salmon (serves four)

6 tablespoons butter, melted
4 salmon steaks, about ¾ inch (2 cm) thick
Salt to taste
Freshly ground pepper to taste
1 tablespoon mixed chopped parsley, chives, and
   dill
Juice of 1 lemon
Lemon wedges

Preheat the broiler. Brush 2 tablespoons of the butter over the salmon steaks. Mix remaining butter with salt, pepper, herbs, and lemon juice. Place salmon steaks on the broiler pan and put it on the highest level under the broiling element. Cook 5 minutes each side. For the last minutes of cooking, pour on the remaining butter mixture. Serve with accumulated pan juices and surround with lemon wedges.

Broiled Scrod (serves four)

Scrod is young cod. It is most delicious when very fresh, split down the back and broiled quickly with a crusty topping to contrast with the tender flesh.

Four ½-pound (225-g) pieces split scrod
6 tablespoons butter, melted
Salt
Freshly ground pepper
½ cup (1 dL) fresh bread crumbs
¼ cup (½ dL) grated Swiss cheese
Lemon wedges

Preheat the broiler. Oil the broiler pan, and place the scrod on it. Sprinkle with half the melted butter, salt, and pepper, and place beneath the broiling element. Cook 6 minutes on one side. Turn, cook 4 minutes, and then sprinkle on the bread crumbs mixed with cheese. Top with the remaining butter and broil another minute or two until nicely browned. Garnish with lemon wedges.

Shad Roe with Bacon (serves two)

The roe of the shad, sold in pairs, is one of our finest culinary treasures. It is often broiled with bacon, which tends to dry and toughen it. It is much more delicate and tender cooked this way, either done at the table or in a kitchen skillet.

2 pairs shad roe
6 tablespoons butter
Salt
Freshly ground pepper
1 lemon
2 tablespoons chopped parsley
4 slices bacon, fried

Sauté the shad roe in the butter in a chafing dish or skillet. Using moderate heat, cover and cook for 15 minutes, turning several times. Season with salt and pepper and squeeze on the juice of half the lemon, slicing the other half to use as garnish. Sprinkle with parsley and serve with crisp bacon.

Sole with Butter, Lemon, and Parsley (serves four)

All species of sole are members of the flounder family: the most common are Dover, grey, lemon, rex, and petrale. Sole is a lean fish, usually sold in fillets, whose white delicate meat lends itself to all kinds of adornment.

⅓ cup (50 g) flour
1¼ teaspoons salt

¼ teaspoon freshly ground pepper
1½ pounds (675 g) sole fillets
6 tablespoons butter
1 tablespoon oil
2 tablespoons lemon juice
1½ tablespoons minced parsley

Preheat the oven to 225°F (110°C). Put in an oven-proof platter. Combine the flour, salt, and pepper, spread it on wax paper, and drag each of the fillets through it so they are well coated. Shake off excess flour. In a large skillet, heat 3 tablespoons of the butter with the oil. Without crowding, put some of the fillets in the skillet and pan fry over medium heat until golden. Unless they are unusually thick, this should take 1–2 minutes on each side. Transfer to the warm platter and cook the rest of the fillets, adding the remaining butter as needed. When all the fish is cooked, turn the heat to high, stir in the lemon juice, and cook for a few seconds. Add the parsley, stir, and drizzle over the fillets.

Sole with Almonds. Omit the parsley and, after the fillets are done, sauté *½ cup sliced almonds* in *2 tablespoons butter* until they are golden. Distribute over the fish before serving.

Seviche   (serves four)

An unusual cool and refreshing dish from South of the Border which has become popular in the States in recent years. Don't be put off by the fact that the fish is raw: it really "cooks" in its marinade of lime and lemon juices, becoming firm and white. Delicious as a first course, seviche also makes a nice summer lunch, served in small chilled bowls or plates garnished with avocado slices and watercress.

1 pound (450 g) fillets of sole, halibut, or other lean white fish
½ cup (1 dL) freshly squeezed lime juice
¼ cup (½ dL) freshly squeezed lemon juice
1 teaspoon finely chopped ginger root
½ teaspoon salt
Freshly ground pepper
1 clove garlic, minced
½ large red onion, sliced thin
1 tablespoon minced seeded canned green chili pepper, or ¼ teaspoon pepper flakes
3 tablespoons chopped Chinese parsley

Slice fillets in half lengthwise and cut into ½-inch pieces. Spread in one layer in a dish. Combine the remaining ingredients, reserving 1 tablespoon of Chinese parsley. Pour over the fish, cover with plastic wrap, and refrigerate for at least 6 hours, turning once. Sprinkle with reserved Chinese parsley before serving.

Whole Striped Bass, Steamed
(serves six)

Striped bass is one of the most highly prized of Atlantic fish. The flesh is so delicate and succulent that it is good hot or cold, poached, steamed, or baked. Served whole with the head and tail on, the large black-striped silvery-skinned bass makes a handsome dish.

4½-pound (2-kg) striped bass, or 2 bass, 2¼
    pounds (1 kg) each
Salt
Freshly ground pepper

Season the fish inside and out with salt and pepper. Lightly oil the steaming rack. Wrap the fish in cheesecloth and place on the rack. Pour in enough boiling water to cover the bottom of the pot without touching the rack. Put on the cover and steam 25–30 minutes for the larger fish (you may have to replenish the water) and 15 minutes for the smaller. Remove carefully, pouring juices that accumulate on the platter back into the water remaining in the steamer. Reduce this, if necessary, to about 2 tablespoons and use it in making Hollandaise Sauce (p. 157) if you are serving the fish warm. If you are serving it cold, chill for several hours and serve with Green Mayonnaise (p. 284).

Poached Striped Bass. Follow the recipe for Poached Salmon (p. 58), cooking 25 minutes for a 4½-pound bass, 15 minutes for a 2-pounder.

Baked Stuffed Striped Bass. Follow the recipe for Red Snapper, Stuffed and Baked (p. 57), baking a 4½-pound bass 45 minutes, and 2-pound bass 25 minutes.

Broiled Swordfish (serves four)

Even people who don't like fish like swordfish, because its firm, oily flesh so resembles meat. Swordfish steaks should be cut about 1 inch thick for broiling. Thicker than that, the outside is apt to get too dry while the inside is under-cooked; thinner than that, the steaks dry out completely and are better pan-fried. Swordfish is also very good cooked on an outdoor grill.

2-pound (900-g) swordfish steak
4 tablespoons butter, melted
Salt
Freshly ground pepper
½ teaspoon anchovy paste (optional)
Lemon wedges

Preheat the broiler. Brush both sides of the swordfish with some of the melted butter, and season with salt and pepper. Broil on the highest level for 5 minutes; then turn, pour on a tablespoon of butter, and broil another 4–5 minutes. Mix the remaining butter with the anchovy paste, if you like a sharper accent, and pour it over the fish. Surround with lemon wedges.

Pan-fried Brook Trout (serves four)

Fresh-water trout is unequaled when cooked straight from the stream, but it is beautiful eating any time.

4 brook trout, cleaned, with head and tail left on
2 tablespoons flour
Salt
7 tablespoons butter
3 tablespoons oil
2 tablespoons lemon juice
2 tablespoons minced chives

Rinse the fish under cold running water and pat dry with paper towels. Dust lightly with flour, and sprinkle with salt. In a large skillet, melt 3 tablespoons of the butter and the oil. When it is hot, put in the trout and fry over medium-high heat. When browned, turn and brown the other side: each side will take about 3 minutes. Melt the remaining 4 tablespoons butter with lemon juice and chives in a small saucepan. When the trout is done, transfer to a warm platter and pour on the sauce.

Steamed Clams (1 quart per serving)

Clams are a bivalve, or two-shelled, mollusk. There are three principal varieties, soft-shelled, hard-shelled, and razor clams from the Pacific. The so-called soft-shelled are oval and come from northern New England. The hard-shelled are round and come in small littlenecks, medium cherrystones, and large quahogs or chowder clams. Small clams are eaten raw, steamed, or on the half-shell; quahogs are good minced and in soups. When buying clams, be sure the shells are clamped tightly together; this indicates that the clam is alive. Discard broken or cracked shells. To get rid of all the sand, scrub under running water and then soak in a salt-water brine for about ½ hour.

1 quart (1 L) clams per serving
¼ cup (½ dL) butter, melted, per serving
Lemon juice or vinegar

Scrub the shells with a brush, changing the water until there is no trace of sand. Put the clams in a deep kettle with 2 tablespoons water for each quart of clams. Cover tightly and cook over low heat until the shells open, about 15 minutes. Don't overcook. Using a slotted spoon, remove the clams to large soup plates. Strain the broth into small glasses and serve with the clams. Set out individual dishes of melted butter, to which you may add a little lemon juice or vinegar, and a small amount of boiling water which will make the butter float to the top and stay hot. To eat, lift the clam from the shell by the black neck. Dip in the clam broth, then in the butter, and eat; some like the neck, some don't.

Stuffed Clams Union League
(serves four)

¼ pound (115 g) butter
1 tablespoon finely chopped shallot or onion
36 small clams in the shell
1 cup (¼ L) dry white wine
3 tablespoons flour
½ cup (1 dL) heavy cream
5–6 drops Tabasco

2 teaspoons finely chopped parsley
1 cup (¼ L) freshly made bread crumbs
½ cup (1 dL) freshly grated Parmesan cheese

Melt 5 tablespoons of the butter in a large sauce-pan. Add the shallot or onion and stir over low heat for 5 minutes. Add the clams and wine, cover, and cook until the shells open, 12–15 minutes. Remove the clams from the shells and chop them. Save the shells. Preheat the oven to 400°F (205°CC). Melt the remaining 3 tablespoons butter in a saucepan. Blend in the flour and cook 1 minute. Slowly add ½ cup of the clam liquid and the cream, and stir until the sauce is smooth. Add the clams and Tabasco and stir constantly until the sauce is thickened. Remove from the heat, add the parsley, and spoon the clams and sauce back into the shells. Mix the bread crumbs and cheese and sprinkle on each clam. Bake for 15 minutes or until the crumbs are lightly browned.

Soft-shelled Crabs, Sautéed
(serves three)

Soft-shelled crabs are a seasonal delicacy. All crabs have hard shells, which they shed as they outgrow them. It is at the time of molting, in late spring and summer, that they are caught and sold as soft-shelled crabs. Buy them alive, whole, and have them killed and cleaned just before you bring them home.

¼ cup (35 g) flour
Salt

Freshly ground pepper
6 soft-shelled crabs
6 tablespoons butter
1 tablespoon oil
Juice of 1 lemon

Season the flour with salt and pepper, dust the crabs with it, and shake off excess. In a large skillet, heat the butter and oil. Toss in the crabs and cook over moderately high heat about 3 minutes each side. Remove to a warm platter. Squeeze in the lemon juice and stir, scraping up all the brown bits. Pour over the crabs.

Soft-shelled Crabs Amandine. Before adding the lemon juice, sauté ⅓ *cup slivered almonds* in the pan, adding additional *butter* if necessary. When the nuts are golden, scatter them over the crabs, and finish with the lemon juice.

Crabmeat Casserole   (serves eight)

1 cup (¼ L) heavy cream
1 cup (¼ L) mayonnaise
1 tablespoon minced parsley
1 tablespoon minced onion
Salt
Freshly ground pepper
3½ cups (⅘ L) crabmeat
6 hard-cooked eggs, chopped
1 cup (¼ L) buttered bread crumbs

Preheat the oven to 350°F (180°C) and butter a shallow baking dish. Combine the cream, mayonnaise, parsley, onion, salt and pepper to taste, crabmeat, and chopped egg. Toss lightly, put into a baking dish, and sprinkle with the bread crumbs. Bake for 30 minutes.

Boiled Live Lobster

Lobsters are found in waters all over the world. They range from one to thirty pounds. The commercial grading is: "chicken," 1 pound; "quarters," under 1½ pounds; "large," 1½–2½ pounds; and "jumbo," over 2½ pounds. When buying a live lobster, look for one that is active and lively and heavy for its size. Killed lobsters should be cooked as soon as possible after purchase. The meat of the claws, body, and tail are wonderful to eat. The green liver or tomalley is a choice morsel, as is the roe or "coral " of the female lobster.

Salt
Lobsters

Fill a kettle with plenty of water to cover the lobsters. Add 2 teaspoons salt for each quart of water used. Bring to a rolling boil and put the lobsters in the pot. Allow 10 minutes cooking time for small lobsters, 15 minutes for medium, and as much as 25 minutes for large. Using tongs, lift from the water and cool just enough to handle. To prepare a boiled lobster to be eaten, first twist off the claws. Break the claws with a hammer or nutcracker so the meat is easily removed. Gently pull apart the tail from the body. Holding the tail with the hard shell down, cut the length of the cartilaginous tail with scissors. Bend it apart so the meat comes loose. Insert a small knife down the center and remove the dark line of intestine. Take the body and carefully remove the meat, discarding the lungs and stomach. Pick carefully for any small shell-like particles.

Coral Butter. Put the lobster coral into a blender or food processor and slowly add *4 tablespoons butter, softened*. Spread on toast or use in a sauce.

Steamed Mussels in White Wine
(serves five)

Another bivalve mollusk like the clam, the mussel in its blue-black oval shell is a great delicacy as well as one of the most abundant of seafoods. Mussels must be very well scrubbed, have their beards scraped away, and any open raw mussels should be discarded. Also, try to move the halves of the shell. If they slide, discard the mussel, for it may be full of mud.

2 cups (½ L) dry white wine, or 1½ cups (3½ dL)
    dry vermouth mixed with ½ cup (1 dL) water
¼ cup (½ dL) finely chopped shallots or scallions
Pinch of thyme
1 bay leaf
4 pounds (1800 g) mussels, scrubbed and scraped
⅓ cup (¾ dL) chopped parsley

Put the wine, shallots or scallions, thyme, and bay leaf in a large pot and boil briskly for 10 minutes. Add the mussels, cover tightly, and boil 3–5 minutes, giving the pot a shake once or twice. If the mussels have opened, they are done; if not, cover and cook 1–2 minutes longer until all are opened. Spoon into large soup plates with a portion of broth. Sprinkle with parsley and serve with crusty bread.

Oysters Casino   (serves four)

Clams are delicious prepared this way, too.

24 oysters on the half-shell
2 tablespoons lemon juice
3 tablespoons minced green pepper
2 tablespoons minced parsley
Salt
Freshly ground pepper
6 strips bacon

Preheat the broiler. Spread 1 inch of rock salt in a shallow baking dish large enough to hold the oyster shells, or use crumbled foil—anything to hold the oysters steady. Arrange the oysters on the salt. Sprinkle each with a few drops of lemon juice. Mix the green pepper, parsley, and salt and pepper to taste, and sprinkle over each oyster. Cut the bacon into 1½-inch lengths and put one piece on each oyster. Broil until the bacon is slightly brown.

Oysters Rockefeller (serves four)

3 scallions, including 1 inch of green tops
¼ cup (½ dL) chopped celery
2 tablespoons chopped parsley
½ cup (1 dL) chopped spinach
2 tablespoons freshly made bread crumbs
Dash of Tabasco
¼ teaspoon Worcestershire sauce
½ pound (225 g) butter, softened
Salt
24 large oysters on the half-shell

Preheat the oven to 450°F (230°C). Combine the scallions, celery, parsley, and spinach and mince them with a knife or chop in a blender or food processor. Put the mixture into a bowl with the bread crumbs, Tabasco, and Worcestershire sauce. Add the butter and salt to taste, and cream all together into a smooth paste. Spread 1 inch of rock salt over a pan or baking dish large enough to hold the oyster shells or use crumpled foil. Arrange the oysters on top. Put 1 tablespoon of butter mixture on each oyster and bake 10 minutes or until the mixture has melted.

Sautéed Scallops (serves four)

Scallops, like oysters and clams, are bivalve mollusks. The part of the scallop we eat is the muscle that opens and closes the shell. Buy tiny bay scallops or larger sea scallops; they should have a shiny moist look and a faint fresh scent of the sea. Scallops, even more than other seafood, tend to toughen and lose their fine character when they are overcooked. Clean by rinsing under cold water; pat dry with paper towels, and then cook them briefly, just until they lose their translucency and become creamy-white.

1½ pounds (675 g) scallops
¼ pound (115 g) butter
1½ tablespoons lemon juice
1 tablespoon minced parsley
Salt

Rinse the scallops and pat dry with paper towels. Melt the butter in a skillet and, when it foams, add the scallops. Cook over high heat about 1 minute each side. Remove to a warm platter and sprinkle with lemon juice, parsley, and salt.

Coquilles Saint-Jacques   (serves six)

1½ pounds (675 g) scallops
6 tablespoons butter
¼ cup (½ dL) finely chopped scallions
2 tablespoons minced parsley
¼ pound (115 g) mushrooms, chopped
1 cup (¼ L) dry white wine
Pinch of cayenne pepper
2 tablespoons flour
1 cup (¼ L) heavy cream
2 egg yolks, lightly beaten
Salt
½ cup (1 dL) freshly grated Parmesan cheese

Butter 6–8 scallop shells or a shallow baking dish. Rinse the scallops and pat dry with paper towels. Cut them in half. Melt 4 tablespoons of the butter in a skillet and add the scallions, parsley, and mushrooms. Stir over medium heat for 3–4 minutes, until the mushrooms have darkened and are soft. Add the scallops, wine, and cayenne, and simmer covered for 3 minutes. Drain and set aside, reserving the liquid. Melt the remaining 2 tablespoons butter in the skillet. Stir in the flour and cook until smooth and blended. Slowly add the reserved liquid and the cream and cook until the sauce is thick. Beat 2 spoonfuls of the sauce into the yolks, then stir the yolk-sauce mixture back into the sauce. Stir and cook until smooth and thickened. Add salt to taste. Spoon the scallops into the buttered shells or baking dish, pour sauce over, sprinkle with Parmesan cheese, and put under the broiler just long enough to brown the cheese.

Scallops Newburg (serves three)

Scallops in a fresh creamy sauce, good with pasta, rice, or in patty shells.

1 pint (½ L) scallops
4 tablespoons butter
1 tablespoon lemon juice
2 teaspoons flour
¾ cup (1¾ dL) heavy cream
2 egg yolks, slightly beaten
2 tablespoons dry sherry
Salt

Rinse the scallops and pat dry with paper towels. Cut them in half. Melt 3 tablespoons of the butter in a skillet and add the scallops and lemon juice. Cook for 1 minute, remove, and set aside. Melt the remaining tablespoon of butter in the skillet, stir in the flour, and cook until smooth and blended. Slowly add the cream, stirring constantly. Stir over low heat until thickened and smooth. Beat 2 spoonfuls of sauce into the yolks, and then stir the yolk-sauce mixture back into the sauce. Add the sherry and cook for 1 minute. Add the scallops and cook 2–3 minutes more. Add salt to taste.

Shrimp in Court Bouillon
(serves two to six)

Shrimp is sometimes cooked in a flavored broth, called a court bouillon, that provides additional taste.

4 tablespoons butter
⅓ cup (¾ dL) chopped carrot
⅓ cup (¾ dL) chopped celery
⅓ cup (¾ dL) chopped onion
4 sprigs parsley
6 peppercorns, crushed
2 cloves
½ bay leaf
2 tablespoons vinegar
1 tablespoon salt
2 pounds (900 g) raw unshelled shrimp

Melt the butter in a large saucepan. Add the carrot, celery, and onion, and cook for 3 minutes. Add the parsley, peppercorns, cloves, bay leaf, vinegar, salt and 2 quarts water. Bring to a boil, add the shrimp, and cook only until they turn pink, 3–5 minutes. Drain, cool, and shell. If you are making a sauce, reduce the court bouillon to 2 cups, strain and use the reduced liquid in the sauce.

Shrimp Jambalaya (serves six)

One version of a fine Cajun dish of Spanish origin.

3 slices bacon, diced
½ cup (1 dL) chopped celery
½ cup (1 dL) chopped onion
½ cup (1 dL) chopped green pepper
1 tablespoon minced garlic
4 cups (1 L) canned tomatoes with liquid
⅛ teaspoon cayenne pepper
1 teaspoon chili powder
¼ teaspoon thyme, crumbled
2 pounds (900 g) shrimp, cooked, shelled, and deveined
¼ cup (½ dL) finely chopped parsley
Salt to taste
4 cups (1 L) hot cooked rice

Fry the bacon in a skillet and, when it is crisp, drain on paper towels. If the skillet is very hot, let it cool down a bit. Put it over medium heat and cook the celery, onion, and green pepper in the bacon fat until the onion is soft. Add the garlic, tomatoes, cayenne pepper, chili powder, and thyme. Lower the heat and simmer 20 minutes. Add the shrimp, parsley, and salt to the tomato sauce and cook for a few minutes until the shrimp is hot. Mound the rice on a platter, spoon the shrimp and tomato sauce over it, and garnish with bits of crisp bacon.

Fried Shrimp (serves six)

Serve with Chili Sauce (p. 160) or Tartar Sauce (p. 168).

1 cup (140 g) flour
½ teaspoon salt
½ teaspoon sugar
1 egg
2 tablespoons oil
2½ pounds (1¼ kg) raw shrimp
Oil for frying

Preheat the oven to 225°F (110°C) and warm an ovenproof platter. Beat the flour, salt, sugar, egg, 2 tablespoons oil, and 1 cup ice water in a bowl and refrigerate. Shell and devein the shrimp. Pat the shrimp dry with paper towels. Heat 3 inches of oil to 365°F (185°C) in a heavy pot or skillet. Dip each shrimp into the batter and drop into the hot oil. Don't crowd the pot. Do a few at a time, frying for about 1 minute or until golden. Proceed until all the shrimp are fried, draining each batch and keeping warm on the platter in the oven.

Meat

Tenderloin Roast
(allow ⅓ pound per serving)

The tenderloin or fillet of beef is very costly because it is the tenderest part of the steer, but you are buying 4–6 pounds of pure meat with no bones and fat to discard.

1 whole tenderloin
¼ cup (½ dL) vegetable oil or butter; or thin
  strips beef fat or blanched salt pork

Preheat the oven to 450°F (230°C). Have the meat at room temperature and place it on a rack in an open shallow pan, tucking the thin end under to make it as thick as the rest of the roast. Brush the meat with vegetable oil, dot with butter, or lay strips of fat over the top. Roast for about 30–35 minutes. A meat thermometer will show 130°F for rare, 140° for medium, and 160° for well done. Take the roast from the oven when the thermometer reads 5 degrees short of the desired temperature. Place the meat on a warm platter, cover loosely with a towel or foil, and let sit for 15 minutes. It will be fork-tender and easy to slice.

London Broil (serves four)

A chewy, flavorful cut of meat that becomes tender when it is carved diagonally across the grain into thin slices. A hearty marinade aids the tenderizing process.

1 clove garlic, peeled (optional)
1½ pounds (675 g) flank steak
1½ tablespoons vegetable oil
Salt
Freshly ground pepper

Preheat the broiler. If you want a garlic flavor, rub the clove of garlic vigorously on both sides of the steak. Rub with oil and place the meat on a rack over a drip pan. Broil 1½ inches beneath the broiling element 4–5 minutes each side for medium, 3–4 for medium-rare. Remove, sprinkle with salt and pepper, and slice as directed above.

Marinated London Broil. Early in the day, mix ¾ *cup red wine, ¼ cup oil, 1 small onion, chopped, 1 tablespoon oregano, crumbled,* and *1 teaspoon salt*. Marinate the steak in this mixture until ready to cook. Remove, pat dry with paper towels, and follow the recipe, elminating the salt, pepper, and garlic.

Pepper Steak (serves four)

A lively way to serve tender steaks, and an exception to the rule against seasoning before cooking.

4 shell or fillet steaks, about ½ pound (225 g) each
1 teaspoon salt
3 tablespoons peppercorns, coarsely crushed
3 tablespoons butter
1 tablespoon oil
4 tablespoons bourbon

Heat the oven to 225°F (110°C) and warm an oven-proof platter. Rub the steaks with salt. Sprinkle with the peppercorns and use a meat pounder or the bottom of a pot to pound the pepper into the steak. Turn the meat over, and repeat seasoning on the other side. Heat the butter and oil in a heavy skillet and sauté the steaks about 4 minutes on each side. Transfer to the warm platter. Add the bourbon and 2 tablespoons water to the skillet and cook rapidly, stirring and scraping, to incorporate the bits of meat and fat in the pan. Boil down for 1 minute and spoon the sauce over the steaks.

Pot Roast (serves eight to ten)

The secret of tender pot roasts lies in keeping the heat below the boil. Violent boiling toughens meat fibers. Cooking ahead allows you to chill the meat and remove the fat on the surface; chilled meat is also easy to slice.

2 tablespoons flour
1½ teaspoons salt
½ teaspoon freshly ground pepper

81

4–5 pounds (2–2¼ kg) boneless chuck or rump
   roast
3 tablespoons shortening
1 onion, sliced
2 teaspoons thyme, crumbled
1 cup (¼ L) tomato juice
¼–½ teaspoon Tabasco

Combine the flour, salt, and pepper. Rub it all over
the roast. Melt the shortening in a heavy casserole
with a lid or a Dutch oven. When the shortening is
hot, add the roast and brown it to a deep rich color
on all sides. Lower the heat and add the onion,
thyme, tomato juice, and Tabasco. Cover and simmer for 3–3½ hours, turning once or twice during
the cooking. When fork-tender, cool. Remove the
fat, slice the meat, and reheat in the degreased
sauce, or skim off the fat, reheat, and bring to the
table to carve.

Beef à la Mode (serves ten)

Call it pot roast, braised beef, or beef à la mode,
but the process is the same: long, slow cooking
in liquid tenderizes and flavors a tough cut of
meat. The savory sauce is the bonus.

⅛ pound (60 g) salt pork, cut in small dice
2 tablespoons flour
4 pounds (1¾ kg) boneless round or chuck roast
⅓ cup (¾ dL) diced carrot
⅓ cup (¾ dL) diced turnip
⅓ cup (¾ dL) diced celery
Salt

Freshly ground pepper
3 sprigs parsley
1 bay leaf

Place a Dutch oven or heavy pot with a lid over medium-high heat. Add the salt pork and cook, stirring often, until the bits are crisp and golden. Remove and drain on paper towels, leaving fat from the pork on the bottom of the pot. Flour the beef on all sides and brown in the melted pork fat. Remove and set aside. Spread the diced vegetables on the bottom of the pot. Place the beef on top and sprinkle with salt and pepper. Add the parsley, bay leaf, and 2 cups of water. Cover closely and simmer for 3 hours. Remove the meat. Slice it and sprinkle with bits of salt pork. Strain the juices, spoon some over the meat, and serve the rest as a sauce.

New England Boiled Dinner
(serves six to eight)

Serve this American classic with Mustard Sauce (p. 159), corn muffins, and sweet butter. Plan for some leftovers for corned beef hash.

4–5 pounds (2–2¼ kg) corned beef brisket
4 medium onions, outer skins removed
6 medium potatoes, peeled
8 small young beets
6 carrots, scrubbed and peeled
6 small turnips, scrubbed
1 medium head green cabbage, quartered and cored

Rinse the corned beef under cold running water to remove the brine. Place in a large pot, cover with cold water, and bring to a boil, skimming off the scum that rises to the surface during the first 10 minutes. Cover and simmer for 2 hours. Then add the onions and potatoes, and continue to simmer. Meanwhile, bring a quantity of water to boil in another saucepan and add the beets. Boil them for 30–40 minutes, or until they are barely tender when pierced with a knife. Drain and put them in a 250°F (120°C) oven to keep warm. When the onions and potatoes have cooked for 15 minutes, add the carrots and turnips to the pot and simmer for 30 minutes more. Remove and slice the meat and arrange, surrounded by vegetables, on an ovenproof platter. Place in the warm oven, along with the dish of beets. Turn up the heat under the broth and, when it boils, add the cabbage. Boil for 3 minutes, drain, and place in a separate serving bowl. Serve the beef surrounded by carrots, turnips, onions, and potatoes, with the beets and cabbage in separate bowls.

Beef Stroganoff (serves six)

Tender beef in a lightly tangy sauce with the flavor of mushrooms: good over brown rice. If your pocketbook can't manage tenderloin, try making it with thin slices of flank steak, cut diagonally across the grain, or very rare leftover roast beef or steak. Incidentally, if you freeze the meat for an hour or so—just enough for it to firm up—it will be easier to slice thin.

6 tablespoons butter
2 tablespoons minced onion
2 pounds (900 g) beef tenderloin, cut thin in 1 ×
   2½-inch strips
½ pound (225 g) mushrooms, sliced
Salt to taste
Freshly ground pepper to taste
⅛ teaspoon nutmeg
1 cup (¼ L) sour cream, at room temperature

Melt 3 tablespoons of the butter in a heavy skillet. Add the onion and cook slowly until transparent. Remove and set aside. Turn the heat to medium-high, add the beef, and cook briefly, turning to brown on all sides. Remove the beef and set aside with the onions. Add the remaining 3 tablespoons butter to the skillet. Stir in the mushrooms, cover, and cook 3 minutes. Season with salt, pepper, and nutmeg. Whisk the sour cream and add to the pan, but do not allow it to boil. Return the beef and onions to the pan and just heat through.

Hungarian Goulash (serves four)

Goulash can resemble stew or soup: this one must be eaten in bowls with a spoon to manage its abundant paprika and onion sauce.

3 tablespoons butter
1 onion, chopped
2 tablespoons sweet Hungarian paprika
2 pounds (900 g) beef round, in 1½-inch cubes
2 tablespoons flour
Salt

¾ teaspoon marjoram, crumbled
4 cups (1 L) beef broth
1½ cups (3½ dL) potato cubes
1½ tablespoons lemon juice

Melt the butter in a covered casserole. Add the onion, stir, and cook until soft. Stir in the paprika and
cook slowly 1–2 minutes. Roll the meat in flour and
add to the onion, cooking only long enough to
brown lightly. Sprinkle with a little salt, and add
marjoram. Pour in broth and bring to a boil. Cover
and simmer for about 1 hour, or until tender. Add
the potato cubes and cook 15–20 minutes, until
done. Remove from heat, stir in the lemon juice,
and add more salt if necessary.

Old-fashioned Beef Stew (serves four)

A stew you will serve in soupbowls: dark-brown
beef and vegetables in lots of rich gravy.

⅓ cup (50 g) flour
1 teaspoon salt
¼ teaspoon freshly ground pepper
2 pounds (900 g) stewing beef plus bones
4 tablespoons shortening
1 tablespoon lemon juice
1 tablespoon Worcestershire sauce
1 large onion, sliced
2 bay leaves
¼ teaspoon allspice
12 small carrots, trimmed and scraped
12 small white onions, trimmed
8 small new potatoes, peeled

Mix the flour, salt, and pepper and roll the beef cubes in the mixture. Shake off excess. Melt the shortening over high heat in a Dutch oven or heavy-bottomed pot with a cover. When the fat is very hot add the beef, about 5 or 6 pieces at a time so as not to crowd them, brown on all sides, and remove. When the last batch of meat is a richly dark color, return all to the pot and pour on 4 cups boiling water. Stand back when you do it, because it will spit and sputter. Stir and add the lemon juice, Worcestershire sauce, onion, bay leaves, and allspice. Lower the heat, cover, and simmer for 1½–2 hours, or until the meat is tender. Add the carrots, onions, and potatoes and cook another 20–25 minutes or until they can be pierced easily with a fork.

Burgundy Beef (serves four)

Beef and red wine just seem to go together. Steamed potatoes, salad, and crusty bread finish off the meal.

⅛ pound (60 g) salt pork, diced fine
1 large onion, chopped
3 tablespoons flour
½ teaspoon salt
¼ teaspoon freshly ground pepper
2 pounds (900 g) stewing beef plus bones
½ teaspoon marjoram, crumbled
1 teaspoon thyme, crumbled
1 cup (¼ L) Burgundy or other red wine
1 cup (¼ L) beef broth

12 small white onions, trimmed and peeled
½ pound (225 g) mushrooms

Melt the salt pork over medium heat in a heavy Dutch oven or covered casserole. When crisp and golden, remove and drain on paper towels. Add the chopped onions to the melted fat in the pan, slowly cook them to a light golden brown, remove, and set aside. Mix the flour, salt, and pepper on a dinner plate and roll the meat in the mixture. Brown the beef, a few pieces at a time, and add the marjoram, thyme, wine, and beef broth. Return the pork and onions to the pot, cover, and simmer for 1½ hours. Add the small onions and cook 20 minutes, then add the mushrooms and cook 10 minutes more. Correct seasoning. When the onions are fork-tender, the stew is done.

Braised Short Ribs (serves four)

Meat with lots of bone makes an especially tasty and juicy stew, and you have the fun of nibbling at the bones! Serve with big napkins.

3 tablespoons flour
1½ teaspoons salt
½ teaspoon freshly ground pepper
4 pounds (1¾ kg) beef short ribs
4 tablespoons shortening
8 small carrots, scraped
2 large onions, peeled and quartered
1 cup (¾ L) sliced celery
4 parsley sprigs

2 bay leaves
1 teaspoon marjoram, crumbled
1 cup (¼ L) red wine

Preheat the oven to 350°F (180°C). Combine the flour, salt, and pepper in a brown paper bag. Shake the short ribs in the bag with the flour, coating it on all sides. Melt the shortening in a heavy casserole or Dutch oven. When it is hot, add the meat and brown to a rich dark color. Pour off the fat in the pan, reduce the heat, and add 1 cup water and remaining ingredients. Cover and cook in the oven for 1½–2 hours. Since this is very fatty meat, it is good to chill it and remove the fat if there is time. Then reheat to serve.

Meat Loaf (serves eight)

A hearty family meal, susceptible to many variations. The second day, slice it thin and make sandwiches on rye bread with sweet pickles.

2 cups (½ L) freshly made bread crumbs
1 onion, chopped fine
2 eggs, slightly beaten
2 pounds (900 g) ground beef
2 tablespoons Worcestershire sauce
1½ teaspoons dry mustard
1½ teaspoons salt
½ teaspoon freshly ground pepper
¾ cup (1¾ dL) milk

Preheat the oven to 350°F (180°C). Butter a loaf pan. Combine all the ingredients in a large bowl;

your freshly washed hands are the best tools for the job. Pat into the loaf pan and bake for 45 minutes.

Meat Loaf with Parsley and Tomato. Omit the Worcestershire sauce and mustard; in place of the milk, use ¾ *cup of juice from a can of tomatoes* and add ¼ *cup minced parsley* plus ½ *teaspoon basil, crumbled.* Pat into pan and cover with ¾ *cup of the tomatoes* from the can, roughly chopped, or ¾ *cup tomato sauce.*

Meat Loaf with Cheese. Omit the Worcestershire sauce and add ½ *cup grated cheese.*

Meat Loaf with Bacon. After patting the loaf into the pan, cover with *4 strips uncooked bacon.*

Meat Loaf with Three Meats. Instead of 2 pounds ground beef, use *1 pound ground beef* mixed with ⅔ *pound ground veal* and ⅓ *pound ground pork. Red wine* may be used instead of milk if desired. Bake 1 hour.

Individual Muffin-Size Meat Loaves. Instead of using a loaf pan, pack the meat into muffin tins or Pyrex baking cups, top each with a square of *bacon,* and bake for only 25 minutes at 400°F (205°C). Turn out and serve with *tomato sauce.*

Chili con Carne (serves six)

In Texas, where this dish originated, strong men have been known to do battle over the proper way to cook chili con carne. This recipe can be made with ground beef, but cubed beef has more character. Serve in the traditional manner, with red pinto beans and fluffy rice.

2 pounds (900 g) beef chuck, in 1-inch cubes
2 tablespoons flour
4 tablespoons shortening
2 cloves garlic, minced
2 tablespoons chili powder
Salt

Roll the beef cubes in the flour. Heat the shortening in a heavy pot or covered skillet and brown the meat, turning to color it on all sides. Lower the heat, add the garlic, and cook for 1 minute, stirring so that it doesn't burn. Add 1 cup water and the chili powder, stirring to blend. Cover and simmer for 2 hours. Add salt to taste.

Cannelon of Beef (serves six)

This moist loaf will be dense, smooth-textured, and easy to slice.

2 pounds (900 g) lean ground beef
Grated rind of ½ lemon
2 tablespoons minced parsley
1 egg
2 tablespoons minced onion
2 tablespoons butter, melted
1 teaspoon nutmeg
½ teaspoon salt
¼ teaspoon freshly ground pepper
4 slices salt pork
1 recipe Mushroom Sauce (p. 153)

91

Preheat the oven to 400°F (205°C). Combine the beef, lemon rind, parsley, egg, onion, melted butter, nutmeg, salt, and pepper (you can do it all in a food processor). Mix until very well blended. Chill, then shape into a roll 6 inches long. Place on a rack in a roasting pan, arrange the slices of salt pork over the top, and bake for 30 minutes. Remove to a warm platter. Serve with the mushroom sauce, garnished with the salt pork cut into small dice.

Swedish Meatballs   (30 meatballs)

These small meatballs, faintly flavored with allspice and nutmeg in a creamy sauce, would be good at a cocktail buffet speared with toothpicks. They are equally good served six to a person over noodles for dinner.

1 pound (450 g) lean beef
¼ pound (115 g) salt pork
5 slices whole-wheat bread
1 egg, lightly beaten
1 teaspoon sugar
¾ teaspoon allspice
¾ teaspoon nutmeg
½ teaspoon salt
¼ teaspoon freshly ground pepper
2 tablespoons shortening
1½ cups (3½ dL) beef broth
½ cup (1 dL) heavy cream

Preheat the oven to 325°F (165°C). Grind the beef, salt pork, and bread together twice, using a meat grinder or food processor. Combine with the egg, sugar, allspice, nutmeg, salt, and pepper. Shape into 1-inch balls. Melt the shortening in a skillet and brown the meatballs. Transfer to a shallow casserole, pour on the beef broth, cover with foil, and bake for 45 minutes. Add the cream and cook without a cover for 15 minutes more.

Meatballs in Sauce for Spaghetti (serves four to six)

This family favorite is particularly good made from scratch with your own homemade tomato sauce, prepared only yesterday or frozen months earlier when tomatoes were ripe and plentiful.

1 pound (450 g) ground beef
½ cup (1 dL) dried bread crumbs
1 clove garlic, minced
2 tablespoons minced parsley
1 tablespoon basil, crumbled
1 egg, lightly beaten
½ teaspoon salt
¼ teaspoon freshly ground pepper
2 tablespoons oil
4 cups (1 L) Tomato Sauce (p. 154)
½ pound (225 g) grated Parmesan cheese

Combine the beef, bread crumbs, garlic, parsley, basil, egg, salt, and pepper. Mix thoroughly and shape into balls 1½ inches in diameter. Melt the oil in a saucepan. Brown the meatballs lightly on all sides; drain off the fat. Add the tomato sauce, cover, and simmer 40 minutes. Serve over spaghetti, and pass the grated cheese.

Beef, Brown Rice, and Feta
Casserole (serves four)

6 large dried mushrooms, or ¼ cup (½ dL) pieces
1 onion, chopped
1 tablespoon oil
1½ cups (3½ dL) canned tomatoes
1 clove garlic, minced
Salt
Freshly ground pepper
2 cups (½ L) cooked brown rice
1½ cups (3½ dL) cooked beef in medium chunks
3 ounces (90 g) feta cheese, crumbled
6 black olives, pitted and sliced
2 tablespoons grated Parmesan cheese

Put the dried mushrooms in ½ cup hot water and let stand 20 minutes. Sauté the onion in the oil slowly for 5 minutes, then add the tomatoes and garlic, and let cook gently uncovered about 10 minutes. Salt and pepper to taste, then add the dried mushrooms, cut in quarters if large, with any tough stems removed, and the mushroom soaking liquid. Cook another 5 minutes. Preheat oven to 400°F (205°C). Line the bottom of 1½-quart casserole with 1 cup of the rice, add the cooked beef, and strew over the top the feta cheese, the olives, and half the sauce. Add the remaining rice and the rest of the sauce, and sprinkle with Parmesan. Bake 20 minutes.

Oven-roasted Veal (serves six to eight)

If you have your butcher remove the bone, you can fill the cavity with any desired stuffing, such as Savory Bread Stuffing (p. 163). A 6-pound roast will then serve eight or ten hungry people.

Pork fat for barding, or 6 tablespoons oil
4–6 pound (1¾–2¾-kg) veal roast, leg or loin
1 recipe Onion Sauce (p. 151)

Preheat the oven to 325°F (165°C). Tie strips of fat over the roast or rub it with oil. Place meat on a rack in a shallow pan in the oven. Roast 30 minutes per pound, basting frequently with drippings, until the veal registers 160°F on a meat thermometer. Serve with the sauce.

Braised Veal Chops (serves six)

2 tablespoons butter
2 tablespoons vegetable oil
6 veal chops (¾ inch thick)
Salt
Freshly ground pepper
¾ cup (1¾ dL) cream

Heat the butter and oil in a frying pan large enough to accommodate the chops. Brown the meat 2–3 minutes on each side; if this cannot be done without crowding, brown a few chops at a time. Return all the meat to the pan. Season with salt and pepper to taste, add the cream, cover, and cook over low heat. This will take anywhere from 20 minutes for

95

tender young chops to 40 minutes for tough older ones. Serve with pan juices.

Braised Veal Chops with Mushrooms. Before adding the cream, toss in *¾ pound quartered mushrooms*. Saute briefly, then add the cream.

Braised Veal Chops with Vegetables. Parboil *16 small white onions*. When the chops are brown, remove and set aside. Pat the onions dry and brown lightly in the pan. Return the chops, omitting the cream and adding instead *½ cup chicken broth*. Cover and cook until tender, adding up to *¼ cup chicken broth* if needed. Serve, sprinkled with *1 tablespoon grated lemon peel*. Or, instead of the onions, cut *1 fennel bulb* into julienne strips (these will not require parboiling). Toss into the pan and cook gently.

Braised Veal Chops with Artichoke Hearts. Parboil *1 package frozen artichoke hearts,* drain, and pat dry. Add to the pan along with *¾ cup diced carrots* and *½ cup chopped scallions* and cook for 1 minute. Omit the cream and add *½ cup chicken broth* and *2 tablespoons butter*. Cover and cook until tender, adding up to *¼ cup chicken broth* if needed. Serve, sprinkled with *¼ cup chopped parsley*.

Breaded Veal Cutlets (serves four)

3 tablespoons flour
2 eggs, lightly beaten
1½ cups (3½ dL) bread crumbs
1 teaspoon salt

½ teaspoon freshly ground pepper
1 pound (450 g) veal cutlets, about ¼–⅓ inch thick, pounded
1½ tablespoons butter
1½ tablespoons oil
1 tablespoon finely chopped parsley
1 lemon, in 4 wedges

Put the flour, eggs, and crumbs in three separate shallow dishes. Mix the salt and pepper into the crumbs. Dip the cutlets one at a time into the flour, shaking off any excess, then into the beaten eggs, letting any excess drip off. Then drag the cutlet lightly through the seasoned crumbs. Set aside for 15 minutes so that the coating can dry. Heat the butter and oil in a skillet, and fry the cutlets over medium heat, 3–5 minutes on each side, or until brown and cooked through. Sprinkle with parsley and serve with lemon wedges.

Veal Cutlets in Wine (serves three)

1 pound (450 g) veal cutlets
1 tablespoon butter
1 tablespoon oil
2 tablespoons finely chopped onion
1 tablespoon chopped parsley
2 tablespoons finely chopped ham
1 clove garlic, split
¼ cup (½ dL) dry red wine

Pound the veal cutlets with a meat mallet or the edge of a saucer until they are ¼ inch thick. Melt the butter and oil in a skillet. Add the cutlets and

97

brown lightly on both sides. Add the onion, parsley, ham, and garlic. Cover and simmer for 20 minutes. Add the wine and ¼ cup water, cover, and cook 10 minutes more. Remove the veal and keep warm in the oven. Boil down the pan juices to reduce by a third, and pour over the meat before serving.

Scaloppine of Veal Marsala
(serves three)

1 pound (450 g) veal cutlets, trimmed and
   pounded thin
⅓ cup (¾ dL) freshly grated Parmesan cheese
3 tablespoons butter
1 tablespoon oil
1 clove garlic, peeled
¼ cup (½ dL) beef broth
¼ cup (½ dL) Marsala wine

Cut the veal into 2-inch pieces. Dip in Parmesan cheese to coat both sides. Melt the butter and oil in a skillet, add the garlic and the veal, and cook until lightly browned on both sides. Discard the garlic. Remove the veal to a warm platter. Turn the heat up and add the beef broth, stirring and scraping the bits of meat clinging to the bottom of the skillet. Cook 1 minute over high heat, then add the wine and cook 1 minute more. Pour over the veal and serve.

Blanquette of Veal (serves six)

Serve gently sautéed spring vegetables and fried bread triangles or rice with this creamy veal stew.

2 pounds (900 g) stewing veal in 2-inch pieces
6 small white onions
1 medium onion, stuck with 2 cloves
2 carrots, in thick slices
1 bay leaf
2 teaspoons thyme, crumbled
3 tablespoons butter
3 tablespoons flour
3 egg yolks
Juice of 1 lemon
¼ teaspoon nutmeg
Salt
Freshly ground pepper

Put the veal into a pot and cover with cold water. Add the small onions, onion with cloves, carrots, bay leaf, and thyme. Bring to a boil, then simmer, covered, for 1½ hours or until tender. Skim off the scum as it rises. Remove the meat and keep warm. Strain the broth. Melt the butter in a saucepan. Stir in the flour and cook over medium heat for a few minutes, then slowly add 3 cups of the veal broth. Stir constantly over medium heat until well blended, smooth, and thick. In a separate bowl, beat the egg yolks with the lemon juice. Pour a spoonful or two of the hot sauce into the egg mixture, then remove the sauce from the heat and briskly stir the egg mixture into the remaining sauce. Add nutmeg, salt and pepper to taste, put the meat in a serving dish, and pour the sauce over it.

Veal Loaf (serves six)

Expensive milk-fed veal is not necessary for this dish.

2 pounds (900 g) ground veal
½ pound (225 g) ground pork
½ green pepper, chopped fine
1 onion, chopped fine
1 tablespoon lemon juice
1 teaspoon salt
½ cup (1 dL) cracker crumbs
1 egg
½ cup (1 dL) milk
2 teaspoons Worcestershire sauce

Preheat the oven to 325°F (165°C). Combine all ingredients and mix until well blended, using a large spoon or your hands. Press into a loaf pan. Cover with foil and bake for 40 minutes. Uncover and bake 20 minutes more to brown the top.

Vitello Tonnato (serves six)

This Italian favorite (it means veal tuna) makes a marvelous summer dish, lovely with an accompanying platter of freshly sliced tomatoes, cucumbers, blanched green beans. You can also substitute an equal amount of skinned turkey breast for the veal.

12-ounce (340-g) can oil-packed tuna
3 pounds (1⅓ kg) boned veal roast
1 onion, chopped
2 carrots, chopped
2 ribs celery, chopped
2 bay leaves
½ teaspoon thyme, crumbled
2 tablespoons anchovy fillets, drained and
  mashed
1½ cups (3½ dL) chicken broth
3 tablespoons lemon juice
1 cup (¼ L) homemade Mayonnaise (p. 282)
3 tablespoons capers, drained
Salt

Heat a heavy casserole and add the oil drained from the can of tuna, then sear the meat, browning on all sides. Remove and set aside. Add a little vegetable oil to the pan if less than 3 tablespoons remain, and cook the onion, carrots, and celery in it, stirring often, until soft. Add the bay leaves, thyme, mashed anchovy fillets, chicken broth, and lemon juice, and mix well. Add the meat, cover, and lower heat to simmer; cook for about 1 hour, or until tender. Remove the meat, cover, and refrigerate until needed. Meanwhile turn the heat up to reduce the juices in the casserole until quite thick. Remove from the heat and cool. Put the reduced juices and vegetables through a food mill or processor to purée along with the mayonnaise, tuna, capers, and salt to taste. Refrigerate until ready to serve. Slice the meat rather thin and spoon some of the sauce over. Pass remaining sauce in a bowl.

Roast Leg of Lamb   (serves six)

Allow about a pound per person when cooking a leg of lamb with the bone in; if it has no bone, a 4-pound roast will serve twice as many people.

5–6-pound (2¼–2¾-kg) leg of lamb
Oil
Salt
Freshly ground pepper
½ teaspoon rosemary, crumbled
2 cloves garlic, in slivers (optional)

Preheat the oven to 350°F (180°C). Have the meat at room temperature. Place the lamb, fat side up, in a shallow open roasting pan. Rub with oil, salt, pepper, and the rosemary. If using garlic (and it's delicious with lamb) make 8–10 slits in the meat with the point of a paring knife, and tuck a sliver of garlic into each slit. Roast for about 1½ hours, or until a meat thermometer registers 145°F for medium-rare, 165°F for well done. Let the roast rest for 5–10 minutes, then carve at the table.

Shish Kebab   (serves eight)

Start your marinade early in the day or the night before. Shish kebab is at its best if it can be cooked over coals, but if that isn't possible, broiling works very well. You cannot, incidentally, use cheaper cuts because they'll be too tough cooked this way. Be sure to push the cubes of meat together on the skewer, so they do not dry out while they cook. Try separate skewers of vegetables—the cooking time will be different from the lamb. Serve with rice.

1 leg of lamb, boned, in 1½-inch cubes
2 medium onions, sliced
2 teaspoons salt
½ teaspoon freshly ground pepper
½ cup (1 dL) dry sherry
1 tablespoon vegetable oil
⅛ teaspoon oregano, crumbled

Trim most of the fat from the meat. Mix remaining ingredients in a small bowl and blend well. Spread the meat in a shallow dish and cover with the marinade, tossing so meat is well coated. Cover the dish with foil and refrigerate several hours or overnight. When you are ready to cook, place the lamb on skewers, pushing the pieces snugly together. Cook over charcoal or place on a rack 3 inches under the broiler and broil 4–5 minutes on each side. Serve either on the skewers or pushed off on a plate.

Shish Kebab with Vegetables. On two separate skewers, place *4 small onions, parboiled 5 minutes, 4 large mushrooms, 4 cherry tomatoes or tomato quarters, 4 squares green pepper,* and *4 chunks canned pineapple* or other vegetables. Brush with *1 tablespoon oil* and cook for 2 minutes on each side. Serve with the skewers of lamb.

103

Fricassee of Lamb (serves six)

A succulent dish to serve with parslied boiled potatoes.

2 pounds (900 g) boneless shoulder of lamb, in 1½-inch cubes
2 tablespoons flour
2 tablespoons vegetable shortening
2 cups (½ L) boiling tomato juice
1 medium onion, chopped
2 carrots, chopped
4 parsley sprigs, chopped
1 bay leaf
4 cloves
Salt
Freshly ground pepper

Trim off most of the lamb fat. Dust the lamb cubes with the flour. Melt the shortening in a heavy pot with a cover or a Dutch oven. Brown the lamb pieces on all sides. Pour the boiling tomato juice over the meat, then add the onion, carrots, parsley, bay leaf, and cloves. Lower the heat, cover, and simmer for 1½–2 hours, or until lamb is very tender. Salt and pepper to taste. Remove the bay leaf and serve.

Irish Stew (serves six)

The simple goodness of lamb and roast vegetables tasting of themselves. Try that fine old-fashioned twosome—Irish Stew and Dumplings (p. 133).

2 pounds (900 g) boneless shoulder of lamb, in
    1½-inch cubes
2 tablespoons shortening
1 cup (¼ L) ½-inch carrot slices
1 cup (¼ L) cubed white turnip
1 potato, peeled and cubed
1 onion, sliced
Salt to taste
Freshly ground pepper

Take care to trim off most of the lamb fat. Melt the shortening in a heavy pot, add the lamb cubes, and brown them well on all sides. Stand back while you pour 2 cups of boiling water over the lamb—it will sizzle and sputter. Cover and simmer for 1 hour. Add the carrot, turnip, potatoes, onion, salt and pepper, cover, and simmer 30 minutes more. Taste, correct for seasoning, and serve.

Braised Lamb Shanks (serves four)

The meat on lamb shanks is particularly succulent from lying close to the bone. You will need one per person because there is not actually much meat on them.

4 lamb shanks
2 fat cloves garlic, each in 8 slivers
2 tablespoons flour
3 tablespoons shortening
1 bay leaf
1 tablespoon grated lemon rind
⅓ cup (¾ dL) lemon juice

Salt
Freshly ground pepper
4 carrots, in ½-inch pieces
8 small onions, peeled

Cut four slits in the flesh of each lamb shank; insert a sliver of garlic in each slit. Lightly dust the shanks with flour. Heat the shortening in a Dutch oven or a heavy pot with a lid. Put the shanks in and brown on all sides. Remove all but 1 tablespoon fat. Add the bay leaf, lemon rind, lemon juice, and ¼ cup water, and sprinkle salt and pepper over all. Lower the heat, cover, and simmer for 1½–2 hours, depending on the tenderness of the shanks. Add the carrots and onions for the last 40 minutes of cooking. Remove shanks and vegetables to a platter and keep warm. Serve with the pot juices.

Lamb Curry   (serves six)

A mild curry: add more curry powder if a spicy dish is desired. If you use leftover lamb, substitute beef broth for the lamb broth. Serve with rice and chutney.

2 pounds (900 g) boned lean lamb, in 1½-inch cubes
3 onions, sliced
1 teaspoon thyme, crumbled
2 parsley sprigs
3 tablespoons butter
3 tablespoons flour
2 teaspoons curry powder

Salt
Freshly ground pepper

Put the meat in a heavy pot with a lid or a Dutch oven and cover with 1 quart of boiling water. Add the onions, thyme, and parsley. Simmer for 1 hour, skimming the scum that rises to the top during the first 15 minutes. Remove the meat, strain the liquid, and set aside. In a skillet, melt the butter and gradually stir in the flour and curry powder. Cook over low heat, stirring constantly, for 3 minutes. Slowly add the lamb broth and stir. Add salt and pepper to taste, and cook, stirring, for several minutes, until the sauce thickens.

Moussaka (serves six to eight)

Pronounced "*moo*-sah-kah," this is a traditional Greek dish. Make it with either uncooked or leftover lamb. For best results when frying eggplant, see p. 236.

6 tablespoons vegetable oil
¼ cup (½ dL) chopped onion
1 pound (450 g) fresh or cooked ground lamb
½ teaspoon allspice
½ teaspoon salt
½ teaspoon freshly ground pepper
1 cup (¼ L) tomato sauce
3 eggplants
3 eggs, lightly beaten
2 cups (½ L) light cream
2 tablespoons minced parsley

107

1 cup (¼ L) freshly made dry bread crumbs
4 tablespoons butter, melted

Preheat the oven to 350°F (180°C). Grease a 2½-quart baking dish. Heat 2 tablespoons of the oil in a skillet, add the onion, and cook, stirring, until soft. If using fresh lamb, add to the onion and cook, stirring, until most of the pinkness disappears. Add the allspice, salt, pepper, and tomato sauce to the skillet, along with the cooked lamb if you are using it. Cover and simmer for 30 minutes. Heat the remaining 4 tablespoons of oil in a skillet. Cut the eggplants into ¼-inch slices. Have the oil very hot, and quickly brown each side of the eggplant slices, then pat them dry of excess oil. Mix the eggs, cream, parsley, and ½ cup of the bread crumbs. Put a layer of eggplant on the bottom of the casserole and spread a layer of the lamb mixture over it. Continue layering, ending with eggplant on top. Pour the egg mixture over all, sprinkle the remaining ½ cup of crumbs on top, and drizzle the butter over. Bake 40 minutes or until the egg custard is set.

Roast Pork (serves four)

Ask the butcher to cut through the chine bone, and the roast will be easy to carve. If you want to do a 5- to 7-pound roast, it will need three or more hours of cooking time. Serve with hot applesauce and horseradish.

4-pound (1¾-kg) loin of pork
Salt

Freshly ground pepper
½ teaspoon thyme, crumbled

Preheat the oven to 350°F (180°C). Put the roast, fat side up, on a rack in a shallow open pan. Rub lightly with salt, pepper, and thyme. Roast 1¾–2 hours, or until the internal temperature is 160°F. Remove from the oven and let rest for 15 minutes for easy carving.

Pork Tenderloin Teriyaki   (serves six)

Add flavor to pork tenderloin with this Oriental marinade, mixed early in the day.

4 tablespoons soy sauce
1 clove garlic, minced
½ teaspoon freshly ground pepper
2 teaspoons light-brown sugar
2 tablespoons olive oil
1 teaspoon ground ginger
2 pork tenderloins, about ¾ pound (340 g) each

Combine the soy sauce, garlic, pepper, brown sugar, oil, and ginger in a jar. Cover tightly and shake until all the ingredients are well blended. Pour over the tenderloins and let them marinate for several hours. Drain and place on a rack over a shallow pan 4 inches beneath the broiler element. Broil for 12–15 minutes. Slice and serve.

Skillet-fried Pork Chops (serves six)

Fried pork chops retain their tenderness and moisture when they aren't cooked to death. Cook ½-inch chops 5 minutes each side; ¾-inch chops only 8 minutes; 1-inch chops 10 minutes a side. Anything thicker should be lightly browned and then braised in liquid. All are especially nice served with a snowdrift of mashed potatoes.

6 pork chops, cut ½–¾ inch thick
2 tablespoons flour
Salt
Freshly ground pepper
3 tablespoons shortening
½ cup (1 dL) cider or chicken broth

Lightly dust the pork chops with flour, shaking off the excess. Sprinkle with salt and pepper. Heat the shortening in the skillet and brown the chops over medium heat for 5–8 minutes, as directed above. Remove to a warm platter. Pour off all but 2 tablespoons of fat. Splash in the cider or broth, cook down 1 minute, and spoon over the chops.

Braised Pork Chops with Sweet Potatoes (serves six)

4 sweet potatoes
6 pork chops, cut 1½ inches thick
2 tablespoons flour
Salt

Freshly ground pepper
3 tablespoons shortening

Parboil the sweet potatoes for 20 minutes in boiling water. Peel, cut into ½-inch slices, and set aside. Lightly dust the chops with flour, shaking off the excess. Sprinkle with salt and pepper. Melt the shortening in the skillet and brown the chops over medium-high heat for 1 minute on each side. Add the sweet potatoes to the pan, cover, and cook over medium heat for 30 minutes.

Braised Pork Chops with Apples. Omit the sweet potatoes and add *4 apples, peeled, cored, and sliced,* to the chops in the skillet.

Braised Pork Chops with Cabbage. Omit the sweet potatoes and add *4 cups finely shredded cabbage and ½ teaspoon caraway seeds* to the chops in the skillet.

Braised Pork Chops with Sauerkraut. Omit the sweet potatoes and add *2 cups sauerkraut* and *6 juniper berries* to the chops in the skillet.

Rib Chops with Celery Stuffing and Apples (serves six)

Apples and meat juices add flavor to the stuffing.

2 tablespoons shortening
6 thick rib pork chops, trimmed
Salt
Freshly ground pepper

1 recipe Celery Stuffing (p. 166)
3 firm red apples, cored and halved

Preheat the oven to 350°F (180°C). Grease a 1½-quart covered casserole. Melt the shortening in a skillet and brown the chops on each side. Sprinkle with salt and pepper. Spread the stuffing on the bottom of the casserole and place the browned pork chops over it. Put one half-apple, cut side down, on top of each pork chop. Cover snugly and bake about 45 minutes.

Barbecued Spareribs (serves six)

Marinate these ribs for several hours before cooking.

1¼ cups (3 dL) tomato juice
2 tablespoons soy sauce
¾ cup (1¾ dL) vinegar
1 teaspoon dry mustard
1 tablespoon Worcestershire sauce
2 tablespoons finely grated onion
1 cup (¼ L) vegetable oil
¾ cup (145 g) sugar
6 pounds (2¾ kg) spareribs in 1 or 2 pieces or racks

Combine all ingredients except spareribs in a blender or large lidded jar, and blend or shake until the mixture is thoroughly combined. Place the spareribs in a large shallow baking pan and cover them with the sauce. Cover with aluminum foil and marinate at room temperature for several hours.

Preheat the oven to 350°F (180°C). Leave the foil in place and bake for 45 minutes; uncover and bake another 30–40 minutes. Serve, cut in portions of 2–3 ribs.

Baked Ham (allow ½ pound per serving)

Be sure to read the label on the ham: some are precooked, some partially cooked. If the ham has not been precooked at all, allow 20 minutes per pound in a 350°F oven, then use a meat thermometer to be sure that the internal temperature is 160°F. If the ham is precooked, you must still allow 10 minutes per pound to warm the meat and melt the glaze.

1 ham
1 cup (200 g) brown sugar
¼ cup (½ dL) honey, maple syrup, or cider
 vinegar
2 teaspoons dry mustard
15 or more cloves
1 can pineapple rings (optional)

Basting Sauce (optional)

1 cup (200 g) brown sugar
1 teaspoon dry mustard
1 cup (¼ L) orange juice

Preheat the oven to 350°F (180°C). Place the ham on a rack in a shallow roasting pan, fat side up. Bake the ham unglazed until the thermometer reads 130°F (54°C), or until 1 hour before the ham is done. Prepare for glazing by scoring the outside fat in a diamond pattern, cutting ¼ inch deep with a sharp knife. Combine the brown sugar with the honey, syrup, or vinegar and the mustard. Mix well and spread over the outside of the ham. Stud with whole cloves set decoratively in the center of each diamond. Or if you like pineapple rings, set them in place with toothpicks, putting the cloves in the holes. Return to the oven for 1 hour to finish baking, brushing, if you wish, every 15 minutes with basting sauce. Let it rest and carve at the table.

Boiled Country Ham
(allow ½ pound per serving)

Begin preparing home-cured ham the day before you serve it. Long soaking and cooking make country ham a special treat.

1 home-cured Smithfield or Virginia ham
1 cup (200 g) dark-brown sugar
8 cloves

Soak the ham overnight in cold water to cover. Drain, scrub with a stiff brush, and place in a large pot. Cover with water, heat, and simmer for 25 minutes per pound, or until an instant meat thermometer shows an internal temperature of 150°F. Add more water as it cooks away. Allow the ham to cool in the water in which it cooked, then remove it and peel or cut off the tough outer skin and most of the fat. The ham is now ready to eat, but a brief glazing and baking will make it even better.

114

Preheat the oven to 350°F (180°C). Place the ham on a rack in a shallow roasting pan, and rub it all over with the brown sugar. Stud with cloves and bake for 10 minutes per pound, until the meat is heated through and the glaze is melted and shining.

Ham with Red-eye Gravy
(allow ⅓ pound per serving)

In this regional southern dish, the fried ham lends a slightly reddish tint to pan gravy. Often a few drops of coffee are added for a richer color. Serve with grits or hot biscuits.

⅓-pound (150 g) slice of ham
1 tablespoon flour
Salt
1½ tablespoons coffee

Cut a piece of fat from the ham and melt it in a skillet. Add the ham and fry over medium heat until the edges are slightly brown. Remove and keep warm. Turn the heat to high and stir in the flour. Cook flour slowly until golden, then add 1 cup water, stirring constantly. Sprinkle in salt and the coffee. Turn the heat to medium-low and cook 5–7 minutes, stirring often to keep the gravy smooth. Return meat to the gravy to heat through.

Ham Croquettes   (about 15 croquettes)

3½ cups (8 dL) ground cooked ham
2 cups (½ L) Thick White Sauce (p. 147)

1 tablespoon minced parsley
1 tablespoon Dijon mustard
3 tablespoons minced onion
¼ teaspoon freshly ground pepper
1½ cups (3½ dL) freshly made bread crumbs
1 egg
Vegetable oil

Combine the ham, sauce, parsley, mustard, onion, and pepper, in a bowl and blend well. If mixture is slightly warm, chill in the refrigerator until firm. Put the bread crumbs in a shallow dish, and in another dish beat the egg with 1 tablespoon water. Shape the meat into 1½-inch balls or cylinders. Roll them in the crumbs, then dip into the egg, and again roll in the crumbs. Let the croquettes dry in the refrigerator for at least 30 minutes to set the coating. Fill a skillet halfway with vegetable oil and heat to about 360°F (181°C). Fry a few croquettes at a time to golden brown, turning to brown on all sides. Remove with a slotted spoon and dry on paper towels.

Liver Sautéed in Butter (serves four)

1 pound (450 g) liver, in ⅛–¼-inch slices
3 tablespoons flour
3 tablespoons butter
1 tablespoon oil
Salt
Freshly ground pepper

Dip the liver in flour and shake off any excess. Heat the butter and oil in a skillet until foaming,

116

then add the liver. Cook about 1 minute—or less for very thin pieces—on each side or until the red color is gone. Sprinkle with salt and pepper.

Liver and Bacon. Fry *8 slices of bacon,* drain on paper towels, and keep warm. Remove all but 3 tablespoons bacon fat from the skillet, and use this instead of butter and oil to sauté the liver. Serve with the cooked bacon.

Liver and Onions. Slice *2 large onions* thin, and separate the rings. Melt *2 tablespoons butter* in a skillet over medium heat, and cook the onions until light golden. Remove and keep warm. In sautéing the liver, omit the oil. Serve covered with onions.

Poultry

Roast Stuffed Turkey
(1 pound per serving)

Before you place the turkey on its V-shaped rack, cover the rack with heavily greased parchment, foil, or brown paper to keep the skin from tearing when you turn the turkey.

1 turkey
Stuffing (pp. 163–164)
¼–½ pound (115–225 g) butter, depending on size
   of turkey
Salt
Freshly ground pepper

Preheat the oven to 325°F (165°C). Rinse the turkey and pat it dry. Stuff the body and neck cavities before trussing. Soften ⅛–¼ pound butter and rub all over the turkey, depending on its size—it should be thoroughly buttered. Sprinkle with salt and pepper and place, breast down, on the paper-covered rack in a roasting pan. Put in the oven. Melt the remaining butter (about ¼ pound) with ¼ cup water and baste the turkey every 20 minutes with this mixture until enough pan drippings for basting have accumulated in the bottom of the roasting pan. Cook 15 minutes per pound if the turkey weighs less than 16 pounds; 12 minutes per pound if it is heavier. Turn breast up after 1 hour if the turkey weighs less than 12 pounds; after 1½ hours if it weighs more. When a meat thermometer registers 170°F in the breast meat and 185°F in the thigh meat, remove the turkey to a warm platter and cover loosely with a towel or foil. Let rest 15 minutes before carving.

Unstuffed Roast Turkey. Omit the stuffing. Sprinkle the body cavity with *1 teaspoon salt* and *½ teaspoon poultry seasoning,* then place in the cavity *5 sprigs parsley, 4 stalks celery,* and *3 onions, peeled and quartered.*

Basic Chicken or Turkey Gravy (2 cups)

Two factors help make a lovely deep-brown gravy: the drippings on the bottom of the roasting pan and the slow browning of the flour in the fat.

4 tablespoons fat from poultry pan drippings
3 tablespoons flour
Salt
Freshly ground pepper
2 cups (½ L) liquid: stock, giblet broth, water, or milk

When the bird has been removed from the roasting pan, skim off all but 4 tablespoons of fat in the pan. If there is not enough fat in the drippings, add butter. Place the pan over a burner and heat it, scraping the bottom of the pan to loosen all the browned bits. (If the roasting pan is clumsy to handle, scrape and pour the drippings into a saucepan.) Stir in the flour and blend well over medium heat for 3 minutes or more, until lightly browned. Add salt and pepper to taste, and slowly pour in the liquid, stirring constantly, until smooth. Simmer for 10 minutes to develop the flavor.

Giblet Broth

In general "giblets" refers to all the loose parts—the neck, heart, liver, and gizzard of poultry. A broth made of giblets and vegetables will add richness to gravy, as will the chopped giblets themselves. Because of its strong flavor, the liver should not be cooked in the broth, but separately.

Giblets
1 teaspoon thyme, crumbled
1 thick slice onion
1 rib celery with leaves, sliced
Salt
Freshly ground pepper
Butter (optional)

Rinse the gizzard, heart, and neck, and trim all fat, membranes, and blood. Put the giblets in a saucepan, cover with cold water, and add the thyme, onion, celery, and a sprinkle of salt and pepper. Bring to a boil and simmer 45 minutes, or until the gizzard is tender. Meanwhile, cook the liver under the roasting bird 5–10 minutes or sauté lightly in some butter. Strain the giblets, reserve the broth, and finely dice the gizzard, liver, and heart. Using this broth, make the gravy following Basic Chicken or Turkey Gravy and add the giblets at the end.

Roast Chicken   (1 pound per serving)

Although a 3–5-pound chicken is called a roaster, small broiler-fryers can also be cooked this way. Use a roasting pan that accommodates the bird comfortably; if the pan is too big, the good pan drippings will spread out and cook away.

2½–5-pound (1¼–2¼-kg) chicken
Stuffing (p. 163, optional)
¼–⅓ pound (85–115 g) butter
Salt
Freshly ground pepper

Preheat the oven to 325°F (165°C). Rinse the chicken and pat it dry. Stuff the body and neck cavities, if desired, before trussing. Soften 3–4 tablespoons of the butter and rub it all over the chicken. Sprinkle with salt and pepper and place the chicken in the oven, breast up, on a V-shaped rack in a roasting pan. Melt the remaining butter in a saucepan. Baste every 15 minutes with the melted butter until enough pan drippings for basting have accumulated in the bottom of the roasting pan. Cook about 25 minutes a pound, or until a meat thermometer registers 170°F in the breast meat and 185°F in the thigh meat. Remove the chicken to a warm platter and cover loosely with a towel or foil. Let rest 10 minutes to distribute the juices and settle the meat for carving.

Thyme-roasted Chicken. Omit the stuffing and rub *½ teaspoon salt* in the body cavity before inserting *1 carrot, sliced,* and *1 rib celery with leaves, sliced.* Add *1 teaspoon thyme, crumbled,* to the butter rubbed on the chicken. Make basic gravy (p. 119),

using *1 cup chicken broth* and *1 cup water* and adding the *juice of 1 lemon* before serving.

Oven-broiled Chicken (serves four)

Unlike real broiled chicken, fowl cooked by this
simple method does not require careful watching. It is good when hot, and unequaled later in
salads or sandwiches.

2½–3-pound (1¼–1½-kg) chicken, in halves or
  quarters
3 tablespoons oil
Salt
Freshly ground pepper

Preheat the oven to 400°F (205°C). Lightly oil a
shallow pan. Coat the chicken with oil and season
with salt and pepper. Place skin side up in the pan.
Bake for 35–45 minutes, or until a meat thermometer reads 170°F in the breast meat, 185°F in the
dark meat.

Pan-fried Chicken (serves four)

Remember all the nice things that go with this:
biscuits with butter and maybe honey, cream
gravy—and mustard greens cooked with salt
pork for a real southern dinner.

2½–3-pound (1¼–1½-kg) chicken, in 8 pieces
Milk
¾ cup (1¾ dL) flour

1 teaspoon salt
½ teaspoon freshly ground pepper
Oil for frying
Cream Gravy

Wash and dry the chicken pieces. Place them snugly together in one layer in a shallow dish. Pour on milk to cover, and soak 1 hour, turning once. Mix the flour, salt, and pepper on a piece of wax paper or in a paper bag. Remove chicken from the milk and roll it in the seasoned flour or shake vigorously in the paper bag. Pour oil into a large skillet to a depth of ½ inch. Heat until a small cube of bread browns in 60 seconds or a frying thermometer registers 375°F. Put the dark meat into the pan first, adding the white meat 5 minutes later. Do not crowd the chicken; if necessary, cook in two batches. Fry about 20–30 minutes, turning often with a pair of tongs. Remove, drain on paper towels, and keep warm while you make the gravy. Serve hot with the gravy.

Cream Gravy (1¾ cups)

A must with all types of fried chicken!

3 tablespoons pan drippings and butter
3 tablespoons flour
1½ cups (3½ dL) cream
Salt
¼ teaspoon freshly ground pepper

Heat the pan drippings in the skillet, adding butter, if necessary, and scraping up any brown bits in the pan. Stir in the flour and blend, cooking over low heat until lightly browned. Slowly add the cream, stirring constantly until smooth. Season with salt to taste and pepper, and cook for about 7 minutes.

Maryland Fried Chicken (serves four)

In Maryland, it seems, they dip their chicken in flour, egg, and soft bread crumbs before frying it.

½ cup (70 g) flour
1 teaspoon salt
½ teaspoon freshly ground pepper
2 cups (½ L) freshly made bread crumbs
1 egg
2½–3-pound (1¼–1½-kg) chicken, in 8 pieces
Oil for frying
Cream Gravy (p. 123)

Mix the flour with the salt and pepper on wax paper. Spread the bread crumbs on another piece of wax paper. Lightly beat the egg in a shallow bowl with 2 tablespoons of water. Wash and dry the chicken pieces. Coat them with flour, dip in the egg, then roll them in the bread crumbs. Heat ½ inch of oil until a small cube of bread browns in 60 seconds or a frying thermometer registers 365°F. Using tongs, put the chicken in the hot oil and fry for about 20 minutes, turning often, until brown and done. Drain on paper towels and keep warm while you make the gravy.

Coq au Vin (serves six)

A wonderfully robust dish, full of friendly flavors in a rich dark sauce—and a good way to use a middle-aged hen.

6 tablespoons butter
2 tablespoons oil
5-pound (2¼-kg) chicken, in 8 pieces
½ cup (1 dL) chopped ham
10 small white onions
2 cloves garlic, crushed
1 teaspoon thyme, crumbled
3 parsley sprigs
2 bay leaves
10 whole mushrooms
1 teaspoon salt
½ teaspoon freshly ground pepper
4 tablespoons Cognac or other brandy
1 cup (¼ L) dry red wine

Preheat the oven to 275°F (135°C). Melt the butter and oil in a large pot. Brown the chicken pieces on all sides. Remove and place in a casserole with the drippings. Add the ham, onions, garlic, thyme, parsley, bay leaves, mushrooms, salt, and pepper. Warm the brandy slightly in a small saucepan. Ignite it with a match and pour it, flaming, over the chicken. When the flames die, pour on the red wine. Cover and bake 1½–2 hours.

Delmonico's Deviled Chicken
(serves four)

"Deviled" here means that the chicken is split, seasoned, and then sprinkled with crumbs.

2½–3-pound (1¼–1½-kg) chicken, in quarters
4 tablespoons butter, softened
1 tablespoon prepared mustard
1 tablespoon vinegar
½ teaspoon salt
½ teaspoon paprika
1 cup (¼ L) freshly made bread crumbs

Preheat the oven to 375°F (190°C). Wipe the chicken with a paper towel. Mix the butter, mustard, vinegar, salt, and paprika, and rub the mixture all over the skin side of the chicken. Place the quarters, skin side up, in a shallow roasting pan. Sprinkle evenly with the crumbs and bake for about 40 minutes or until a meat thermometer registers 170°F in the breast meat, 185°F in the dark meat.

Chicken Cacciatore   (serves four)

An Italian dish—*cacciatore* meaning "hunter's"—which has a good earthy taste. The final garnish adds wonderful zest to the finished dish—and those shy of garlic *can* always leave the garlic out.

1 ounce (30 g) dried mushrooms
4 tablespoons olive oil

1 medium chicken, cut in 8 pieces
1 large onion, chopped
½ cup (1 dL) dry white wine
1 clove garlic, minced
1 tablespoon tomato paste
2 cups (½ L) fresh tomatoes, peeled, seeded, and
   chopped or canned drained
½ teaspoon allspice
Freshly ground pepper
2 bay leaves
½ teaspoon thyme, crumbled
Salt to taste

Garnish

Grated rind of 1 lemon
½ clove garlic, minced
3 tablespoons minced parsley

Put the mushrooms to soak for ½ hour in a cup with just enough warm water to cover. Heat the oil in a large skillet and cook the chicken until lightly browned on all sides. Add the onion and sauté a minute or two, then splash in the wine and let it boil up. Lower the heat and add the garlic, paste, and tomatoes, the soaked mushrooms and their liquid, carefully strained, and the seasonings. Cover and cook slowly for about 40 minutes, or until done. Remove bay leaves, taste and correct the salt. Mix together the lemon rind, minced garlic, and parsley and scatter over the top.

Chicken Jambalaya (serves six)

From the South: chicken, ham, and vegetables in tomato-flavored rice.

4–5-pound (2–2¼-kg) chicken, in quarters
2 tablespoons oil
2 tablespoons bacon fat
Salt
Freshly ground pepper
⅛ teaspoon cayenne pepper
1 cup (¼ L) diced ham
½ cup (1 dL) chopped green pepper
½ cup (1 dL) chopped celery
1 large onion, chopped
2 cloves garlic, minced
5 cups (1¼ L) chicken broth
¼ cup (½ dL) minced parsley
1 bay leaf
1½ teaspoons thyme, crumbled
1 cup (¼ L) chopped canned or fresh tomatoes
2 cups (½ L) rice

Preheat the oven to 325°F (165°C). Rinse the chicken pieces and wipe dry. Heat the oil and bacon fat in a large skillet. Brown the chicken pieces and sprinkle them with salt, pepper, and cayenne pepper. Remove from the pan and set aside. Add the ham, green pepper, celery, onion, and garlic to the pan and cook until the vegetables are soft. Add the chicken broth, parsley, bay leaf, and thyme; bring to a boil and cook uncovered until the broth is reduced to 4 cups. Remove the chicken meat from the bones in large pieces. Put the chicken meat, the unstrained broth, the tomatoes, and rice

128

in a casserole. Stir, cover, and bake for 1 hour, checking every 20 minutes and adding more hot broth or water if it dries out. Remove the bay leaf before serving.

Chicken Marengo   (serves four)

4–5-pound (2–2¼-kg) chicken, in 8 pieces
⅓ cup (¾ dL) olive oil
Salt
Freshly ground pepper
1 onion, chopped
2 cloves garlic, crushed
½ cup (1 dL) dry white wine
1 cup (¼ L) chopped canned or fresh tomatoes
½ pound (225 g) mushroms, sliced

Rinse the chicken and wipe dry. Heat the oil in a skillet. Add the chicken, brown lightly on all sides, and sprinkle with salt and pepper. Remove the chicken and set aside. Cook the onion and garlic until soft. Return the chicken to the pan with the wine, tomatoes, and mushrooms. Cover and simmer 30–40 minutes.

Chicken Paprika   (serves four)

A Hungarian dish that is good served with wide noodles.

3-pound (1⅓-kg) chicken, in quarters
4 tablespoons butter

½ cup (1 dL) chopped onion
Salt
2 tablespoons sweet Hungarian paprika
1 tomato, peeled and chopped
½–1 cup (⅛–¼ L) chicken broth
3 tablespoons flour
¼ cup (½ dL) heavy cream
½ cup (1 dL) sour cream, at room temperature

Rinse the chicken and pat it dry. Melt the butter in a heavy pan. Cook the onion until lightly browned, then add the chicken and sprinkle with salt. When the chicken pieces are browned, remove them from the pan and set aside. Mix in the paprika and cook for 1 minute; add the tomato and ½ cup chicken broth, lower the heat, and simmer for 7 minutes. Return the chicken to the pan, cover, and cook 30–40 minutes. Remove the chicken to a warm platter. Sprinkle the flour over the pan drippings, stirring briskly to smooth and blend, and cook for 3 minutes. Gradually add enough chicken broth to make 1 cup of liquid, then stir in the heavy cream. When it is heated through, turn off the heat, whisk the sour cream in a small bowl, and add it to the sauce, blending it quickly without letting it boil. Spoon over the chicken pieces to serve.

Chicken Fricassee (serves six)

A great old-fashioned dish, the essence of chicken in a creamy sauce.

5-pound (2¼-kg) chicken, cut in large pieces
¼ pound (115 g) butter
2 tablespoons oil
1 small onion, sliced
2 ribs celery with leaves, cut in pieces
1 carrot, sliced
1 bay leaf
4 tablespoons flour
1 cup (¼ L) heavy cream
2 tablespoons lemon juice
Salt
Freshly ground pepper

Rinse the chicken and pat it dry. Heat 4 table-spoons of the butter with the oil in a Dutch oven, and brown the chicken on all sides. Lower the heat, pour on boiling water to cover the chicken, and add the onion, celery, carrot, and bay leaf. Cover and simmer 40–45 minutes. Remove the chicken to a platter and keep warm. Strain the broth and remove any surface fat. Bring the broth to a boil and reduce to 1½ cups. Melt the remaining 4 tablespoons of butter in a saucepan. Stir in the flour and cook for 2–3 minutes. Slowly add the cream and broth, continuing to stir and simmer for 4–5 minutes until thickened and smooth. Add the lemon juice and salt and pepper to taste, spoon over the chicken, and serve.

Chicken Fricassee with Mushrooms. Add *1 cup mushrooms* sautéed in *2 tablespoons butter* to the sauce just before adding the lemon juice.

Chicken Gumbo (serves four)

Use fresh okra if you can get it, frozen okra if you can't.

3-pound (1⅓-kg) chicken, in 8 pieces
Salt
Freshly ground pepper
3 tablespoons bacon fat
½ onion, chopped
4 cups (1 L) sliced okra
½ cup (1 dL) chopped sweet red pepper
1½ cups (3½ dL) chopped fresh or canned
 tomatoes
2 teaspoons basil, crumbled
1 cup (¼ L) cooked rice

Rinse the chicken, pat it dry, and sprinkle with salt and pepper. Melt the bacon fat in a large skillet and brown the chicken on all sides. Remove from the pan and set aside. Add the onion, okra, and pepper and cook over medium heat, stirring constantly, for 5 minutes. Stir in the tomatoes, basil, and 3 cups of boiling water. Mix in the chicken and about a teaspoon of salt. Cover and simmer 30–40 minutes. Add the cooked rice, mix well, and cook 5 minutes more to heat through. There will be lots of spicy liquid to serve in soupbowls.

Poached Chicken (serves four)

Chicken prepared this way stays juicy and moist for salads and sandwiches. The broth may be

132

saved and used for stock, for boiling noodles or rice, or for poaching another chicken.

3-pound (1⅓-kg) chicken, whole
Salt

Wash the chicken with cold water. Truss and place in a large saucepan. Add water halfway up the chicken, with ½ teaspoon salt for every quart of water used. Cover and simmer over medium-low heat for 1 hour, turning the chicken over once or twice during the cooking. Cool the chicken in the broth and refrigerate until needed.

Chicken with Dumplings (serves six)

Serve in soupbowls: pieces of chicken in broth with a dumpling floating on top.

4–5-pound (2–2¼-kg) chicken, in 8 pieces
2 carrots, sliced thin
2 ribs celery with leaves, sliced fine
1 large onion, chopped
1½ teaspoons thyme, crumbled
½ teaspoon rosemary, crumbled
2 teaspoons salt
½ teaspoon freshly ground pepper

Dumplings

2 cups (285 g) flour
3 teaspoons baking powder
1 teaspoon salt
2 tablespoons minced parsley

4 tablespoons shortening
¾–1 cup (1¾ dL–¼ L) milk

Rinse the chicken pieces, put them in a large pot, and cover with water. Add the carrots, celery, onion, thyme, rosemary, 2 teaspoons salt, and pepper. Bring to a boil and reduce to a simmer. Combine the flour, baking powder, 1 teaspoon salt, and parsley in a bowl. Cut in the shortening until the mixture resembles coarse meal. Add ¾ cup milk and stir briefly with a fork. Add only enough of the remaining ¼ cup milk to make the dough hold together. When the chicken has simmered for 20 minutes, drop spoonfuls of dough on top of the bubbling broth. Cover and steam for 20 minutes without lifting the cover.

Sautéed Chicken Breasts (serves four)

Buy 3 pounds of unboned chicken breasts if you are boning them yourself. This is equally good made with thin slices of turkey breast.

⅓ cup (¾ dL) flour
1½ pounds (675 g) skinned and boned chicken breasts
4 tablespoons butter
2 tablespoons oil
Juice of 1 lemon
Salt
Freshly ground pepper
1 tablespoon minced parsley

Spread the flour on a piece of wax paper and dredge each chicken breast. Melt the butter and oil in a skillet. When it foams, add the chicken, and cook over medium-high heat for about 3 minutes on each side. Remove to a warm platter. Pour off all but 2 tablespoons of fat from the pan, and stir in the lemon juice and salt and pepper to taste. When it is very hot, spoon this sauce over the chicken and sprinkle with parsley.

Baked Chicken Breasts. Omit the flour. Season each breast with salt and pepper, place in a shallow pan, and dot with *4 tablespoons butter.* Cover with foil and bake in a preheated 375°F (190°C) oven for 20 minutes or until done. Remove the foil, drizzle on the lemon juice, and sprinkle with the parsley.

Mushroom-stuffed Chicken

Breasts   (serves four to six)

¼ pound (115 g) plus 4 tablespoons butter
½ pound (225 g) mushrooms, chopped fine
½ teaspoon salt
¼ teaspoon freshly ground pepper
1½ cups (3½ dL) freshly made bread crumbs
¼ teaspoon nutmeg
4 chicken breasts, skinned, boned, and halved
1 cup (¼ L) heavy cream

Preheat the oven to 350°F (180°C). Melt ¼ pound of the butter in a skillet. Add the mushrooms, salt, and pepper, and cook, stirring often, until the mushrooms turn very dark and absorb all the butter. Remove from the heat and stir in ¾ cup of the bread crumbs and the nutmeg. Divide the mushroom stuffing into 8 portions and place a portion in the center of each piece of chicken. Fold the chicken around the stuffing, and place, seam side down, in a shallow casserole. Melt the remaining 4 tablespoons butter and brush over the chicken. Sprinkle with the remaining ¾ cup of bread crumbs. Pour on the cream and bake for 30 minutes until lightly brown.

Sautéed Chicken Livers with Madeira   (serves four)

Serve the livers and sauce spooned over toast with broiled tomato halves.

2 tablespoons butter
2 tablespoons oil
1 pound (450 g) chicken livers
4 tablespoons Madeira
Salt
Freshly ground pepper

Heat the butter and oil in a skillet, toss in the chicken livers, and cook very quickly, shoving them about in the pan, until dark brown; remove to a warm platter. Turn the heat up very high and add the Madeira. Let it come to a boil as you scrape up the pan juices. Add salt and pepper to taste.

Chicken Livers with Mushrooms (serves four)

1 pound (450 g) chicken livers
5 tablespoons butter
2 cups (½ L) sliced mushrooms
3 shallots or scallions, minced fine
1½ tablespoons lemon juice
¾ cup (1¾ dL) beef broth
Freshly ground pepper
1 tablespoon minced parsley

Trim the chicken livers of any discolored membranes or tough connective tissue, and wipe with a paper towel. Melt the butter in a skillet. Add the mushrooms and cook, stirring, over medium heat for 1½ minutes. Add the livers, shallots or scallions, lemon juice, broth, and salt and pepper to taste. Turn the heat to high and cook, stirring, for another 1½ minutes. Serve, sprinkled with the parsley.

Roast Duck (serves four)

For a crisp brown duck, try this recipe: the secret is basting it with water.

5-pound (2¼-kg) duck
Salt
Freshly ground pepper

Preheat the oven to 450°F (230°C). Rub the inside of the duck with salt and pepper. Prick the skin all over, especially along the sides under the breast, to allow the fat to run out while the duck roasts. Place the duck breast up on a rack in a shallow roasting pan. Baste every 15 minutes, pouring off the fat from the pan as it accumulates. Turn the duck breast down after the first 45 minutes of roasting. Turn it breast up again after the second 45 minutes. Roast the duck for 1¼ hours, then baste it with 3–4 tablespoons of ice water and roast another 15 minutes—1½ hours altogether or until a meat thermometer reads 180°F in the thigh. If you like your duck very well done, roast it another 20–30 minutes, but be forewarned, the meat is going to be dry. Remove from the oven and let rest for 15 minutes before carving.

Duck à l'Orange   (serves four)

5-pound (2¼-kg) duck
Salt
Freshly ground pepper
5 oranges
2 lemons
3 tablespoons sugar
3 tablespoons wine vinegar
2 cups (½ L) beef broth
1 tablespoon cornstarch
2 tablespoons red currant jelly
4 tablespoons dry white wine

Preheat the oven to 350°F (180°C). Prick the duck skin all over and rub the cavity with salt and pepper. Roast for 1¾ hours (or until interior temperature is 180°F in the thigh) on a rack in a shallow roasting pan, pouring off the fat every 20 minutes. Using a vegetable peeler, remove the colored part, or "zest," of the skins of 2 of the oranges and 1 of the lemons. Cut the zest into thin strips. Squeeze the juice from the peeled fruit and set aside. Bring a pan of water to a boil and add the strips. Steep them 5 minutes, drain, and set aside. Cut the pieces of fruit free from the membranes of the remaining 3 oranges and 1 lemon. Put the sections in a bowl and set aside. In a small heavy-bottomed pan, cook the sugar over medium-high heat. Caramelize it by moving the pan over the heat so that the sugar turns golden, taking care that it does not burn. Add the vinegar, orange juice, and lemon juice, and boil rapidly until the liquid is reduced by half. Stir in the broth and simmer for 5 minutes more. In a small bowl, dissolve the cornstarch in 2 tablespoons water. Add it to the caramelized sauce with the currant jelly, stirring until the sauce is clear and thickened. When the duck is roasted, put it on a warm platter. Pour off the fat from the roasting pan and place it over a burner. Add the wine, scrape up the bits from the bottom of the pan, and boil rapidly for 1 minute. Strain into the sauce. Sprinkle the duck with the fruit rind strips, surround with fruit sections, and pour enough of the rich brown sauce over to glaze the duck, serving the rest in a sauceboat.

Roast Goose with Apples and Prunes   (serves six)

2 dozen prunes, pitted
1 cup (¼ L) red wine
5 tart green apples
8–10-pound (3½–4½-kg) goose
Salt
Freshly ground pepper
2 tablespoons flour
1½ cups (3½ dL) chicken or goose* broth

Soak the prunes in wine for 30 minutes. Peel, core, and quarter the apples. Preheat the oven to 325°F (165°C). Rub the goose inside and out with salt and pepper. Drain the prunes, toss with the apple sections, and stuff into the goose cavity. Sew up or skewer the opening. Place the goose on a rack in a shallow pan, pricking the skin all over to release the fat as the bird roasts. Cook 3–3½ hours, until the juices run clear when the skin is cut at the upper thigh or a meat thermometer registers 185°F. During the roasting, pour off the fat every 20 minutes, using a bulb baster or spoon. Remove the goose to a platter and keep warm. Remove all but 1 tablespoon fat from the roasting pan. Set it over a burner, stir in the flour, and brown it lightly. Slowly add the chicken broth, stirring until thickened. Season the gravy with salt and pepper, strain it, and pass with the goose.

*If the neck and gizzards come with the goose, simmer them with a small carrot and onion in about 4 cups water for 1½–2 hours, it will reduce to about 1½ cups.

Rock Cornish Game Hens with Wild Rice Stuffing (serves six)

Serve one hen to a person, garnished with watercress.

¼ pound (115 g) butter
½ onion, chopped fine
1 cup (¼ L) chopped mushrooms
1½ cups (3½ dL) cooked wild rice
½ teaspoon thyme, crumbled
½ teaspoon marjoram, crumbled
Salt
Freshly ground pepper
6 Rock Cornish game hens
1 cup (¼ L) chicken broth
½ cup (1 dL) dry vermouth

Preheat the oven to 400°F (205°C). Melt 4 tablespoons of the butter in a saucepan. Add the onion and mushrooms and cook over medium heat until soft. Mix in the rice, thyme, and marjoram. Stuff loosely into the cavities of the hens. Rub them all over with the remaining butter and sprinkle with salt and pepper. Place the hens, not touching, in a shallow pan and roast, basting every 10–15 minutes with a mixture of chicken broth and vermouth. After 15 minutes, reduce the heat to 300°F (150°C) and cook another 30–40 minutes, or until the juices run clear when a small slit is made in the upper thigh. Serve with pan juices as a natural sauce.

141

Chicken Pie (serves six)

6 tablespoons butter
6 tablespoons flour
2 cups (½ L) chicken broth
1 cup (¼ L) heavy cream
½ teaspoon freshly ground pepper
Salt
4 cups (1 L) cooked chicken, cut in large chunks
12 small white onions, cooked
¾ cup (1¾ dL) peas, cooked
1 recipe Basic Pastry for 9-inch shell (p. 390)

Preheat the oven to 425°F (220°C). Melt the butter in a saucepan, stir in the flour, and cook, stirring, for 2 minutes. Slowly add the broth, cream, pepper, and salt to taste. Cook for 5 minutes, until thickened and smooth. Put the chicken pieces in a deep pie plate or casserole, cover with sauce, and stir in the small onions and peas. Place the prepared piecrust over the casserole, allowing enough overhang so that the edges can be crimped. Cut vents in the crust to allow the steam to escape. Bake for 25–30 minutes or until the crust is nicely browned.

Louisburg Chicken Pie. Add to the cooked onions and peas *1 cup sliced mushrooms, sautéed in butter,* and *½ pound sausage meat* that has been shaped into tiny balls and sautéed.

Chicken Pie, Country Style. Use *1 recipe Baking Powder Biscuits* (p. 311) instead of Basic Pastry. Roll out the biscuit dough ½ inch thick, cut into 2-inch rounds, and place them, edges touching, all over the top of the pie. Bake at 450°F (230°C) for 15–20 minutes until browned.

Chicken and Noodles   (serves four)

A golden sauce, sharp with the tang of cheese.

¼ pound (115 g) broad egg noodles or green noodles
¾ cup (1¾ dL) freshly grated Parmesan cheese
2 tablespoons butter
2 tablespoons flour
1 cup (¼ L) heavy cream
1 cup (¼ L) chicken broth
2 cups (½ L) cubed cooked chicken
2 egg yolks, lightly beaten
Salt

Preheat the oven to 375°F (190°C). Butter a 2-quart baking dish. Cook the noodles until just done. Drain them, and, while they are still hot, stir in all but 2 tablespoons of the cheese. Melt the butter in a saucepan, add the flour, and cook for 2–3 minutes. Gradually stir in the cream and broth. Cook over low heat, stirring often, for 5 minutes. Add the chicken and cook another minute. Beat ¼ cup of the hot sauce into the egg yolks, then return the yolk-sauce mixture to the chicken mixture. Stir briskly for 1 minute, remove from the heat, and add salt to taste. Place the chicken mixture over the noodles. Sprinkle with the reserved 2 tablespoons of cheese, and bake 20–30 minutes, until golden.

Chicken à la King   (serves two to three)

Serve in flaky patty shells.

½ cup (1 dL) sliced mushrooms
2 tablespoons butter
1½ cups (3½ dL) Velouté Sauce (p. 149)
1 cup (¼ L) cubed cooked chicken
4 tablespoons canned pimientos, in strips
1 egg yolk, lightly beaten
2 tablespoons dry sherry
Salt to taste

Sauté the mushrooms in butter. Mix them into the sauce together with the chicken and pimientos in a saucepan over low heat. When it is hot, add ¼ cup of this mixture to the egg yolk, beating constantly. Return the yolk-sauce mixture to the saucepan with the sherry and salt and blend well.

Chicken-Almond Supreme
(serves three to four)

2 cups (½ L) cooked chicken in large pieces
3 tablespoons butter
1½ cups (3½ dL) sliced mushrooms
1 cup (¼ L) canned water chestnuts, sliced thin
1 tablespoon soy sauce
1 recipe Supreme Sauce (p. 149)
⅓ cup (¾ dL) slivered almonds

Preheat the oven to 350°F (180°C). Spread the chicken pieces in a shallow baking dish. Melt the butter in a skillet, add the mushrooms, and cook

144

until soft. Sprinkle the mushrooms and water chestnuts over the chicken. Add the soy sauce to the supreme sauce, and pour over the chicken mixture. Sprinkle with the almonds and bake 20–25 minutes or until heated through.

Chicken Croquettes (6–8 croquettes)

A firm, creamy blend of chicken and crisp brown crumbs. Tradition dictates that they be shaped like small upside-down ice cream cones, but other shapes taste just as good.

2 cups (½ L) finely diced cooked chicken
½ teaspoon salt
2 teaspoons minced celery with leaves
Pinch of cayenne pepper
2 teaspoons lemon juice
2 teaspoons minced onion
1 teaspoon minced parsley
1 cup (¼ L) Thick Cream Sauce (p. 148)
2 eggs, lightly beaten
2 cups (½ L) freshly made bread crumbs
Oil for frying

Mix the chicken, salt, celery, cayenne pepper, lemon juice, onion, parsley, and cream sauce until well blended. Cover with foil, refrigerate until chilled, then form into small cones, 1½ inches at the base and about 2 inches high. Dip them into the beaten eggs, then roll them in the crumbs. Set them to dry on a piece of wax paper. Heat 3 inches of oil in a heavy pot, until medium hot—360°F. Add the croquettes, let them brown, turn, and brown on the other side. Don't crowd the pot; do in two batches, if necessary. Drain on paper towels. Place on a warm platter and serve with White Sauce.

Chicken and Almond Croquettes. Add *½ cup blanched, chopped almonds* to the mixture. Serve with *Brown Sauce* (p. 000).

Chicken and Mushroom Croquettes. Sauté *1 cup chopped mushrooms* in *2 tablespoons butter* and add to the chicken mixture. Serve with White Sauce.

Sauces, Stuffings, Preserves & Pickles

White Sauce or Béchamel Sauce
(1 cup)

This used to be one of the first lessons in home economics classes; invariably white and pasty, it coated many a bland dish. When well made, however, it has a proper place in homey, creamed dishes, often making leftovers stretch or giving cooked foods new life. And it is important as a base for soufflés. The French term for this medium-thick white sauce is *béchamel*. The foolproof way to attain a perfectly smooth sauce is to have the milk hot when added to the butter and flour. It uses an extra pot and as you become more proficient, this cautionary measure may not be necessary.

2 tablespoons butter
2 tablespoons flour
1 cup (¼ L) milk, heated

Salt
Freshly ground pepper

Melt the butter in a heavy-bottomed saucepan. Stir in the flour and cook, stirring constantly, until the paste cooks and bubbles a bit, but don't let it brown—about 2 minutes. Add the hot milk, continuing to stir as the sauce thickens. Bring to a boil. Add salt and pepper to taste, lower the heat, and cook, stirring, for 2–3 minutes more. Remove from the heat. To cool this sauce for later use, cover it with wax paper or pour a film of milk over it to prevent a skin from forming.

Thick Cream Sauce. Use *3 tablespoons flour* to *1 cup milk*. This is the consistency needed as a base for croquettes and for soufflés.

Curry Cream Sauce. Add *1 teaspoon curry powder* and *¼ teaspoon ground ginger*.

Mock Hollandaise. Just before serving, beat in *2 egg yolks, 6 tablespoons butter* (1 tablespoon at a time), and *1 tablespoon lemon juice*.

Cheese Sauce. Stir in *½ cup grated Cheddar cheese* during the last 2 minutes of cooking, along with a *pinch of cayenne pepper*.

Mornay Sauce. Add *2 tablespoons grated Parmesan cheese* and *2 tablespoons grated Swiss cheese* during the last 2 minutes of cooking. Stir until blended. Just before removing from the heat, beat 2 tablespoons of the sauce into *1 lightly beaten egg yolk*. Stir the sauce-yolk mixture back into the sauce and add *2 tablespoons butter.* Cook, stirring, 1 minute more.

Egg Sauce. Add *2 hard-boiled eggs* in ¼-inch slices and thin sauce with ¼ cup additional milk, or *chicken or fish stock,* depending on what it is served with.

Velouté Sauce (1½ cups)

Another basic sauce: creamy with a background taste of well-flavored broth.

2 tablespoons butter
3 tablespoons flour
1 cup (¼ L) hot chicken broth
⅓ cup (¾ dL) heavy cream
Salt to taste

Melt the butter in a heavy-bottomed pan. Stir in the flour and blend over moderate heat until smooth. Continue to cook, stirring constantly, for 2 minutes. Add the chicken broth, continuing to stir as the sauce thickens. Bring to a boil, lower the heat, and cook 2 minutes more. Pour in the cream, add salt, and heat thoroughly.

Supreme Sauce. Just before serving, lightly beat *2 egg yolks* in a small bowl. Beat 2 tablespoons of the sauce into the yolks, then stir the sauce-yolk mixture back into the sauce with *¼ teaspoon nutmeg* and the *juice of ½ lemon.*

Lobster Velouté Sauce. Cover the *shells of 1 (or more) lobster* with water and simmer for 1 hour. Strain the broth and return to the boil, reducing to 1 cup. Omit the chicken broth and use the lobster broth instead. If a richer sauce is desired, beat *2 egg yolks* in a small bowl. Beat 2 tablespoons of the sauce into the yolks, then stir the sauce-yolk mixture back into the sauce. Add *1 tablespoon lemon juice*. Stir to blend.

Russian Sauce. Before adding cream, add *½ teaspoon finely chopped chives, ½ teaspoon prepared Dijon mustard, 1 teaspoon grated horseradish (or prepared horseradish)*. Cook 2 minutes, then add the cream and *1 teaspoon lemon juice*.

Bercy Sauce (1 cup)

Creamy yellow, with the flavor of shallots. A good sauce for heating leftover chicken or veal; also good on fish.

3 tablespoons butter
1 tablespoon minced shallots
2 tablespoons flour
1 cup (¼ L) hot chicken broth
Salt

Melt 1 tablespoon of the butter in a small pan. Add the shallots and cook, stirring, for 2–3 minutes. Add the flour, blend well, and cook, stirring for 2 minutes more. Slowly pour in the chicken broth, stir until smooth, and simmer for 15 minutes. Strain the sauce through cheesecloth or a fine sieve, and add the remaining 2 tablespoons of butter and salt to taste.

Onion Sauce or Soubise   (2 cups)

3 medium onions, chopped
4 tablespoons butter
1½ recipes White Sauce (p. 147)
¼ teaspoon nutmeg
½ cup (1 dL) heavy cream
Salt to taste

Preheat the oven to 350°F (180°C). Bring a pan of water to a boil and plunge in the chopped onions. Cook for 1 minute, then remove and drain the onions on paper towels. Melt the butter in a saucepan and, when it bubbles, stir in the onions. Cover and cook over very low heat, shaking the pan often to keep the onions from sticking or scorching. Cook until tender. Put the onions in a shallow baking dish, add the white sauce and nutmeg, and stir to blend. Cover with foil and bake 30 minutes or until the onions are mushy. Remove and put through a food processor or press through a sieve. Stir in the cream and salt, and heat thoroughly without boiling.

Parsley Butter   (½ cup)

Good on steaks, chops, broiled fish, as well as vegetables.

¼ pound (115 g) butter, softened
⅛ teaspoon freshly ground pepper
2 tablespoons finely chopped parsley
1 tablespoon lemon juice
Salt

151

Put the butter into a bowl with the pepper and parsley and blend with the back of a spoon. Or spin the ingredients in a food processor. Slowly add the lemon juice, a few drops at a time, then salt to taste. Form into a cylinder, wrap in wax paper or foil, and chill in the refrigerator. Once it is chilled, cut it into slices and place a slice or two to melt on each serving of meat or fish.

Herb Butter. Omit the parsley. Substitute a combination of herbs, making approximately *1 tablespoon fresh herbs* or *1–1½ teaspoons dry herbs*. For example, use *1½ teaspoons chopped chives*, *½ teaspoon dried thyme* or *tarragon*, and *½ teaspoon chopped parsley*.

Brown Sauce (1 cup)

2 tablespoons butter
1 slice onion
⅛ teaspoon freshly ground pepper
2 tablespoons flour
1 cup (¼ L) beef stock
Salt to taste

Melt the butter in a saucepan and add the onion. When the butter is barely brown, stir in the pepper and flour, and cook slowly until the flour is brown. Gradually add the stock, stirring, and boil gently for 1 minute. Remove the onion, add salt, turn the heat to simmer, and cook 15 minutes. Add more liquid if the sauce is too thick.

Onion-Brown Sauce. Omit the onion slice. Cook *4 tablespoons finely chopped onion* in the butter, and do not remove.

Bordelaise Sauce. Omit the onion slice. After adding the broth, stir in *2 green onions, minced, 1 tablespoon minced carrot, 1 sprig parsley, ½ bay leaf, 1 whole clove,* and *1½ teaspoons Worcestershire sauce.* After cooking 15 minutes, strain.

Brown Curry Sauce. Add *1 teaspoon curry powder* and *½ teaspoon dry mustard* to the flour-butter mixture.

Currant Jelly Sauce. Omit the onion slice. After adding the broth, stir in *3 tablespoons currant jelly* and *2 tablespoons cider vinegar.*

Sauce Piquante. Omit the onion slice. After adding the broth, stir in *1 tablespoon vinegar, 2 teaspoons minced green onions, 2 teaspoons capers, 1 tablespoon minced dill pickle,* and a *dash of cayenne pepper.*

Mushroom Sauce   (1½ cups)

Unless mushrooms are very dirty, trim off the hard end of the stems and just wipe them clean with a damp cloth or paper towel.

5 tablespooons butter
½ pound (225 g) mushrooms, sliced
2 tablespoons flour
Juice of ½ lemon

1 cup (¼ L) heavy cream
Salt to taste

Melt the butter in a large skillet. Stir in the mush-rooms and cook for 2–3 minutes, until they darken a little. Stir in the flour, blend to smooth and cook 2 minutes. Slowly stir in the lemon juice, cream, and salt, and cook only until hot.

Sauce Robert   (1 cup)

A lively, robust flavor—good with beef, liver, and leftover lamb.

1 tablespoon butter
2 tablespoons minced shallots or scallions
1 teaspoon flour
1 tablespoon vinegar
1 cup (¼ L) chicken broth
2 tablespoons minced dill pickle
1 teaspoon dry mustard
Salt to taste

Melt the butter in a saucepan. Add the shallots or scallions and the flour, and cook and stir for 3 min-utes. Add remaining ingredients. Simmer, stirring often, for 5 minutes.

Tomato Sauce   (4 cups)

This is a simple sauce with no onions or garlic; the grated carrot adds a little sweetness, but if you prefer, use a little sugar to counter the acidity of the tomatoes. For a more robust flavor, try one of the variations.

2 tablespoons olive oil
¾ cup (1¾ dL) tomato paste
2½ cups (6 dL) peeled and chopped fresh or canned tomatoes
1 carrot, grated, or 1 teaspoon sugar
½ teaspoon freshly ground pepper
1 tablespoon basil, crumbled
5 tablespoons butter
Salt to taste

Heat the oil in a heavy-bottomed saucepan. Stir in the tomato paste, tomatoes, carrot, pepper, and basil. Simmer for 30 minutes. If the sauce becomes too thick, add a little water. Cook 15 minutes more, then stir in the butter and salt. Serve with cooked pasta.

I. Italian Tomato Sauce with Ground Beef. Add *1 pound ground beef* to the heated oil. Cook, stirring and breaking the beef into tiny pieces, until the meat loses its pinkness. If the beef is fat, spoon off all but 3 tablespoons of fat and proceed as directed.

II. Italian Tomato Sauce with Garlic and Onions. Cook *1 onion, chopped,* and *2 cloves garlic, minced,* in the heated oil for 3 minutes before adding the remaining ingredients.

Truman's Sauce for Pasta (4 cups)

2 slices bacon, diced
1 cup (¼ L) chopped green pepper

1 onion, chopped
2 cloves garlic, cut in half
1 pound (450 g) lean ground beef
1½ cups (3½ dL) tomato paste
1½ cups (3½ dL) canned consommé, undiluted
1 tablespoon Worcestershire sauce
4 tablespoons freshly grated Parmesan cheese
Salt to taste
¼ teaspoon freshly ground pepper
1 teaspoon oregano, crumbled

Fry the bacon in a saucepan until some of the fat is melted. Add the green pepper, onion, and garlic, and cook until soft. Add the beef and break it into tiny pieces with a fork until it loses its pinkness. Stir in the tomato paste, consommé, Worcestershire sauce, cheese, salt, pepper, and oregano. Simmer for 1½ hours, adding water if it becomes too thick. Serve with cooked pasta.

Mexican Tomato Sauce (1 cup)

Not really a sauce, but a wonderfully fresh-tasting combination of vegetables. Just right with fish.

2 tablespoons butter
1 onion, chopped fine
1 red pepper, chopped fine
1 green pepper, chopped fine
1 clove garlic, minced
2 tomatoes, peeled and chopped
2 teaspoons Worcestershire sauce
Salt to taste

Melt the butter in a saucepan. Add the onion and cook 3–4 minutes. Add the red pepper, green pepper, garlic, and tomatoes. Partially cover and simmer for 15 minutes. Stir in the Worcestershire sauce and salt. Remove and serve, or refrigerate in a tightly covered jar.

Hollandaise Sauce (1 cup)

There's no reason to fear this classic sauce, yellow with butter and egg and tart with lemon juice. Made the traditional way, or whirred in the blender (following recipe), it should cause no problems for the careful cook.

3 egg yolks
1 tablespoon lemon juice
¼ pound (115 g) butter, melted
Dash of cayenne pepper
Salt to taste

Use a double boiler or a metal bowl placed over hot, but not simmering, water. Put the egg yolks in the boiler top, and beat with a wire whisk until smooth. Add the lemon juice and gradually whisk in the melted butter, pouring in a thin stream. Slowly stir in 2 tablespoons hot water, the cayenne, and salt. Continue to mix for 1 minute. The sauce should be thickened. Serve immediately, or hold over warm water for an hour or two, but don't try to keep it too long without refrigerating.

Béarnaise Sauce. Cook *1 tablespoon minced shallots* or *white ends of scallions* with *2 tablespoons* *vinegar* and *½ teaspoon dried tarragon* until reduced to 1 tablespoon; then strain. Use this in place of the lemon juice. Add *1 teaspoon minced parsley* and, if available, *1 teaspoon minced fresh tarragon* to the sauce when thickened.

Sauce Mousseline. Fold in *⅓ cup heavy cream, whipped,* just before serving. This is a good way to stretch the sauce.

Blender or Food Processor Hollandaise   (1¼ cups)

Smooth, buttery, tart, and easy. Fish, broccoli, asparagus, and eggs all benefit from a cover of hollandaise. The same variations as in the preceding recipe can be made with this Hollandaise and the same rules about storage apply.

2 egg yolks
½ pound (225 g) butter, melted
1 tablespoon lemon juice
Dash of cayenne pepper
Salt to taste

Put the egg yolks in the electric blender or food processor. If using the blender, turn to low speed. Slowly add 1½ tablespoons boiling water, and then add the butter very slowly in a thin stream. Add the lemon juice, cayenne, and salt. Taste and correct the seasonings.

Mustard Sauce (1½ cups)

Adds sharpness to beef, ham, spinach, and sausage.

2 tablespoons dry mustard
1 teaspoon flour
1 cup (¼ L) light cream
1 egg yolk
1 teaspoon sugar
½ cup (1 dL) vinegar, heated
Salt to taste

Blend the dry mustard, flour, and ¼ cup of the cream. Put the remaining ¾ cup cream in a heavy-bottomed pan. Heat, then stir in the mustard mixture. Beat the egg yolk in a small bowl. Beat in 2 tablespoons of the hot mustard mixture, then stir the yolk-sauce mixture into the saucepan. Add the sugar, and cook, stirring constantly, until thickened. Stir in the heated vinegar and salt.

Raisin Sauce (2½ cups)

Very good with ham or tongue.

½ cup (1 dL) dark-brown sugar
1½ teaspoons dry mustard
1 tablespoon flour
2 tablespoons vinegar
2 tablespoons lemon juice
¼ teaspoon grated lemon rind
⅓ cup (¾ dL) raisins
Salt to taste

Combine the brown sugar, dry mustard, and flour in a heavy-bottomed pan off the heat. Slowly stir in the vinegar, lemon juice, lemon rind, and 1½ cups water. Place over medium heat and bring to a boil, stirring constantly. Lower the heat and add the raisins and salt. Cook and stir until the sauce is thick.

Tartar Sauce (1 cup)

Traditional with fish and seafood—and so much superior when you make it yourself.

¾ cup (1¾ dL) mayonnaise, preferably homemade (p. 282)
2 teaspoons minced scallion
1 teaspoon capers
1 teaspoon minced sweet pickle
1 teaspoon minced parsley
1 tablespoon vinegar

Combine all ingredients in a bowl. Stir until well blended.

Orange Sauce (1 cup)

Pleasing with lamb.

⅓ cup (¾ dL) currant jelly
3 tablespoons sugar
Grated rind of 2 oranges

2 tablespoons Port wine
2 tablespoons orange juice
2 tablespoons lemon juice
⅛ teaspoon cayenne pepper
Salt

In a saucepan, combine the jelly, sugar, and grated orange rind and beat until smoothly blended. Stir in the wine, orange juice, lemon juice, and cayenne pepper. Heat through to melt the jelly. Add salt to taste.

Mint Sauce (½ cup)

A slightly sweet sauce of fresh mint in tart vinegar: so much better than the bright-green commercial mint jelly.

½ cup (1 dL) white vinegar
¼ cup (½ dL) sugar
½ cup (1 dL) minced fresh mint leaves

Put the vinegar and sugar in a small pan. Heat until it boils and the sugar dissolves. Pour the hot sauce over the mint and let stand at least 1 hour.

Wine Marinade (2 cups)

Red wine is good with beef and lamb. Let the meat marinate for at least 3 hours before cooking, turning it several times in the marinade.

1 cup (¼ L) red wine
1 cup (¼ L) olive oil

3 cloves garlic
1 teaspoon salt
½ teaspoon marjoram, crumbled
½ teaspoon rosemary, crumbled
1 teaspoon thyme, crumbled
4 tablespoons minced parsley
1 teaspoon coarsely ground pepper

Mix the wine and oil together in a jar with a tight-fitting lid. Crush and chop the garlic with the salt until almost a paste. Add to the wine and oil, along with remaining ingredients. Cover tight and shake until all ingredients are well blended.

Barbecue Sauce (about 2 cups)

A basic barbecue sauce, good on pork chops, spareribs, hamburgers.

2 tablespoons butter
1 onion, grated
2 cloves garlic, minced
¼ teaspoon salt
1 tablespoon chili powder
4 tablespoons brown sugar
4 tablespoons vinegar
4 tablespoons Worcestershire sauce
1 cup (¼ L) catsup
1 teaspoon Tabasco

Melt the butter in a saucepan and cook the onion and garlic until soft. Add 2 cups of water and remaining ingredients. Stir until well mixed. Place over medium-low heat and simmer for 30 minutes.

Chicken Barbecue Sauce   (1½ cups)

Brush on chicken parts as they cook over the coals. Also good with pork.

1 egg, well beaten
½ cup (1 dL) cooking oil
1 cup (¼ L) cider vinegar
1 tablespoon salt
1 teaspoon sage, crumbled
¼ teaspoon freshly ground pepper

Combine all ingredients in a jar. Shake well and let stand for several hours before using.

Bread Stuffing   (about 3 cups)

A pleasant basic stuffing.

¼ pound (115 g) butter
4 tablespoons finely chopped onion
4 tablespoons finely chopped celery
4 cups (1 L) dry bread crumbs
¼ teaspoon freshly ground pepper
Salt to taste

Melt the butter in a skillet and stir in the onion and celery. Cook over low heat until the onion is soft. Add this mixture to the crumbs and toss lightly with plenty of pepper and salt.

Savory Bread Stuffing. Add *1 teaspoon sage, crumbled,* or *1 teaspoon poultry seasoning.*

Raisin-Nut Stuffing. Add *½ cup raisins* and *½ cup walnuts.*

Giblet Stuffing. Cover the *giblets* with 1 quart cold water in a saucepan. Bring to a boil and simmer. When the liver is tender, remove it. Continue to cook the gizzard until it is tender, about 45 minutes. Drain the giblets and chop into small bits, and add to the stuffing. Save the liquid for soup.

Herb Stuffing. Add *1 teaspoon thyme, crumbled, 1 teaspoon basil, crumbled,* and *½ teaspoon marjoram, crumbled.*

Mushroom Stuffing. Omit the celery and cook *2 cups chopped mushrooms* with the onions. Add *½ teaspoon nutmeg.*

Onion Stuffing. Add *6 onions,* boiled until barely tender, drained, and chopped.

Oyster Stuffing. Add *2 cups oysters,* in bite-size pieces, and use about *¼ cup of oyster liquor* for moistening the crumbs.

Corn Bread Stuffing. Substitute *2 cups corn bread crumbs* for 2 cups of the bread crumbs. For *Corn Stuffing,* add *1 cup cooked whole-kernel corn.*

Apple Stuffing (2½ cups)

The apples, which turn lightly brown and tender, are mixed with spices and crumbs to make a fine Christmas stuffing.

4 tablespoons bacon fat
2 cups (½ L) diced unpeeled tart apples
2 teaspoons sugar
½ cup (1 dL) dry bread crumbs

¼ teaspoon nutmeg
¼ teaspoon cinnamon

Melt the bacon fat in a skillet. Add the apples and sugar and cook over medium-low heat, stirring, for 5 minutes. Remove from the heat and toss in the crumbs, nutmeg, and cinnamon.

Mushroom Duxelles   (1½ cups)

A French method of preserving mushrooms for use in fillings, soups, and sauces. Duxelles should be cooked until all moisture is absorbed.

4 tablespoons butter
½ onion, finely chopped
1 pound (450 g) mushrooms, finely chopped
Salt
Freshly ground pepper

Melt the butter in a very large skillet over medium heat, add the onion, and cook, stirring, for 2 minutes. Add the mushrooms and continue to cook over low heat, stirring occasionally, until all the moisture has evaporated—about 20 minutes. Season to taste. Cool, then put in a container and close tightly. Refrigerate or freeze until needed.

Wild Rice and Mushroom Stuffing   (3 cups)

1 cup (¼ L) wild rice
4 tablespoons butter

2 cups (½ L) chopped mushrooms
1 small onion, chopped fine
¼ teaspoon freshly ground pepper
¼–½ teaspoon ground nutmeg
Salt to taste

Steam the rice. Melt the butter in a saucepan, add the mushrooms and onion, and cook over low heat until soft. Toss in the rice with the pepper, nutmeg, and salt.

Celery Stuffing (6 cups)

This is a more moist stuffing.

4 tablespoons butter
1 cup (¼ L) chopped celery
4 tablespoons finely chopped onion
4 tablespoons minced parsley
4 cups (1 L) dry bread crumbs
¼ teaspoon freshly ground pepper
¼ cup (½ dL) chicken broth
Salt to taste

Melt the butter in a skillet. Stir in the celery and onion and cook over low heat for 3–4 minutes. Remove from the heat and blend in the parsley, crumbs, pepper, chicken broth, and salt.

Sausage Stuffing (8 cups)

1 pound (450 g) sausage meat
4 tablespoons minced onion

8 cups (2 L) freshly made dry bread crumbs
1 teaspoon freshly ground pepper
2 tablespoons minced parsley
Salt to taste

Heat a skillet and add the sausage, crumbling it into small bits as it cooks. Brown lightly and remove to a bowl, leaving the drippings in the skillet. Add the onion and cook, stirring, for 2 minutes. Add the crumbs, pepper, and parsley, and cook 1 minute more, stirring to mix well. Toss with the sausage meat and salt.

Fried Apple Rings (serves four)

Serve these instead of applesauce with ham, pork dishes, or duck.

2 tart apples
4 tablespoons butter
2 tablespoons sugar

Core the apples. Peel them only if the skins are very tough. Cut them in ½-inch slices and sauté the slices in butter until just barely tender. Sprinkle with sugar, cover the pan, and cook a few minutes more, until they are glazed and golden.

Cranberry Sauce (serves eight–ten)

1 pound, 450 g (4 cups, 1 L) fresh cranberries
1½ cups (275 g) sugar

Wash the cranberries. Bring 2 cups of water to a boil, then add the cranberries and sugar. Cook for 10 minutes or until the skins pop. Skim off the white froth and cool. Refrigerate until ready to serve.

Cranberry and Orange Relish
(serves six)

½ pound, 225 g (2 cups, ½ L) cranberries
1 small orange
¾ cup (1¾ dL) sugar

Wash the cranberries. Cut the orange in pieces and remove the seeds; do not peel. Chop the cranberries and orange with a food chopper or in a food processor. Add the sugar and stir well. Let stand at least 30 minutes before serving.

Chili Sauce (1½ cups)

2 cups (½ L) canned tomatoes
1 onion, chopped
Dash of cayenne pepper
⅛ teaspoon ground cloves
⅛ teaspoon cinnamon
1 tablespoon sugar
¼ cup (½ dL) vinegar
2 tablespoons chopped green pepper
About ½ teaspoon salt

In a heavy-bottomed saucepan, combine the to-matoes, onion, cayenne, cloves, cinnamon, sugar, and vinegar. Simmer, uncovered, for 1 hour. Add the green pepper and simmer 30 minutes more. Add salt to taste. Chill before serving.

Mustard Relish (3 cups)

A food processor makes light work of preparing the chopped vegetables for this relish.

2 cups (½ L) shredded cabbage
1 sweet red pepper, chopped fine
½ large green pepper, chopped fine
⅓ cup (¾ dL) chopped onion
1½ cups (3½ dL) vinegar
Salt
¼ cup (50 g) sugar
3 tablespoons flour
2 teaspoons dry mustard
¼ teaspoon turmeric
¼ teaspoon celery seed

Mix the cabbage, red pepper, green pepper, onion, 1 cup of the vinegar, 1 cup of water, and 2 table-spoons salt, and let stand for several hours. In a heavy-bottomed pan, whisk the sugar, flour, mus-tard, turmeric, and celery seed. Slowly add the re-maining ½ cup of vinegar with ½ cup of cold water. Stir and cook over low heat until thick; cover and cook gently 10 minutes. Drain the vegetables. Add them to the dressing and simmer 5 minutes more. Taste, and add more salt if you wish. Chill before serving.

169

Basic Method for Preparing Fruit
Jam (2–3 pints)

The basic proportions for jam are ¾ cup sugar for each cup of prepared fruit.

4 cups (1 L) prepared fruit
3 cups (600 g) sugar

Wash the fruit thoroughly. Peel and remove cores, pits, stems, and seeds. Berries and small fruits may be crushed in the pan. Other fruits should be cut into small pieces. Measure the fruit before putting it into the pan. Cook until tender, adding just enough water to prevent burning. Add the sugar to the fruit, stirring until it dissolves. Boil rapidly until the jam is thick, stirring to prevent sticking. Test for the jellying point, using a thermometer, the sheet test, or the freezer test (see below). Pour into hot, sterilized jars and seal.

Testing for the Jellying Point

Since jellies and jams thicken as they cool, it is often difficult to determine when the hot jelly or jam has reached the proper consistency. There are three ways to test the jellying point:

Thermometer Test. A jelly or candy thermometer is probably the most accurate way to test for the jellying point. First it is necessary to know the boiling point of water in your locality, which can be determined by taking the temperature of water with your jelly thermometer. Jelly should register 8 degrees higher than the boiling point of water to assure the proper amount of jell.

Sheet Test. Using a cool metal spoon, scoop up a bit of the boiling jelly mixture. Tip the spoon and let the jelly run off the side. When the jelly separates from the spoon in a sheet, rather than in separate drops, it is done.

Freezer Test. Remove the jelly from the heat while making this test. Put a few drops on a plate and cool it quickly in the freezer to see if it will jell when cool.

Raspberry Jam (about 2 pints)

Since it's easy to overcook this jam, it's best to use a jelly thermometer when you make it.

4 cups (1 L) raspberries
3 cups (600 g) warm sugar

Clean the raspberries, put them in a large pot, and crush them with a potato masher. Cook for 15 minutes to reduce the juices. Add the sugar and bring to a boil. Cook stirring, until the mixture registers 214°F degrees on a jelly thermometer. Skim off the foam and let stand until cool. Pour into hot, *sterilized* jars and seal.

Blackberry Jam. Substitute *4 cups blackberries* for the raspberries. If you prefer to remove the seeds, put the cooked berries through a food mill or coarse sieve.

Raspberry Currant Jam. Use *3 cups raspberries* and *1 cup currants*.

Strawberry Preserves (about 2 pints)

3 cups (600 g) sugar
1 quart (1 L) strawberries

Cook the sugar and 1 cup water together until the mixture reaches 238°F on a jelly thermometer. Wash and hull the berries, add to the syrup, cover, and remove from heat. Let stand for 10 minutes. Skim off any foam. Remove the berries and set aside. Cook the syrup to 238°F again, add the berries, and let stand over very low heat for 15 minutes. Skim, remove the berries, and reheat again to 238°F. Add the berries once more and cook slowly until the syrup is thick. Let stand for 24 hours before putting into *sterilized* jars and closing them. Refrigerate, freeze, or process in a simmering-water bath at 185°F for 10–15 minutes.

Peach Preserves (about 7 half-pint jars)

10 large peaches, peeled, pitted, and sliced
6 cups (1200 g) sugar

Combine the peaches and the sugar and let stand in a cool place overnight. Boil gently, stirring frequently, until the fruit is clear and the syrup thick, about 45 minutes. Pour into hot, *sterilized* jars and seal.

Grape Conserve (about ten 6-ounce jars)

5 pounds (2¼ kg) Concord grapes

½ orange, in thin slivers
Sugar
½ cup (1 dL) walnut pieces

Wash the grapes, remove the stems, and separate the pulp from the skins; reserve the skins. Heat the pulp gently to free the seeds, stirring to prevent sticking. Put through a sieve or food mill and discard the seeds. Add the orange to the grape pulp and skins and measure. Add an equal amount of sugar to the grape mixture. Cook slowly in a large, flat skillet, in two batches, if necessary. Use the freezer test (p. 171) to see if the conserve is thick, then add the walnuts. Spoon into hot, *sterilized* jars and seal.

Cranberry Conserve
(about three 6-ounce jars)

4 cups (1 L) cranberries
⅔ cup (1½ dL) boiling apple or pineapple juice
¼ pound (115 g) seedless raisins
1 orange, sliced, seeded, and cut small
1½ pounds (675 g) sugar
½ pound (225 g) walnut or filbert meats, cut in pieces

Wash the cranberries and put them in a large pot. Add ⅔ cup cold water and cook until the skins break. Force through a strainer or food mill. Add the apple or pineapple juice, raisins, orange, and sugar. Bring to a boil, then simmer for 20 minutes. Add the nuts and let cool. Spoon into clean jars, close the jars, and process in a simmering-water bath at 185°F for 10–15 minutes.

Cranberry Ginger Conserve. Add *½ cup preserved ginger, cut small,* along with the raisins and orange.

Orange Marmalade   (about 3 pints)

6 large oranges
2 lemons
Sugar

Peel the oranges and cut the peel into very thin slices. Cut up the orange pulp. Slice the lemons very thin. Combine the fruit in a large pot and add 1½ quarts water. Bring to a boil and simmer for about 10 minutes; then let stand overnight in a cool place. Bring to a boil again and cook rapidly until the peel is tender. Measure the fruit and liquid. For each cup of undrained fruit measure ¾ cup sugar and add it to the fruit. Heat, stirring, until the sugar is dissolved, then cook rapidly until the jellying point is reached (p. 170), about 30 minutes. Pour into hot, *sterilized* jars and seal.

Ginger Marmalade. Add *2½ cups chopped preserved ginger* to each quart of fruit before boiling to the jellying point.

Apple Butter (about ten 6-ounce jars)

This recipe works for other fruit butters as well: use fresh apricots, peaches, plums, or the pulp in the jelly bag after the juice has been extracted. When using fruits that are juicier than apples, crush them and add just enough water, not cider or vinegar, to keep the fruit from sticking.

4 pounds (1¾ kg) tart apples
2 cups (½ L) cider, cider vinegar, or water
Sugar
Salt
About 2 teaspoons cinnamon
About 1 teaspoon ground cloves
About ½ teaspoon allspice
Grated rind and juice of 1 lemon

Cut the apples into pieces without peeling or coring them. Put them in a pot, cover with the cider, vinegar, or water, and cook until soft. Put through a sieve or food mill. Measure. Add ½ cup sugar for each cup of apple pulp. To the whole mixture, add a dash of salt and the cinnamon, cloves, allspice, and lemon rind and juice. Cook, covered, over low heat until the sugar dissolves, taste, and adjust the seasonings. Uncover and cook quickly, stirring constantly to prevent burning, until thick and smooth when a bit is spooned onto a cold plate. Pour into hot, *sterilized* jars and seal.

Brandied Peaches (2 or 3 pint jars)

Use perfect peaches for this. If the skins are thin, it is not necessary to peel them: simply rub off the fuzz with a clean cloth and prick each peach twice with a fork. Store these for a month before using.

6 peaches
2 cups (400 g) sugar
Brandy

Peel the peaches, if you wish, dipping them quickly in hot water before removing the skins. Combine the sugar with 3 cups water and boil for 10 minutes. Cook the peaches, a few at a time, in the sugar syrup until tender when pricked with a toothpick, about 5 minutes. Pack into clean, hot jars, adding 2 tablespoons of brandy to each pint jar. Fill the jars with syrup, close the jars, and process in a simmering-water bath at 185°F for 10–15 minutes.

Brandied Cherries. Substitute *2 pounds firm cherries* for the peaches.

Bread-and-Butter Pickles
(about 4 pints)

Use Kirby cucumbers or other small, unwaxed cucumbers, and tiny white onions, if possible.

6 cups (1½ L) thin-sliced cucumbers
1 pound (450 g) onions
1 green pepper, shredded
¼ cup (½ dL) salt
2 cups (½ L) brown sugar
½ teaspoon turmeric
¼ teaspoon ground cloves
1 tablespoon mustard seed

1 teaspoon celery seed
2 cups (½ L) cider vinegar

Mix the cucumbers, onions (sliced if large), green pepper, and salt. Cover and let stand for 3 hours. Mix the remaining ingredients in a large pot, bring slowly to the boiling point, and boil for 5 minutes. Drain the vegetables in a colander and rinse them well with cold water. Add them to the hot syrup and heat to just below the boiling point. Spoon into hot *sterilized* jars, fill with the cooking syrup, leaving ⅛-inch headspace, and seal. Or, if you prefer, process in a boiling-water bath for 10 minutes.

Dill Pickles (6–8 quarts)

About 50 unwaxed 3–4-inch cucumbers
1 quart (1 L) cider vinegar
¾ cup (1¾ dL) salt
Fresh dill sprigs
Garlic cloves, peeled

Put the cucumbers in the sink, cover with cold water and let stand overnight. Drain and pack them into hot, *sterilized* jars. Combine the vinegar and salt with 2 quarts water in a pot and bring to the boiling point. Pour over the cucumbers, leaving ¼-inch headspace. Add a sprig or two of dill and a clove of peeled garlic to each jar and seal. Or close the jars and process in a boiling-water bath for 15 minutes.

Mustard Pickles (8 pints)

Be careful not to overcook so these pickles remain crisp.

3 pounds (1½ kg) small cucumbers, sliced
3 large cucumbers, cubed
2 pounds (900 g) green tomatoes, diced
1½ pounds (675 g) small white onions, peeled
4 green peppers, diced
1 large cauliflower, in small pieces
½ cup (1 dL) salt
1 cup (140 g) flour
6 tablespoons dry mustard
1 tablespoon turmeric
2 quarts (2 L) cider vinegar
2 cups (400 g) sugar

Put the cucumbers, tomatoes, onions, peppers, and cauliflower in a large bowl. Mix the salt with 4 quarts cold water, pour over the vegetables, cover, and let stand for 8 hours or overnight. Drain and rinse under cold water. Put the vegetables in a pot, cover them with fresh cold water, bring to the boiling point, and drain in a colander once again. Put the flour, mustard, and turmeric in the pot. Stir in enough vinegar to make a smooth paste, then gradually add the remaining vinegar and the sugar, stirring well. Bring to a boil, stirring constantly, and cook until thick and smooth. Add the vegetables and cook, stirring, until heated through. Spoon into hot, *sterilized* jars, leaving ¼-inch headspace, and seal. Or close the jars and process in a boiling-water bath for 10 minutes.

Corn Relish (about 6 pints)

Use sweet pimiento for a mild relish, hot red pepper for a spicy one. A food processor will be handy here.

18 ears of corn
1 head green cabbage, chopped fine
8 white onions, chopped fine
½ cup (1 dL) chopped pimiento, or 4 small hot red peppers
6 green peppers, chopped fine
2 quarts (2 L) vinegar
2 cups (400 g) sugar
¼ cup (½ dL) salt
2 teaspoons celery seed
2 teaspoons mustard seed

Cut the kernels from the corn ears. Combine them with the remaining ingredients in a large pot, bring to the boiling point, and simmer for 40 minutes. Spoon into hot, *sterilized* jars, leaving ⅛-inch headspace, and seal. If you wish, process in a boiling-water bath for 15 minutes.

Red or Green Pepper Relish
(6–7 pints)

You can chop the vegetables for this and other relishes coarse or fine, according to your preference. Use a food processor, if you have one, to save time and effort.

24 sweet red or green peppers or a combination
12 onions, peeled

6 stalks celery
1 quart (1 L) cider vinegar
2 cups (400 g) sugar
3 tablespoons salt
1 tablespoon mustard or celery seed

Chop the peppers, onions, and celery, cover with boiling water, then drain. Put them in a pot, cover with cold water, bring to the boiling point, then drain again. Mix the vinegar, sugar, salt, and mustard or celery seed in a pot, heat to the boiling point, add the vegetables, and simmer for about 10 minutes, adjusting the seasonings if necessary. Spoon into clean, hot jars, fill with the cooking liquid, leaving ⅛-inch headspace, and seal. If you wish, process in a boiling-water bath for 10 minutes.

Piccalilli   (6 pints)

Sweet and spicy.

12 green tomatoes
4 green peppers
2 sweet red peppers
6 onions, peeled
1 small cabbage
¼ cup (½ dL) salt
3 cups (¾ L) light-brown sugar
1½ teaspoons celery seed
1 tablespoon mustard seed
1 tablespoon cloves
2-inch stick cinnamon
1 tablespoon whole allspice
2 cups (½ L) cider vinegar

Chop the tomatoes, peppers, onions, and cabbage coarsely. Sprinkle them with the salt, cover, and let stand overnight. Cover with cold water and then drain. Mix the remaining ingredients in a large pot. Add the vegetables and bring to the boiling point. Reduce the heat and simmer for about 15 minutes. Spoon into hot, *sterilized* jars, fill with the cooking liquid, leaving ⅛-inch headspace, and seal. If you wish, process in a boiling-water bath for 10 minutes.

Green Tomato Relish (4 pints)

4 pounds (1¾ kg) green tomatoes, chopped (about 8 cups, 2 L)
¼ cup (½ dL) salt
1 teaspoon freshly ground pepper
1½ teaspoons dry mustard
1½ teaspoons cinnamon
½ teaspoon allspice
1½ teaspoons ground cloves
¼ cup (½ dL) mustard seed
1 quart (1 L) cider vinegar
1 cup (¼ L) light-brown sugar
2 sweet red or green peppers, chopped
1 onion, chopped

Mix the tomatoes with the salt, cover, and let stand overnight or for 24 hours. Wash in cold water and drain. Mix the remaining ingredients in a pot, add the tomatoes, and bring to a boil. Cook gently for about 15 minutes. Spoon into hot, *sterilized* jars, leaving ⅛-inch headspace, and seal. If you wish, process in a boiling-water bath for 10 minutes.

181

Tomato Relish (2 pints)

This is a tart, red tomato relish. Add more sugar if you want it to be sweet.

1 bunch celery
2 large green peppers
1 onion
6 large tomatoes, peeled and cut in pieces
1 tablespoon salt
1 tablespoon sugar
1¼ cups (3 dL) cider vinegar

Chop the celery, peppers, and onion and mix in a large pot. Add the tomatoes, salt, sugar, and vinegar and simmer, stirring occasionally, until thick, about 1½ hours. Spoon into hot, *sterilized* jars, leaving ⅛-inch headspace, and seal. If you wish, process in a boiling-water bath for 10 minutes.

Sweet Chili Sauce (3–4 pints)

Good with hamburgers and steak.

3 pounds (1⅓ kg) (about 4 cups, 1 L) ripe
   tomatoes, peeled and cut up
2 green peppers, chopped fine
2 onions, chopped fine
2 apples, cored and chopped fine
½–1 cup (100–200 g) sugar
1 tablespoon salt
½ teaspoon freshly ground pepper

1 teaspoon cinnamon
1 teaspoon ground cloves
½ teaspoon allspice
1 teaspoon nutmeg
1 cup (¼ L) cider vinegar

Cook the tomatoes slowly for about 30 minutes, until they are soft. Stir in the peppers, onions, and apples and cook 30 minutes more. Add the remaining ingredients, adjusting the amount of sugar to taste. Boil until thick, about 10 minutes, stirring frequently and taking care not to let the mixture burn. Spoon into hot, *sterilized* jars, leaving ⅛-inch headspace, and seal. If you wish, process in a boiling-water bath for 15 minutes.

Peach Chutney (three or four 6-ounce jars)

2 cups (½ L) cider vinegar
3 cups (600 g) sugar
4 cups (1 L) (about 2 pounds, 900 g) peaches, peeled, pitted, and cut up
½ pound (225 g) currants or raisins
2 cloves garlic, minced
2 tablespoons candied ginger, cut fine

Combine the vinegar and sugar in a pot and bring to a boil. Add the remaining ingredients, and cook slowly for about 2 hours, stirring occasionally to prevent sticking. Spoon into hot, *sterilized* jars, leaving ¼-inch headspace, and seal. If you wish, process in a boiling-water bath for 10 minutes.

Apple Chutney (7 pints)

A splendid sweet-and-spicy partner to ham and other pork dishes. Use ripe, red tomatoes, if you wish. You may add ½ cup of finely cut mint leaves, if you have them.

1½ pounds (675 g) green tomatoes, chopped (about 3 cups, ¾ L)
4 tablespoons salt
1 quart (1 L) cider vinegar
1 pound (450 g) dark-brown sugar
12 large, tart apples, cored and chopped
2 Spanish onions, peeled and chopped
1 pound (450 g) raisins
2 tablespoons ground ginger

Put the tomatoes in a bowl, toss them with 2 tablespoons of the salt, cover, and let stand for about 12 hours. Drain and soak them in cold water for a few minutes, then drain again. Heat the vinegar, the remaining 2 tablespoons of salt, and the sugar in a large pot. Add the drained tomatoes, the apples, onions, raisins, and ginger, and cook over low heat for about 30 minutes, until the apples and onions are tender. Spoon into hot, *sterilized* jars, leaving ¼-inch headspace, and seal. If you wish, process in a boiling-water bath for 10 minutes.

Ginger Apple Chutney. Omit the ground ginger and substitute *6 ounces preserved ginger, cut small.*

Watermelon Pickle (2 quarts)

Sweet and spicy, this will appeal to thrifty souls because it uses the watermelon rind that would otherwise go uneaten.

Rind from 1 large watermelon
½ cup (1 dL) salt
2½ cups (6 dL) cider vinegar
2 cups (400 g) sugar
2 teaspoons cloves
1 small stick cinnamon, in pieces
2 tablespoons whole allspice

Remove the pink pulp from the watermelon and cut the rind into manageable pieces. Cover with boiling water and boil for 5 minutes; drain and cool. Cut off the green outer skin of the watermelon rind and remove any remaining bits of pink pulp. Cut the rind into 1-inch strips or squares or any shape you prefer. You should have about 8 cups of cut-up rind. Mix the salt with 1½ quarts cold water and pour over the rind. Let stand at room temperature for about 6 hours. Drain, soak in several changes of fresh, cold water, and drain again. Cover with fresh, cold water, bring to a boil, and simmer until just tender when pierced with a fork; drain. Mix the vinegar, 1 cup water, and the sugar in a pot, then add the cloves, cinnamon, and allspice tied in a cheesecloth bag. Simmer until the sugar dissolves. Add the watermelon rind and simmer until it is clear, adding more water only if necessary. Remove the spice bag. Pack in hot, *sterilized* jars and cover with the boiling liquid, leaving ¼-inch headspace, and seal. If you wish, process in a boiling-water bath for 10 minutes.

Ginger Watermelon Pickle. Add *1–2 tablespoons chopped preserved ginger* to the vinegar mixture.

Rice, Beans, Pasta & Crêpes

Boiled Rice (3 cups white rice or 2 cups brown rice)

There is no reason to worry about failures if you cook rice like pasta in lots of boiling salted water and watch the timing.

1 teaspoon salt
1 cup (¼ L) rice

Bring about 3 quarts water and salt to a boil in a deep pot. Trickle the rice slowly into the water so that it doesn't stop boiling. Don't stir, but give the pan a shake so the rice levels. Keep the water boiling over medium-high heat. White rice will be done in 15–18 minutes; brown rice will be done in 35–40 minutes. Test at the minimum time by removing a few grains with a slotted spoon; bite into the kernel—it should be firm, not mushy and splayed out at the ends. If in doubt, it is better to undercook the rice slightly and steam it longer at the end, particularly if you are planning to hold the rice 10 or 15 minutes before serving. Drain the rice in a colander. Keep warm by placing the colander over gently boiling water, covering the rice with a dish towel.

Baked Rice (serves four)

A nice way to serve rice when the meat is rather plain and the casserole, popped in the oven about a half an hour before serving, is all ready to come to the table.

⅓ cup (¾ dL) chopped onion
2 tablespoons butter
1 cup (¼ L) rice
2 bouillon cubes, chicken or beef

Preheat the oven to 375°F (190°C). Sauté the onion in the butter about 3 minutes. Add the rice and stir, cooking just long enough to coat it, 2 or 3 minutes. Pour in 2 cups water, bring to the boil, stir in the bouillon cubes, dissolve, and mix well. Turn into a 1-quart casserole, cover, and bake for 30 minutes.

Baked Rice with Pepper and Ham. Add *½ cup chopped green* or *red pepper* along with the onion. After the rice has been coated, add up to *1 cup chopped ham*. Sprinkle the top with *2–3 tablespoons Swiss* or *Parmesan cheese* and remove the cover for the last 5 minutes of baking.

Saffron Rice with Raisins and Pine Nuts. Before turning the mixture into the casserole, remove ¼ cup of the hot liquid and pour over *⅛ teaspoon crumbled saffron;* let steep 5 minutes. Remove to the casserole and stir in *½ cup raisins* and *2 tablespoons pine nuts.*

Turkish Pilaf   (serves four)

Pilaf is a seasoned rice dish common to many Eastern countries. It can be a whole meal made with fish, poultry, or meat, or a simple side dish made with herbs, spices, nuts, or raisins.

3 tablespoons olive oil
3 tablespoons finely chopped onion
1 cup (¼ L) long-grain rice
½ teaspoon salt
¼ teaspoon freshly ground pepper
2 cups (½ L) beef broth

Heat the oil in a saucepan. Add the onion and cook, stirring often, until soft. Add the rice and cook over low heat, stirring constantly, for 3 minutes. Add the salt, pepper, and beef broth. Cover and simmer 20 minutes or transfer to a covered casserole and bake in a 350°F (180°C) oven for 1 hour.

Mushroom Pilaf. Add the broth to *1 cup chopped mushrooms* that have been sautéed in *2 tablespoons butter.*

Chicken Pilaf. Substitute *2 cups chicken broth* for the beef broth, and with the broth add *1 cup diced cooked chicken* and *½ teaspoon tarragon, crumbled.*

Spanish Rice   (serves four)

4 tablespoons olive oil
1 onion, chopped
1 small green pepper, chopped

189

2 cloves garlic, minced
1 rib celery, diced
1 cup (¼ L) chopped mushrooms
2 large tomatoes, peeled and chopped
1 cup (¼ L) long-grain rice
½ teaspoon salt
¼ teaspoon freshly ground pepper
2 cups (½ L) chicken broth

Preheat the oven to 375°F (190°C). Lightly oil a 2-quart casserole. Heat the olive oil in a skillet and add the onion, green pepper, garlic, celery, and mushrooms. Cook over medium-low heat, stirring often, for 5 minutes. Transfer to a casserole and add the tomatoes, rice, salt, and pepper. Pour in the broth, stir, cover, and bake 30 minutes. Stir again and bake for another 30 minutes.

Fried Rice (serves four)

Add cooked diced shrimp, pork, or chicken, if you wish, and serve as a supper dish.

4 tablespoons oil
4 cups (1 L) cooked rice
4 tablespoons chopped scallions
1½ tablespoons soy sauce
¼ teaspoon freshly ground pepper
2 eggs, slightly beaten

Heat the oil in a large skillet, and add the rice, scallions, soy sauce, and pepper. Cook over medium-high heat, stirring often, for 6 minutes. Add the eggs and stir briskly so they cook and break into small bits throughout the rice. As soon as the egg is set, remove and serve.

Rice and Pecan Loaf (serves six)

An old southern tradition, utterly simple and delicious.

1½ cups (3½ dL) cooked brown rice
1½ cups (3½ dL) coarsely chopped pecans
1½ cups (3½ dL) cracker crumbs
1 egg, well beaten
1¼ cups (3 dL) milk
1 teaspoon salt
½ teaspoon freshly ground pepper
3 tablespoons butter, melted
1 recipe Onion Sauce (p. 151)

Preheat the oven to 350°F (180°C). Butter a 2-quart loaf pan or casserole. Mix rice, pecans, crumbs, egg, milk, salt, and pepper until well blended. Turn into the loaf pan or casserole and pour melted butter on top. Bake 50–60 minutes and serve with the sauce.

Curried Rice (serves four)

3 tablespoons oil
1 onion, chopped fine
1 cup (¼ L) long-grain rice
2 teaspoons curry powder
½ teaspoon salt

2 tablespoons butter
½ cup (1 dL) raisins
2 cups (½ L) chicken broth

Preheat the oven to 375°F (190°C). Butter a 1½-quart casserole. Heat the oil in a skillet, add the onion, and cook until it is soft. Stir in the rice and cook, stirring, for 3 minutes. Add the curry powder, salt, butter, and raisins, and cook 1 minute more. Transfer to a casserole, pour in the chicken broth, stir, cover, and bake for 1 hour.

Wild Rice (3 cups)

Wild rice is expensive and special. Cook it simply to enjoy its distinctive flavor and texture.

1 cup (¼ L) wild rice
1 teaspoon salt
4 tablespoons butter

Rinse the rice several times in cold water and remove any foreign particles. Boil 3 cups water with the salt and slowly add the rice. Simmer for 45–50 minutes or until the grain is tender and has absorbed all the water. Stir in the butter, toss with a fork, and serve.

Preparing Dried Beans for Cooking

Wash beans by covering them with cold water and picking out any pebbles or floating particles. Soak them overnight to reduce the cooking time, or, if you forget to do this or are short of time, use the following short method: put 2 cups of beans in a pot, cover with 6 cups water, bring to a boil, and cook for 2 minutes; remove from the heat, cover the pot, and let stand for 1 hour before cooking.

Lentils do not have to be soaked before cooking, nor do those beans with package directions that say "no soaking necessary."

Boston Baked Beans (serves eight)

2 cups (½ L) navy beans, small white beans, or
   Great Northern beans
About 1 teaspoon salt
¼ pound (115 g) salt pork
2 teaspoons dry mustard
5 tablespoons dark-brown sugar
4 tablespoons molasses

Wash the beans. Soak overnight or use the short method (above). Add salt, stir and drain, reserving the liquid. Preheat the oven to 300°F (150°C). Cut off a third of the salt pork and place the piece on the bottom of a bean pot. Add the beans to the pot. Blend the mustard, brown sugar, and molasses with the reserved bean liquid and pour over the beans. Cut several gashes in the remaining piece of salt pork and place on top of the beans. Cover and bake for about 6 hours, adding water as needed. Uncover for the final hour of cooking so the pork will become brown and crisp. Taste and correct seasoning.

Chili Beans (serves eight)

A touch of cayenne pepper heightens the taste of this old favorite.

2 cups (½ L) red, pink, or pinto beans
¼ pound (115 g) salt pork, diced fine
2 large onions, chopped
2 cloves garlic, chopped
2 tablespoons bacon fat, if needed
1 teaspoon freshly ground pepper
About 1 teaspoon salt
¾ teaspoon oregano, crumbled
½ teaspoon sage, crumbled
½ teaspoon cumin
2 tablespoons chili powder
¼ teaspoon cayenne pepper (optional)
2 tablespoons cornmeal
1 cup (¼ L) peeled and chopped fresh or canned tomatoes

Wash the beans. Soak overnight. Or use the short method (p. 192), in either case do not drain. Sauté the salt pork; after 5 minutes, add the onions and garlic and cook until the onions are golden. If the pork does not render enough fat, add 2 tablespoons bacon fat. Add black pepper, salt, oregano, sage, cumin, chili powder, cayenne pepper (if you wish), cornmeal, tomatoes, and 1 cup of the bean liquid. Cook, stirring constantly, for 5 minutes and add to the pot of beans and liquid. Stir to blend, and simmer for 2 hours, checking frequently to see if the liquid needs replenishing. Taste, and correct seasoning.

Refried Beans with Cheese
(serves eight)

A classic dish south-of-the-border. "Refried" means that they are first simmered and then fried.

2 cups (½ L) pink or pinto beans
About 1½ teaspoons salt
½ teaspoon freshly ground pepper
5 tablespoons bacon fat
1½ cups (3½ dL) cubed Cheddar or Monterey
   Jack cheese

Wash the beans. Soak overnight or use the short method (p. 192). Return to the heat and simmer about 1½ hours, or until tender. Add salt and pepper. Heat the bacon fat in a skillet. Drain 1 cup of beans and put in the skillet. Mash thoroughly, adding ½ cup of the reserved liquid. Stir and cook for 1–2 minutes. Add and mash more beans with more of the reserved liquid. Repeat until all the beans and liquid have been used and the mixture is creamy. Add the cheese, blend, and cook until the cheese is melted.

Lima Beans Fermière   (serves six)

2 cups (½ L) dried lima beans
1 teaspoon salt
¼ teaspoon freshly ground pepper
¼ pound (115 g) salt pork, diced
1 onion, chopped

1 cup (¼ L) finely diced carrot
2 tablespoons butter

Wash the lima beans. Soak overnight or use the short method (p. 192). Drain the beans and put in a casserole, reserving the liquid. Stir in the salt and pepper. Preheat the oven to 300°F (150°C). Cook the salt pork in a skillet until it is golden brown. Add the onion and carrot, and cook, stirring, until the vegetables are golden. Mix the vegetables and butter into the casserole with the lima beans. Pour in 1 cup reserved bean liquid, cover, and bake for 2 hours, adding more bean liquid as needed.

Lentils and Lamb (serves six)

This classic combination is a harbinger of spring.

1 cup (¼ L) dried lentils
1 onion, chopped
2 tablespoons finely chopped parsley
2 cloves garlic, minced
½ cup (1 dL) chopped celery
¼ teaspoon freshly ground pepper
1 teaspoon salt
2 tomatoes, peeled, seeded, and chopped
2 cups (½ L) cooked lamb, in bite-size pieces

Wash the lentils. Add 5 cups water with the onion, parsley, garlic, celery, pepper, salt, and tomatoes. Bring to a boil and simmer 30 minutes, or until the lentils are tender. Drain, reserving the liquid, and put the lentils into a casserole. Preheat the oven to 350°F (180°C). Put 2½ cups of liquid into a saucepan and boil briskly until it is reduced by half, about 15 minutes. Pour over the lentils, stir in the lamb, cover, and bake 1 hour.

Lentils and Ham. Omit the lamb and salt and add *2 cups chopped cooked ham.*

Lentils and Sausage. Omit the lamb and add *1 pound sausage meat,* browned in a skillet. Cover the lentils with *3 strips of bacon* and uncover the pot for the last 30 minutes of cooking so the bacon will crisp.

Alfredo's Noodles (serves three to four)

You may know this creamy, delicate dish as Fettucine Alfredo. As a first course, which is the way Italians would serve it, this recipe makes enough for four.

½ pound (225 g) noodles, ¼ inch wide
¼ pound (115 g) sweet butter, melted
1 cup (¼ L) heavy cream, warmed
¾ cup (1¾ dL) freshly grated Parmesan cheese
Salt to taste
¼ teaspoon freshly ground pepper

Have a large bowl warmed and ready before you cook the noodles. Drain the cooked noodles and put them into the bowl. Quickly add remaining ingredients, tossing briskly to coat all the noodles, and serve at once.

Noodles with Poppy Seeds. Omit the Parmesan cheese and add *3 tablespoons poppy seeds.*

Cannelloni (serves eight)

This cannelloni is made with crêpes, which gives the finished dish a delightful texture. It can also be made with the pasta that is sold as cannelloni, if you can find it. The same filling could go into manicotti and ravioli.

1 recipe Crêpes or French Pancakes (p. 318)

Filling

1 onion, chopped fine
3 tablespoons olive oil
1 clove garlic, minced
1 pound (450 g) lean ground beef
2 tablespoons cream
1 teaspoon oregano, crumbled
2 eggs
1½ pounds (675 g) fresh spinach, cooked, drained, and chopped; or one 10-ounce (285-g) package frozen spinach, thawed and drained
Salt to taste
Freshly ground pepper

Sauté the onion in the olive oil until just soft, then add the garlic and cook, stirring, a minute more. Remove to a bowl. Add the beef to the skillet, breaking it up, and cook until it loses its pinkness. Scrape into the onion and garlic, then add the cream, oregano, eggs, spinach, salt, and pepper. Mix vigorously with a wooden spoon or with your hands until the ingredients are well blended. Set aside.

Sauce I

6 tablespoons butter
6 tablespoons flour
1 cup (¼ L) hot milk
1 cup (¼ L) heavy cream
¼ teaspoon nutmeg
Salt to taste
Freshly ground pepper

Melt the butter in a saucepan, add the flour, and cook, stirring constantly, over medium heat 3–4 minutes. Add the milk, stirring until the sauce is smooth and thick, then add the cream and continue to cook gently a few minutes. Sprinkle in the nutmeg, salt and pepper to taste. Set aside.

Sauce II

1½ cups (3½ dL) Tomato Sauce (p. 154)

To Assemble the Cannelloni: Preheat the oven to 375°F (190°C). Film the bottom of a shallow baking dish, about 13 × 9 × 2 inches, with tomato sauce. Fill each crêpe with 4 tablespoons of the filling. Roll up and place each crêpe seam side down in the baking dish. Proceed until the crêpes are filled and in a single layer. Spoon the white sauce, Sauce I, over the top and drizzle the remaining tomato sauce lengthwise in two rivulets over the white sauce. Bake for 40 minutes or until the sauce bubbles around the edges.

Cheese-stuffed Manicotti
(serves four or eight)

Manicotti are large tubular pasta shapes, about 4 inches long and 1½ inches in diameter. Here are three fillings for manicotti: a mild cheese filling, a heartier meat filling (for which you could use cooked beef if you have some leftovers), and a subtle chicken or turkey filling. All are quite rich and the dish will serve eight as a first course or lunch dish, but for a main dinner dish, count on its serving only four with just a green salad.

8 manicotti, cooked, slightly underdone, and drained

Stuffing

2 cups (½ L) ricotta or small-curd cottage cheese
1 egg, slightly beaten
2 tablespoons minced parsley
4 tablespoons freshly grated Parmesan cheese
1 teaspoon basil, crumbled
¼ teaspoon nutmeg
½ teaspoon salt
¼ teaspoon freshly ground pepper

Combine the ricotta or cottage cheese with remaining ingredients. Mix well and use it to stuff the manicotti.

Sauce

¼ pound (115 g) butter
7 tablespoons flour

3 cups (¾ L) chicken broth
1 cup (¼ L) heavy cream
2 cups (½ L) grated Monterey Jack cheese
¼ teaspoon Tabasco
Salt to taste

Melt the butter in a saucepan. Stir in the flour and cook, stirring constantly, for 3 minutes. Slowly stir in the broth and cream and cook 3 minutes more, until sauce is smooth and thickened. Add the cheese, Tabasco, and salt and cook until the cheese melts.

To Assemble the Manicotti: Preheat the oven to 375°F (190°C). Film the bottom of an 11¾ × 7½ × 1¾-inch baking pan with the sauce. Make a single layer of the stuffed manicotti. Cover with the remaining sauce, cover with foil, and bake 1 hour.

Beef-Spinach Stuffed Manicotti

8 manicotti, cooked, slightly underdone, and
    drained
3 tablespoons olive oil
½ pound (225 g) lean ground beef
½ cup (1 dL) minced onion
1 cup (¼ L) freshly made bread crumbs
3 tablespoons freshly grated Parmesan cheese
3 eggs, slightly beaten
1½ pounds (675 g) fresh spinach, cooked,
    drained, and chopped, or 10-ounce (285-g)
    package frozen spinach, thawed, drained, and
    chopped

½ teaspoon salt
¼ teaspoon freshly ground pepper
2 cups Tomato Sauce (p. 154)

Preheat the oven to 375°F (190°C). Heat the olive oil in a skillet and add the beef and onion. Cook, breaking the meat into tiny bits with a fork, until it has lost its pinkness. Put the meat and onion in a bowl and mix with the bread crumbs, cheese, eggs, spinach, salt, and pepper. Stuff the cooked manicotti with the mixture and make a single layer in an 11¾ × 7½ × 1¾-inch baking dish, allowing space between the manicotti for expansion. Spoon the tomato sauce evenly over the top, cover with foil, and bake 45 minutes.

Spaghetti with Clams   (serves four)

¼ pound (115 g) butter
⅓ cup (¾ dL) olive oil
½ teaspoon freshly ground pepper
1 teaspoon oregano, crumbled
2 tablespoons basil, crumbled
3 cloves garlic, minced
1½ cups (3½ dL) minced clams, fresh or canned
1 cup (¼ L) clam juice, fresh or bottled
Salt
1 pound (450 g) spaghetti
½ cup (1 dL) freshly grated Parmesan cheese
3 tablespoons minced parsley

Melt the butter in a skillet and add the olive oil, pepper, oregano, basil, garlic, clams, and clam juice. Simmer for 30 minutes. Add salt to taste. Warm a large bowl while you cook the spaghetti. Drain the spaghetti, put it into the bowl, and add the clam sauce. Toss with the cheese and parsley and serve immediately.

Vermicelli in Fresh Tomato Sauce (serves six)

6 vine-ripened tomatoes, peeled and chopped
1 tablespoon lemon juice
2 teaspoons basil, crumbled
¼ teaspoon freshly ground pepper
4 tablespoons finely chopped parsley
½ cup (1 dL) olive oil
3 cloves garlic, minced
½ cup (1 dL) sliced scallions
Salt to taste
1 pound (450 g) vermicelli

Mix the tomatoes, lemon juice, basil, pepper, and parsley in a bowl. Heat the olive oil in a saucepan. Add the garlic and cook, stirring, for 2 minutes; add the scallions and continue to cook and stir for 1 minute more. Add the tomato mixture and salt, and simmer for 10 minutes as you cook the vermicelli. Drain the pasta, place in a large warm bowl, add the tomato mixture, and mix well.

Macaroni and Cheese (serves four)

It is so easy and inexpensive to make this favorite dish from scratch.

9 ounces (250 g) macaroni, cooked
2 cups (½ L) Cheese Sauce (p. 148)
½ cup (1 dL) grated sharp Cheddar cheese
½ cup (1 dL) freshly made buttered bread crumbs

Preheat the oven to 375°F (190°C). Butter a 1½-quart casserole. Put the cooked macaroni into the casserole, pour the cheese sauce over it, and mix gently with a fork. Sprinkle the grated cheese evenly over the top and spread the crumbs over the cheese. Bake uncovered, until the top is golden and the sauce is bubbling, about 30 minutes.

Macaroni and Cheese with Chipped Beef. Take ¼ *pound dried beef,* separate the slices, cover with boiling water, and let stand 5 minutes. Drain well, chop into coarse pieces, and mix in with the cheese sauce before adding it to the macaroni.

Lasagne (serves six)

3 tablespoons olive oil
½ cup (1 dL) chopped onions
⅓ cup (¾ dL) chopped carrots
3 cloves garlic, minced
1 pound (450 g) lean ground beef
3 cups (¾ L) canned Italian plum tomatoes
3 tablespoons butter, melted
1 teaspoon oregano, crumbled

1 tablespoon basil, crumbled
1 teaspoon salt
½ teaspoon freshly ground pepper
½ pound (225 g) lasagna noodles, cooked
½ pound (225 g) mozzarella cheese, grated
2 cups (½ L) ricotta cheese
¼ pound (115 g) freshly grated Parmesan cheese

Heat the oil in a skillet. Add the onions, carrots, and garlic, and cook, stirring, until they are lightly browned. Push to the side of the pan and add the beef. Break it up into bits, cooking until it loses its pink color. Purée the tomatoes in a blender or food processor, add to the meat, and simmer 15 minutes. Add the butter, oregano, basil, salt, and pepper, partially cover, and simmer 30 minutes. Preheat the oven to 375°F (190°C). Assemble the lasagne by drizzling some sauce over the bottom of a shallow rectangular baking dish. Put in a layer of noodles, sprinkle with some of the mozzarella, and spread on a layer of ricotta. Make another layer of noodles, sauce, mozzarella, and ricotta. Finish with noodles and sauce. Sprinkle Parmesan cheese evenly over the top and bake 20 minutes or until hot and bubbling.

Chicken or Turkey Crêpes

(filling for 12 crêpes)

4 tablespoons butter
2 tablespoons finely chopped shallots or scallions
4 tablespoons flour
1¼ cups (3 dL) light cream

205

¾ cup (1¾ dL) chicken broth
¼ cup (½ dL) dry white wine
¼ teaspoon tarragon, crumbled
2 egg yolks, slightly beaten
2 cups (½ L) diced cooked chicken or turkey
Salt
1 recipe Crêpes or French Pancakes (p. 318)

Melt the butter in a saucepan, add the shallots or scallions, and cook, stirring, for 2 minutes. Add the flour, stir to blend, and slowly add 1 cup of the cream, stirring constantly. Add the broth, wine, and tarragon, and stir over medium-low heat until the sauce thickens. Cook for 5 minutes. Beat 3 tablespoons of hot sauce into the yolks, and then return the yolk-sauce mixture to the saucepan, stirring briskly. Cook 1 minute more, and remove from the heat. Mix half the sauce with the chicken or turkey and add salt to taste. Preheat the oven to 350°F (180°C). Fill each crêpe with 3 tablespoons of the filling. Roll and place seam side down in a baking dish approximately 13 × 9 × 2 inches. Thin the rest of the sauce with the remaining ¼ cup cream and spread it over the crêpes. Bake for 25 minutes, or until the sauce begins to bubble.

Chicken and Mushroom Filling. Omit the shallots or scallions and the tarragon. Sauté *2 cups sliced mushrooms* in the melted butter. Toast *1 cup slivered almonds* and add half of it to the sauce with the chicken. Sprinkle the rest over the crêpes just before serving.

Mushroom Crêpes (serves six)

1¼ pounds (565 g) mushrooms
5 tablespoons butter
4 tablespoons minced shallots or scallions
5 tablespoons flour
1½ cups (3½ dL) hot chicken broth
1½ cups (3½ dL) heavy cream
Salt to taste
Freshly ground pepper
1 recipe Crêpes or French Pancakes (p. 318)

Preheat the oven to 350°F (180°C). Butter a shallow baking dish, approximately 13 × 9 × 2 inches. Slice the mushrooms, including the stems, and sauté them in the butter with the shallots or scallions, for about 4 minutes, until soft. Sprinkle on the flour and cook for 2 minutes. Slowly add the broth, stir until thick and smooth, then add the cream, and season with salt and pepper to taste. Continue cooking, stirring, for 5 minutes to reduce and thicken slightly. Spoon 3 tablespoons of filling in the center of each crêpe. Fold the ends over and place each crêpe end side down in the baking dish. Spoon the remaining mushroom filling over the top of the crêpes. Bake for 25 minutes or until sauce bubbles.

Seafood Crêpes (serves six)

Different varieties or combinations of seafood may be used: chopped shrimp, clams, mussels, scallops, or crabmeat, cooked lean fish, salmon, cod, or sole.

5 tablespoons butter
3 tablespoons minced shallots or scallions
4 tablespoons flour
1 cup (¼ L) hot chicken broth or fish stock
½ cup (1 dL) light cream
3 tablespoons dry sherry
2 cups (½ dL) flaked cooked shellfish and/or fish
Tabasco to taste
Salt to taste
1 recipe Crêpes or French Pancakes (p. 318)
½ cup (1 dL) heavy cream
¼ teaspoon nutmeg
2 tablespoons minced parsley
Lemon slices

Preheat the oven to 350°F (180°C). Butter a baking dish approximately 13 × 9 × 2 inches. Sauté the shallots or scallions in the butter for 2 minutes. Sprinkle on the flour, stir, and cook for 2 minutes. Slowly add the hot broth or stock. Stir until thick and smooth, then add the cream and sherry. Cook for 5 minutes, stirring constantly, until sauce is smooth and thickened. Add the shellfish and/or fish, taste and season with Tabasco and salt. Stir a minute and remove from the heat. Fill each crêpe with 3 tablespoons of filling. Roll and place seam side down in the baking dish. Spoon any extra filling around the edges and between the crêpes. Lightly whip the heavy cream, add the nutmeg, and spread over the crêpes. Bake for 20–25 minutes or just until the sauce bubbles. Sprinkle the parsley on top and serve garnished with lemon slices.

Eggs & Cheese

French Omelet   (serves one)

Read this recipe from beginning to end before starting to cook. A perfectly made omelet is a mass of creamy scrambled eggs enclosed in an envelope of coagulated egg. The keys to making a good omelet are quickness and proper heat. Almost any leftover food makes a good filling, as long as it isn't too liquid. It is always better to make omelets one at a time. You cannot achieve the same result working with more than two or three eggs and a larger pan.

2 "large" eggs
Salt
Freshly ground pepper
Tabasco (optional)
3–4 tablespoons filling (optional: see following)
1 tablespoon butter

Beat the eggs in a bowl only until they are just blended. Add a pinch of salt and pepper or a dash of Tabasco. If a filling is to be used, have it prepared and warm, if necessary. Heat a 7- or 8-inch nonstick skillet until hot. Add butter. When it foams and sizzles, quickly pour in the eggs. Shake the skillet with a short forward and backward motion. Using a fork, pull back a little of the edge of the egg that will have started to curl up and, by tipping the skillet, allow the liquid egg in the center of the pan to run over. Continue to shake and fork around the edges, but work quickly: it should take only 15 seconds from the time the eggs are poured into the skillet until the filling (if you are using one) is added. Spread the filling across the center of the omelet. Have a warm place ready. Use a spatula or the fork and roll one-third of the omelet over onto itself, then out of the skillet onto the plate, encouraging it to make the second fold as it falls. Don't cook the omelet dry; the center of a finished omelet should be moist, which means that you start to roll it when the surface is still a little runny.

Herb Omelet. Add *1 teaspoon minced parsley, 1 tablespoon minced chives,* and *⅛ teaspoon tarragon, crumbled,* to the egg mixture.

Crouton Omelet. Lay *¼ cup freshly made buttered croutons* over the omelet just before folding.

Cheese Omelet. Sprinkle *¼ cup freshly grated Gruyère or Swiss cheese* over the omelet just before folding.

Mushroom Omelet. Spread *½ cup sliced mushrooms,* first sautéed in a little butter, over the center of the omelet just before folding.

Bacon Omelet. Fry *2 slices bacon.* Drain, break into small pieces, and sprinkle over the omelet just before folding.

Other excellent omelets can be made by using ¼–½ cup of any of the following fillings. Heat and spread over the omelet just before you fold it.

210

Chicken or turkey, cooked and creamed
Chicken livers, chopped and sautéed
Fish, cooked and flaked or creamed
Ham, cooked and chopped
Tomato, chopped with onions, peppers, or
    canned green chilies
Cooked vegetables, diced and heated in butter
Lobster, shrimp, tuna, or crabmeat, cooked and
    creamed or heated in butter

Potato and Leek Frittata (serves four)

A frittata is the flat omelet served in Mediterranean countries that is often a background for spicy vegetables. It is easier to make (than separate omelets) for four or more and a most satisfying way to use up bits of cooked vegetables—see suggestions in this recipe.

4 tablespoons butter
1 tablespoon oil
1 cup (¼ L) cooked peeled potatoes, in ½-inch
    cubes
½ cup (1 dL) cooked leeks sliced in thin rounds
1 tablespoon minced parsley
¼ cup (½ dL) freshly grated Parmesan cheese
5 eggs
½ cup (1 dL) heavy cream
¼ teaspoon salt
⅛ teaspoon freshly ground pepper

Heat 2 tablespoons of the butter and the oil in a skillet. Add the potatoes and leeks and cook until the potatoes are lightly browned. Put into a bowl,

211

toss in the parsley and cheese, and set aside. Combine the eggs, cream, salt, and pepper, and add to the potatoes and leeks. Melt the remaining 2 tablespoons of butter in the skillet. Pour in the egg mixture and cook very slowly over low heat, pricking the top with a fork and lifting the bottom gently. Continue to cook until the bottom is brown and set. Slide out onto a dinner plate and invert into the pan. Or else place the frittata under a preheated broiler until the top is brown.

Spinach-Cheese Frittata. Eliminate the potatoes and leeks. Sauté *½ cup chopped spinach* and *½ onion, chopped,* in the butter and add *¼ cup freshly grated Parmesan cheese* to the egg mixture.

Eggs Chasseur (serves four)

2 tablespoons butter
2 shallots, chopped fine, or 2 tablespoons finely chopped onion
6 mushrooms, chopped
½ cup (1 dL) chicken broth
2 tablespoons dry sherry
¼ teaspoon salt
Pinch of cayenne pepper
8 poached eggs
4 tablespoons heavy cream
2 tablespoons freshly grated Parmesan cheese

Preheat the oven to 400°F (205°C). Melt the butter in a saucepan. Add the shallots or onion and cook over low heat for 3 minutes. Add the mushrooms and cook until soft. Add the chicken broth, sherry,

212

salt, and cayenne pepper, bring to the boiling point, and simmer for 10 minutes. Pour the sauce into a shallow baking dish that will accommodate 8 poached eggs. Put the eggs in the sauce and spoon cream over them. Sprinkle with cheese and bake until cheese is melted, about 3–5 minutes.

Eggs Benedict (serves one)

Multiply this recipe according to the number of persons being served, and encourage heartier appetites to have two.

⅓ cup (¾ dL) Hollandaise Sauce (p. 157)
1 slice cooked ham, ⅜ inch thick, the size of the
    muffin, or 1 slice Canadian bacon
½ English muffin
Butter
1 egg

Prepare the Hollandaise and keep it warm. Put the ham in a small skillet and heat thoroughly or fry the Canadian bacon. Spread the English muffin with butter, and toast under the broiler. Poach the egg. To assemble, put the English muffin on a plate, place the ham or bacon on the muffin, carefully place the egg on the ham, and cover with hollandaise sauce.

Cheese Soufflé (serves four)

This is a light fragile soufflé that must be brought to the table as soon as it is ready. Soufflés can be made of many kinds of leftovers—ground meat or poultry that has a good flavor, a bit of fish, finely chopped vegetables that have intense color and taste. Follow the proportions for the Spinach Soufflé variation.

1 cup (¼ L) plus 2 tablespoons grated Cheddar cheese
4 tablespoons butter
4 tablespoons flour
1 cup (¼ L) hot milk
½ teaspoon salt
Pinch of cayenne pepper
4 egg yolks, slightly beaten
5 egg whites

Preheat the oven to 375°F (190°C). Butter a 1½-quart straight-sided soufflé dish and sprinkle 2 tablespoons of the cheese over the bottom and around the sides. Melt the butter in a saucepan, add the flour, and cook gently 2–3 minutes, stirring constantly. Add the milk and continue to cook over low heat 2–3 minutes, stirring, until thick and smooth. Add the salt, cayenne pepper, and the rest of the cheese, blending in the cheese thoroughly; the sauce should be very thick. Beat 3 tablespoons of the hot cheese mixture into the egg yolks and then return to the saucepan, stirring 1 minute over low heat. Remove and pour into a large bowl. Beat the egg whites until they are stiff but not dry. Stir a fourth of the whites into the cheese sauce, then fold in the remaining whites. Spoon into the soufflé

214

dish. Bake on the middle rack of the oven for 35 minutes. Serve immediately.

Herb Soufflé. Omit the cheese and add *1½ tablespoons minced onion, 1 teaspoon basil, crumbled, 1 teaspoon tarragon, crumbled,* and *1 tablespoon minced parsley* to the cream sauce base.

Spinach Soufflé. Instead of the 1 cup Cheddar cheese, use *¾ cup well-drained, finely chopped cooked spinach* and *⅓ cup grated Swiss cheese.*

Eggs à la Suisse (serves two)

A simple dish to make if you keep the heat very low.

1 tablespoon butter
½ cup (1 dL) heavy cream
4 eggs
Salt
Pinch of cayenne pepper
2 tablespoons freshly grated Gruyère or Swiss cheese
2 slices toast, buttered

Melt the butter in a skillet. Add the cream, gently break in the eggs one by one, and sprinkle with salt and cayenne pepper. Cook over very low heat, basting with the cream, until the whites are almost firm. Sprinkle the cheese evenly over the top. Place 2 eggs and a spoonful of cream on each piece of buttered toast.

Welsh Rabbit (serves four)

½ pound (225 g) sharp Cheddar cheese, in small
   dice
1 tablespoon butter
½ teaspoon dry mustard
Cayenne pepper to taste
1 egg, slightly beaten
Salt
½ cup (1 dL) beer
4 slices toast

Combine the cheese, butter, mustard, and cayenne pepper in a heavy-bottomed pan, a chafing dish, or the top of a double boiler. Cook over low heat, stirring constantly, until the cheese has melted. Beat a little of the hot cheese mixture into the egg, and then return the egg-cheese mixture to the pan. Add salt to taste. Add the beer and cook 1–2 minutes more, until very hot but not boiling. Spoon over toast.

Mild Rabbit. Substitute *½ cup milk* for the beer.

Tomato Rarebit (serves six)

2 tablespoons butter
2 tablespoons flour
1 cup (¼ L) light cream, heated
½ cup (1 dL) finely chopped canned or fresh
   tomatoes
⅛ teaspoon baking soda
2 cups (½ L) grated Cheddar cheese
2 eggs, slightly beaten

1 teaspoon dry mustard
Cayenne pepper to taste
Salt
6 slices toast

Melt the butter in a saucepan. Stir in the flour and cook for 2–3 minutes, stirring. Slowly pour in the cream, and cook and stir until the mixture thickens. Add the tomatoes mixed with baking soda, cheese, eggs, mustard, and cayenne pepper. Cook over gentle heat, stirring, until the cheese melts. Salt to taste. Do not boil. Spoon over toast.

Swiss Fondue (serves four)

Make the fondue in a chafing dish, a special fondue dish, or in a heavy earthenware casserole placed over very low heat on an asbestos mat. Then sit around and dunk. If it thickens too much as it cools, thin it with a little more warm wine.

1 clove garlic
1 cup (¼ L) dry white wine
1 pound (450 g), about 2½ cups (6 dL) Swiss cheese, grated or diced small
¼ teaspoon nutmeg
¼ teaspoon freshly ground pepper
3 tablespoons kirsch
Salt to taste
1 loaf French bread, in 1-inch cubes

Vigorously rub the inside of the casserole with the garlic clove. Pour the wine into the casserole and heat until it barely simmers. Over low heat, add the cheese a little at a time, stirring with a wooden spoon until it is melted. Stir in the nutmeg, pepper, kirsch, and salt. Give guests long-handled forks, and let them spear cubes of bread to dunk into the creamy fondue.

New England Cheddar Pie
(serves six)

1½ cups (3½ dL) grated sharp Cheddar cheese
1 recipe Basic Pastry for 9-inch pie shell (p. 390)
4 eggs
2 cups (½ L) heavy cream
2 hearty shakes of the Tabasco bottle
Salt to taste
½ cup (1 dL) coarsely chopped walnuts (optional)

Preheat the oven to 425°F (220°C). Sprinkle the cheese evenly over the bottom of the pie shell. In a bowl, beat the eggs and stir in the cream and Tabasco. Pour over the cheese in the pie shell. Taste and add salt as needed. Bake for 15 minutes, lower the heat to 300°F (150°C), and bake 15–20 minutes more or until a knife inserted in the center comes out clean. Remove from the oven, sprinkle with chopped walnuts, if desired, and let stand for 5 minutes to make it easier to cut and serve.

Cheese and Bacon Quiche (serves six)

10 slices bacon, fried crisp and crumbled
1 partially baked Tart Pastry (p. 391), without
  sugar
4 eggs
2 cups (½ L) light cream
½ teaspoon salt
⅛ teaspoon nutmeg
Pinch of cayenne pepper
1¼ cups (3 dL) grated Swiss cheese

Preheat the oven to 425°F (220°C). Sprinkle the crumbled bacon over the bottom of the tart shell. Combine the eggs, cream, salt, nutmeg, and cayenne pepper in a bowl and beat to mix thoroughly. Sprinkle the cheese over the bacon and ladle the custard over all. Bake for 15 minutes at 425°F (220°C); then lower the heat to 350°F (180°C) and bake for 30 minutes more, or until a knife inserted in the center comes out clean. Serve in wedges, hot or cold.

Spinach Quiche. Omit the bacon and use only ½ cup grated Swiss cheese. Add *1 cup cooked, chopped spinach, well drained,* and *2 tablespoons minced onions* sautéed in *1 tablespoon butter* to the custard mixture.

Onion Quiche. Omit the bacon and add to the custard mixture *2 onions, thinly sliced* and sautéed in *3 tablespoons butter.*

Vegetables

Basic Method for Cooking Artichokes (allow one per person)

Cooked artichoke stems are delicious. Do not detach them until after cooking, and use them in salads or as an hors d'oeuvre.

To prepare for cooking, peel the coarse fibers from the artichoke stem. Remove the tough bottom leaves, then slice off about an inch from the leaves at the top. With scissors, snip off the prickly tops of the remaining side leaves. Plunge the artichokes into a very large pot filled with boiling water and boil them gently until done. Allow 25–40 minutes: they are done when an outer leaf pulls off easily and the bottom is tender when pierced with a fork. Drain them upside down. Serve them hot or warm, with *melted butter* or *Hollandaise Sauce* (p. 157) on the side, or cold with *French Dressing* (p. 279) or *mayonnaise seasoned with lemon juice and a drop of prepared mustard.*

Basic Method for Cooking
Asparagus (serves about four)

The shorter the cooking time, the fresher and greener the color.

24 large asparagus

Wash the asparagus and cut or break off the tough, colorless, woody bottom of each stalk. Peel with a vegetable peeler, lightly near the top and more deeply toward the bottom. Plunge the spears into a large pot of boiling water and boil gently until the bottoms are just tender when pierced with a knife. Begin testing after 5–8 minutes, depending on the thickness of the stalks. Drain well and serve with *melted butter, Hollandaise Sauce* (p. 157), or *Cheese Sauce* (p. 148).

Asparagus Vinaigrette. Spoon ½ *cup French Dressing* (p. 279) over hot or cold asparagus, either ahead of time or just before serving.

Basic Method for Cooking
Green Beans (serves three to four)

If you leave the beans whole, they will be less watery and more flavorful. If they are very thick, however, you may wish to slice them diagonally or "French" them.

1 pound (450 g) green beans
Butter
Salt
Freshly ground pepper

Wash the beans and remove the ends and strings, if there are any. Leave them whole or cut them in diagonal strips. Drop them into a large pot of boiling water and boil them gently until just done, allowing about 5–10 minutes, depending on the size and age of the beans. Taste one to see if it is done; it should still be very crunchy. Drain the beans and rinse them thoroughly in cold water to stop the cooking. Reheat them in lots of butter, salt, and pepper just before serving.

Basic Method for Cooking

Beets (serves three to four)

> Young boiled beets need nothing for embellishment except, perhaps, a little butter. If your beets are old and not very flavorful, try sugaring them or pickling them.

1 pound (450 g) beets
Butter
Salt
Freshly ground pepper
Chopped parsley

Cut off all but 1 inch of the beet tops; do not pare or remove the roots. Drop the beets into enough boiling water to cover them, and cook them, uncovered, until they are tender, allowing 30 minutes to 1 hour, depending on the age of the beets. Drain the beets, drop them in cold water for a minute or two to cool them slightly, then slip off the skins. Leave them whole or quarter them, or slice them with an egg slicer. Toss them with butter, salt and pepper to taste, and some chopped parsley, and reheat them, if necessary, before serving.

Sugared Beets. Toss each pound (about 2 cups) of sliced, cooked beets with *2 tablespoons butter, 1 teaspoon sugar,* and *½ teaspoon salt.* Reheat, if necessary, before serving.

Pickled Beets. Mix *½ cup vinegar* with *¼ cup sugar* and boil for 5 minutes. Add *1 teaspoon caraway seeds* and *¼ teaspoon salt.* Pour over 1 pound (about 2 cups) of sliced, cooked beets and serve cold or at room temperature.

Basic Method for Cooking
Broccoli (serves two to three)

It's true for many vegetables, but especially true with broccoli: Don't overcook!

1 pound (450 g) broccoli
Melted butter
Salt

Cut off and discard the tough end of the stems and coarse outer leaves of the broccoli. Cut the broccoli into flowerets with short stems and peel the stems lightly with a vegetable peeler. Peel more deeply the thick stems cut from the flowerets, and slice them diagonally, so that they will cook quickly. Drop the stems into a large pot of boiling, salted water and boil 3 or 4 minutes, then add the flowerets. Boil until the stems are just tender when pierced with a sharp knife, about 6–10 minutes in all. Drain. Toss with melted butter and salt or serve with *Hollandaise Sauce* (p. 157).

Puréed Broccoli. Put the cooked broccoli through a vegetable mill or purée it in a food processor. Reheat, seasoning to taste with lots of butter, salt, and pepper.

Broccoli in Cheese Custard
(serves six)

This custard recipe may also be used with other cooked vegetables such as cauliflower, corn kernels, onions, spinach, and cabbage.

2 cups (½ L) chopped cooked broccoli
¾ cup (1¾ dL) grated Cheddar cheese
3 eggs
1½ cups (3½ dL) milk or light cream
¾ teaspoon salt
¼ teaspoon freshly ground pepper

Preheat the oven to 350°F (180°C). Butter a 1½-quart baking dish, put the chopped broccoli into it, and sprinkle with the cheese. Beat the eggs lightly in a bowl and stir in the milk or cream, salt, and pepper. Stir into the broccoli-cheese mixture. Put the baking dish in a shallow pan with hot water halfway up its sides. Bake for 45–60 minutes, or until the custard is set.

Basic Method for Cooking Brussels Sprouts (serves four)

Properly cooked Brussels sprouts should be bright green and never overcooked.

1 pound (450 g) Brussels sprouts
Melted butter
Salt

Wash the sprouts in cold water, removing any wilted leaves and cutting off the stems. Drop them into a large pot of boiling, salted water for 8–10 minutes, or until just tender. Taste one to see if it's done; it should still be slightly crunchy. Drain. Toss with melted butter and salt to taste or *Hollandaise Sauce* (p. 157).

Basic Method for Cooking Cabbage (serves three)

1 pound (450 g) cabbage

Cut the cabbage in half; cut away and discard the hard, whitish core. Slice into wedges. Drop them into a large pot filled with boiling, salted water and boil until the cabbage is just tender, about 10–15 minutes. The cabbage should be crisp-tender and retain its color. Drain well.

Braised Red Cabbage and Apples (serves eight)

This is exceptionally good: moist, spicy, and faintly sweet. A roasted loin of pork would be a splendid companion.

4 tablespoons bacon fat
2 tablespoons sugar
1 onion, chopped
2 pounds (900 g) red cabbage, shredded
2 tart apples, peeled, cored, and sliced thin
2 tablespoons cider vinegar
½ teaspoon caraway seeds
¼ teaspoon nutmeg
⅛ teaspoon cayenne pepper
½ cup (1 dL) dry red wine
Salt

Melt the bacon fat in a skillet, add the sugar and cook, stirring, for 2 minutes. Add the onion and cook slowly until lightly colored. Stir in the cabbage, apples, vinegar, caraway seeds, nutmeg, cayenne, and red wine. Cook over low heat, covered, for 10 minutes, then add ½ cup water and cook, with cover askew, stirring occasionally, for 30–40 minutes more. Add salt to taste. Serve hot or cold.

Sauerkraut (serves four)

Sauerkraut, German in origin, is shredded cabbage preserved in a salt-water brine. It is not necessary to wash the brine from the sauerkraut unless a milder taste is desired. Sauerkraut, with its assertive flavor, is very compatible with goose and with pork sausages.

1 pound (450 g) sauerkraut
1 large tart apple, peeled, cored, and diced
1 cup (¼ L) beef bouillon
1 teaspoon caraway seeds
¼ teaspoon freshly ground pepper
Salt

Wash the sauerkraut in several changes of cold water if desired; drain thoroughly. Combine the sauerkraut, apple, bouillon, caraway seeds, and pepper. Cook over low heat, stirring occasionally, for about 30–35 minutes. Add salt to taste. Serve hot.

Braised Chinese Cabbage (serves four)

8 strips bacon
1 head Chinese cabbage, shredded
Salt
Freshly ground pepper
Soy sauce

Cook the bacon in a skillet until crisp; remove and drain. Pour off all but 2 tablespoons of bacon fat. Heat the remaining fat, then add the cabbage. Cover and cook slowly, stirring occasionally, until just tender, about 3 minutes. Crumble the bacon and stir it into the cabbage. Season to taste with salt and pepper and serve with soy sauce.

Stuffed Cabbage Leaves (serves four)

A wonderful way to transform cooked beef or pork, particularly if you save some sauce—meat juices, drippings, or leftover gravy—to add flavor and moisture to the filling. If you use ham or corned beef, add 1 teaspoon mustard in place of leftover gravy. The inner part of the cabbage, chopped and sautéed with a little butter and cream, makes a vegetable course for another meal.

1 head cabbage
2 onions, chopped
4 tablespoons butter
1 teaspoon sweet paprika
2 cups (½ L) minced cooked beef or pork
2 cups (½ L) cooked rice
¼ cup (½ dL) chopped parsley
½ teaspoon rosemary, crumbled
Salt
Freshly ground pepper
¾ cup (1¾ dL) meat sauce—gravy, juice, or
  strong bouillon
16-ounce (450-g) can tomatoes

Preheat the oven to 350°F (180°C). Cut a circle around the core of the cabbage to loosen the leaves, then drop them into a large pot of boiling, salted water. Lift out after 3–4 minutes. Carefully select 8 of the large outer leaves. Lay them out flat, and cut out a small V from the root end to remove the hard spine. Sauté the onions in the butter with paprika until soft. Leaving 2 tablespoons of the onion in the pan, spoon the rest into a bowl and add the meat, rice, parsley, most of the rosemary, some salt and pepper, and ½ cup of the meat sauce or other liquid. Place one-eighth of the filling in the center of each leaf. Fold in the sides, then roll to make a neat sausage-shaped package. Place the rolls, seam side down, in a shallow baking dish that holds them snugly. Add the tomatoes and their juice to the onions remaining in the skillet, breaking them up roughly. Add the remaining ¼ cup meat sauce and boil hard for 5 minutes until the liquid is somewhat reduced. Season to taste with salt, pepper, and a pinch more rosemary, and pour around the stuffed cabbage leaves. Cover loosely with foil and bake for 50 minutes.

Basic Method for Cooking
Carrots (serves three to four)

Cooking times vary greatly with carrots, depending on their size and age.

1 pound (450 g) carrots, trimmed and peeled
2 tablespoons butter
Salt
Freshly ground pepper

Slice or cube the carrots, or leave them whole if they are small. Cook them, covered, in about 2 inches of boiling water until they are tender, about 10–12 minutes if they are sliced, longer if they are whole. Drain. Coat with the butter, season to taste, and reheat, if necessary, before serving.

Candied Carrots. Melt *5 tablespoons butter* in a heavy skillet, stir in *¼ cup brown sugar,* and heat, stirring, until melted. Add the cooked, seasoned carrots and cook slowly until they are well glazed.

Carrots and Peas. Add *cooked green peas* to diced cooked carrots, dot with butter, season to taste with salt and freshly ground pepper, and reheat slowly.

Mashed or Puréed Carrots. Mash the cooked carrots, put them through a food mill, or purée them in a food processor. Season to taste with butter, salt, freshly ground pepper, and a whisper of *nutmeg*. Reheat slowly, preferably in the top of a double boiler.

Baked Carrots (serves three to four)

1 pound (450 g) carrots
3 tablespoons butter
1 small onion, chopped
1 teaspoon sugar
Pinch of nutmeg
Salt
Freshly ground pepper
½ cup (1 dL) broth or stock

Preheat the oven to 350°F (180°C). Peel and grate the carrots and set them aside. Melt the butter in a small casserole, add the onion, and cook until soft and transparent. Stir in the carrots, season with the sugar and nutmeg, and add salt and pepper to taste. Add the broth or stock, cover, and bake until tender, about 30–40 minutes.

Huntington Carrots (serves three to four)

1 pound (450 g) carrots, preferably small
¼ pound (115 g) butter
Salt
½ teaspoon sugar
½ cup (1 dL) heavy cream

Clean and peel the carrots. Leave them whole if they are small, or cut them into 1½-inch strips. Melt the butter in a heavy pan, add the carrots, and turn them over and over in the butter until they are well coated. Season them with salt to taste and sugar, cover, and cook very slowly until the carrots are tender, about 25–35 minutes. Turn them occasionally and be sure that they do not burn. Before serving, adjust the seasonings, add the cream, and reheat.

Basic Method for Cooking Cauliflower (serves four to five)

1 medium cauliflower (about 2 pounds, 900 g)
Melted butter
Salt
Freshly ground pepper

Remove the leaves from the cauliflower. Wash it well, leaving it whole or separating it into flowerets. Steam, covered, in a steamer basket over boiling water until tender, allowing about 10 minutes for flowerets, 20–30 minutes for the whole head. Drain. Pour melted butter over it and season to taste.

Cauliflower with Chopped Walnuts. Before serving, sprinkle with ½ *cup coarsely chopped walnuts.*

Cauliflower au Gratin. Leave the cauliflower whole and put it on a shallow, ovenproof dish. Sprinkle with ¾ *cup freshly grated Parmesan cheese* and ½ *cup buttered bread crumbs.* Bake in a preheated 400°F (205°C) oven until brown on top, about 15 minutes.

Creamed Cauliflower au Gratin. Arrange cooked cauliflower flowerets in a baking dish, season with salt and freshly ground pepper, and cover with *1½ cups White Sauce* (p. 147). Sprinkle ½ *cup grated Cheddar or Parmesan* over the top. Bake in a preheated 400°F (205°C) oven until hot and bubbly throughout and golden on top, 15 to 20 minutes.

Braised Celery   (serves two to three)

Braising celery this way brings out its rich flavor.

1 pound (450 g) celery
2 tablespoons butter
Chicken broth
Salt
Freshly ground pepper

Wash the celery and cut off the leaves and any discolored parts. Cut the stalks in even lengths, about 3 inches long. Sauté in the butter for about 5 minutes, then add about ½ inch of broth, just enough to keep the celery from burning. Season with salt and pepper, unless the stock is already well seasoned. Cover and cook over low heat until the celery is just tender, about 12–15 minutes. Put the celery in a serving dish. Rapidly boil the liquid in the pan until it is reduced to just a few tablespoons. Pour over the celery and serve.

Braised Celery au Gratin. Arrange the braised celery in a shallow baking dish and add a little of the cooking liquid. Sprinkle with *½ cup freshly grated Parmesan cheese* and put under the broiler until the cheese has melted.

Basic Method for Cooking Corn on the Cob (serves four to six)

There is nothing like fresh corn on the cob, quickly boiled, spread with lots of sweet butter, and sprinkled with salt. Two ears per person may seem like a proper serving, but appetites often run high when corn is in season and freshly picked.

12 ears of corn
Butter, softened
Salt

Just before cooking, husk the corn, pull off the silky threads, and cut out any blemishes with a pointed knife. Drop the corn into a large pot filled with boiling, unsalted water. Cover the pot and let the water return to a boil again, then turn off the heat and keep the pot covered. After about 5 minutes, remove enough ears for a first serving. You can keep the remaining corn warm in the water for another 10 minutes without its becoming tough. Serve with lots of butter and salt.

Buttered Corn Kernels. Cut the corn from the cob with a sharp knife. Heat the kernels in butter and season with salt and *freshly ground pepper.*

Foil-roasted Corn on the Cob
(serves four to six)

12 ears of corn
Butter
Salt

Preheat the oven to 400°F (205°C). Husk the corn and wrap each ear in foil, adding 2 teaspoons of butter to each packet. Bake for about 25 minutes. Or roast the foil-wrapped corn over hot coals, turning once during the cooking. Serve with more butter and salt.

Succotash   (serves three)

1 cup (¼ L) cooked corn kernels
1 cup (¼ L) cooked lima beans or other shell
   beans
Butter
Cream
Salt
Freshly ground pepper

Heat the corn and lima beans in butter and a little cream in a saucepan. Season to taste.

Southern Corn Pudding (serves four)

Fresh corn kernels extracted from the cob give this a special quality.

2 cups (½ L) fresh grated or chopped corn kernels
2 eggs, slightly beaten
2 tablespoons butter, melted
2 cups (½ L) hot milk
½ teaspoon salt
⅛ teaspoon freshly ground pepper

Preheat the oven to 350°F (180°C). Butter a 1½-quart casserole. Mix all ingredients together in a bowl. Pour into the casserole and place in a pan of hot water. Bake until firm, about 45 minutes.

Baked Stuffed Eggplant (serves four)

Bake this in a bowl so it holds its shape. The dark skin encasing a moist eggplant filling is most attractive.

1 eggplant (about 1½ pounds, 675 g)
1 cup (¼ L) soft fresh bread crumbs
4 tablespoons butter
1 small onion, chopped fine
Salt
Freshly ground pepper
1 egg, well beaten

Preheat the oven to 375°F (190°C). Put the eggplant in a large pot filled with boiling, salted water and cook for 12–15 minutes. Drain, then cut in half lengthwise. Remove the pulp carefully without breaking the skin. Chop the pulp, including the seeds, and stir in the bread crumbs; set aside. Melt the butter in a skillet. Add the onion and cook until soft; add to the eggplant mixture. Add salt and pepper to taste. Stir in the beaten egg and toss to mix well. Gently place the eggplant shells (skins) in an amply buttered round baking dish to cover the bottom and sides. Spoon the eggplant mixture into the dish and bake for 35–40 minutes. Unmold and serve hot or cold.

Golden Fried Eggplant (serves four)

A simple preparation, good for eggplant lovers.

1 medium eggplant (about 1½ pounds, 675 g)
Salt
Freshly ground pepper
¼ pound (115 g) butter

Cut the eggplant into slices ¼ to ½ inch thick. Sprinkle lightly with salt and pepper and let drain on paper towels for 30 minutes; pat dry. Melt the butter in a large skillet. Cook the eggplant slices over moderate heat, turning them once or twice, until they are golden. Serve hot.

Braised Endive (serves four)

Don't use an iron skillet, or the endive will turn black.

8 small endive
3 tablespoons butter
Chicken broth
Salt

Wash the endive and cut off any discolored spots. Split them lengthwise if they are large; leave them whole if they are small. Sauté them in the butter for about 5 minutes, then add about ½ inch of broth. Cover and cook slowly until just tender when pierced with the tip of a sharp knife, about 20 minutes. Arrange the endive in a serving dish. Boil the cooking liquid rapidly until it is reduced to just a few tablespoons. Add salt to taste. Pour over the endive and serve.

Braised Leeks (serves three)

2 large bunches (about 1 pound, 450 g) leeks
2 tablespoons butter
Chicken broth
Salt
Freshly ground pepper

Wash the leeks thoroughly and trim them, leaving about 1½ inches of the green tops. Sauté them in butter in a skillet for about 5 minutes, then add about ½ inch of broth, enough so that the leeks will not burn. Cover, and simmer slowly until the leeks are tender, about 20–30 minutes. Arrange the leeks on a serving platter. Boil the cooking liquid down to a few tablespoons, season to taste, pour over the leeks, and serve.

Braised Leeks au Gratin. Arrange the cooked leeks in a shallow baking dish, spoon a little of the cooking liquid over them, and sprinkle with *½ cup freshly grated Parmesan cheese.* Put under the broiler until the cheese melts.

Sautéed Mushrooms (serves four)

1 pound (450 g) mushrooms
6 tablespoons butter
2 tablespoons minced shallots or scallions
2 teaspoons minced parsley
Salt
Freshly ground pepper

Wipe the mushrooms clean and slice them. Melt the butter in a pan, add the shallots or scallions, and cook for 3 minutes, stirring often. Add the mushrooms and continue to cook over low heat for 10 minutes. Add the parsley, season to taste, and mix well.

Stuffed Mushrooms (serves four)

12 large mushroom caps
¼ pound (115 g) butter
½ cup (1 dL) dry homemade bread crumbs
1 tablespoon finely chopped parsley
1 tablespoon finely chopped onion
½ teaspoon salt
½ teaspoon pepper

1 egg, lightly beaten
½ cup (1 dL) freshly grated Parmesan cheese

Preheat oven to 350°F (180°C). Generously butter a shallow baking dish. Wipe the mushroom caps clean. Melt 4 tablespoons of the butter in a small pan and let it cool a bit. Using the palms of your hands, thoroughly coat mushroom caps with butter and put them in the baking dish. Mix the bread crumbs, parsley, onion, salt, pepper, and egg together. Fill each mushroom cap with the mixture. Melt the remaining 4 tablespoons of butter. Sprinkle a little Parmesan cheese over each cap, drizzle a little melted butter on top, and bake for 15–20 minutes.

Sautéed Okra (serves four)

When okra is blanched and sautéed in butter, it has good flavor, a velvety outside, and a chewy texture.

1 pound (450 g) okra
6 tablespoons butter
Salt
Freshly ground pepper

Start a large pot of water boiling. Wash the okra and snap or cut off the stems. Drop it in the boiling water for 1 minute; drain. Melt the butter over medium heat. Add the okra and cook for 3 minutes, shaking the pan often to coat the okra with butter. Season lightly with salt and pepper. Serve hot.

Sautéed Okra with Browned Crumbs. Drop the okra into boiling water and let cook 3 minutes. Drain. Sauté *¾ cup freshly made bread crumbs* in the butter until browned. Add the okra, season, and toss together for a minute.

Baked Onions (serves four)

A little sweet, opaque, mostly tender.

4 medium onions, peeled
⅓ cup (¾ dL) seedless white raisins
4 tablespoons butter
Salt

Preheat the oven to 350°F (180°C). Put the onions in a small casserole, sprinkle the raisins around, and put bits of the butter evenly over and around them. Sprinkle with salt and cover with foil. Bake for 45–60 minutes. Serve hot.

Glazed Onions (serves four)

1 pound (450 g) baby white onions
5 tablespoons butter
1½ tablespoons honey
Salt

Bring a pot of water to a boil. Add the onions and boil for 5 minutes; drain and peel. Melt the butter in a skillet and stir in the honey. Add the onions and cook over medium heat, stirring often, for about 10 minutes or until the onions are slightly browned. Sprinkle with salt and serve.

Braised White Baby Onions
(serves four)

Silky texture and a mildly sweet onion taste.

1 pound (450 g) baby white onions
4 tablespoons butter
Salt

Bring a large pot of water to boil. Drop the onions into the boiling water and cook for 3 minutes; drain and remove the outer skin. Melt the butter in a skillet with a lid. Add the onions, cover, and cook over low heat for 20 minutes. Shake the skillet often. Uncover and cook 5 minutes more. Add salt to taste.

Scalloped Onions. Boil the onions for 10 minutes before peeling. Drain and put the onions into a buttered baking dish. Add *1 cup White Sauce* (p. 147) and sprinkle *1 cup grated Cheddar cheese* on top. Bake in a 350°F (180°C) oven for 20 minutes.

Basic Method for Cooking
Parsnips (serves four)

1 pound (450 g) parsnips
2 tablespoons butter

Salt
Freshly ground pepper

Scrape the parsnips and cut them in ½-inch sticks, about 2 inches long. Cook them, covered, in about 2 inches of boiling water until tender, about 10 minutes; drain. Coat them with the butter, season to taste, and reheat them, if necessary, before serving.

Candied Parsnips. Melt *4 tablespoons butter* in a skillet, stir in *2 teaspoons sugar,* and cook, stirring, until the sugar dissolves. Add the parsnips, *½ teaspoon salt,* and *¼ teaspoon freshly ground pepper,* and cook over medium-low heat, stirring often, for 10–15 minutes or until the parsnips are golden. Serve hot.

Mashed or Puréed Parsnips. Mash the cooked, drained parsnips or purée them through a food mill or in a food processor. Stir in *1 tablespoon butter, 1–2 tablespoons heavy cream,* and season to taste with salt and freshly ground pepper. Reheat slowly, preferably in the top of a double boiler.

Basic Method for Cooking
Green Peas (serves four)

2 pounds (900 g) fresh peas (1 pound shelled)
3 tablespoons butter
Salt

Put the shelled peas, 1 cup water, and 1 tablespoon of the butter in a pan, cover, and cook over medium heat. After 6 minutes, check for doneness by pressing or tasting one or two; they should be tender but firm, which may take only a few minutes if young, or up to 20 minutes for older peas. Drain, coat with the remaining 2 tablespoons of butter, and lightly sprinkle salt over all.

Mint-flavored Peas. Add *1 tablespoon finely chopped mint* with the remaining 2 tablespoons of butter.

Purée of Green Peas. Add *1 slice onion* to the water. Add *½ cup heavy cream* with the remaining 2 tablespoons of butter. Put through a food mill or purée in a blender or food processor. Serve hot.

Snow Peas (serves four)

1 pound (450 g) snow peas
3 tablespoons butter
Salt

Wash the snow peas and remove any strings. Bring a large pot of water to boil and drop the snow peas in; boil for 1 minute. Drain and quickly glisten with the butter, sprinkle with salt, and serve.

Stir-fried Snow Peas. Using a wok or a skillet, stir fry whole snow peas, cooking only 2 minutes under cover.

Sautéed Sweet Red and Green Peppers (serves four)

Red and green sweet bell peppers, slightly differ-

ent in taste, are very compatible cooked together.

4 tablespoons vegetable oil
2 sweet red peppers, in ¼-inch strips
2 green peppers, in ¼-inch strips
Salt
Coarsely ground pepper

Heat the oil in a skillet. Put the peppers in the skillet and cook for 5–7 minutes, stirring to coat with
the oil. Sprinkle with salt and pepper to taste.

Stuffed Green Peppers (serves six)

A good way to serve leftover meats in a fresh
way.

3 large green peppers, halved and seeded
3 tablespoons olive oil
1 onion, finely chopped
1 pound (450 g) ground cooked or uncooked beef,
   pork, veal, or lamb
2 tomatoes, peeled and coarsely chopped
2 tablespoons minced parsley
1 tablespoon chopped fresh basil, or 1½
   teaspoons dried, crumbled
Salt
¼ teaspoon freshly ground pepper
1 cup (¼ L) freshly made bread crumbs

Preheat the oven to 350°F (180°C). Oil a shallow
baking dish. Cook the peppers in boiling water for
2 minutes; drain and set aside. Heat the oil in a
skillet and add the chopped onion. Cook, stirring,

until soft. If using uncooked meat, add it and cook lightly for 5–10 minutes. Otherwise, mix the onion and meat together, then add the tomatoes, parsley, basil, salt to taste, and pepper, combining thoroughly. Lightly fill each pepper half with some of the meat mixture. Sprinkle the tops with bread crumbs. Bake for 30–40 minutes.

Parslied New Potatoes, Boiled
(serves six)

12 or more small new potatoes
2 tablespoons finely chopped parsley
6 tablespoons butter
Salt
Freshly ground pepper

Scrub the potatoes—peeling is not necessary unless you prefer to for aesthetic reasons. Cover with cold water in a saucepan, bring to a boil, and boil gently for 15–20 minutes, or until tender when pierced with a knife; drain. Add the parsley and butter, season to taste, and shake the pan to coat the potatoes. Serve hot.

Chantilly Potatoes   (serves four to five)

3 cups (¾ L) mashed potatoes
½ cup (1 dL) heavy cream
½ cup (1 dL) grated Swiss or Gruyère cheese
Salt
Freshly ground pepper

Preheat the oven to 350°F (180°C). Butter a shallow 1½-quart baking dish. Spread the mashed potatoes in the baking dish. Whip the cream until stiff, fold in the cheese, and add salt and pepper to taste. Spread over the potatoes. Bake for 25–30 minutes or until the top is delicately brown.

Cottage-fried or Hashed Brown Potatoes (serves four)

6 tablespoons bacon fat or oil
4 cups (1 L) finely diced potatoes, raw or cooked
1 tablespoon finely chopped onion
Salt to taste
1½ teaspoons coarsely ground pepper

Heat the fat or oil in a large skillet. Spread the potatoes evenly over the bottom and sprinkle the onion, salt, and pepper on top. Cook over low heat, pressing down on the potatoes firmly with a spatula several times. Cook until the bottom side is golden brown, allowing more time if the potatoes are raw; in fact, if you use raw potatoes, cover the pan and cook over a low heat to cook them through; then turn up the heat for a final browning. With the spatula cut down the middle of the potatoes and turn each side over. Cook until golden, again pressing down with a spatula several times. Serve hot.

Potato Pancakes (nine 3½-inch pancakes)

Crisp and brown, good with applesauce and roast pork. Peel and grate the potatoes immediately before cooking, or they will discolor: while this doesn't affect the taste of the pancakes, they will not look as appetizing. If you put grated potatoes in a bowl of cold water, they will not discolor, but you will then have to be especially careful to squeeze out the excess moisture before cooking.

3 medium potatoes
1 tablespoon flour
1 tablespoon heavy or light cream
1 egg, beaten
Salt to taste
4 tablespoons bacon fat or oil

Peel and grate the potatoes. Place them on a double thickness of paper towels, fold the towels around them, and twist and squeeze until most of the moisture is extracted. Put the potatoes in a bowl, add the flour, cream, egg, and salt, and toss until well mixed. Heat the fat or oil in a large skillet. Put about 2 tablespoons of the potato mixture in the pan and press and shape with a spatula into a flat, 3½-inch pancake; repeat until the pan is full but not crowded. Cook each pancake about 5 minutes over medium-low heat until the bottom is crisp and brown; turn and cook the other side 5 minutes more. Keep warm in a 300°F (150°C) oven until all are ready, then serve immediately.

Scalloped Potatoes (serves four)

Little rivers of buttery milk, lots of pepper, and creamy potatoes.

4 medium potatoes, peeled and sliced ¼ inch
  thick
Salt
Freshly ground pepper
3 tablespoons flour
4 tablespoons butter
About 1½ cups (3½ dL) milk

Preheat the oven to 350°F (180°C). Butter a 1½-quart casserole. Cover the bottom of the casserole with a single layer of potatoes. Sprinkle generously with salt, pepper, flour, and a few dots of butter. Repeat until all the potato slices are used. Pour milk over the potato slices until the top is almost covered. Dot with the remaining butter. Bake for 1 hour or until the potatoes are soft.

Scalloped Potatoes with Celery Root or Celeriac. Alternate each layer of potatoes with a layer of *peeled, thinly sliced celery root.*

Delmonico Potatoes (serves six)

6 potatoes, peeled and boiled
1½ cups (3½ dL) White Sauce (p. 147)
Pinch of cayenne pepper
Salt to taste
2 egg yolks, lightly beaten

½ cup (1 dL) grated mild Cheddar cheese
1 cup (¼ L) buttered bread crumbs

Preheat the oven to 375°F (190°C). Butter a 2-quart casserole. Slice the potatoes ¼ inch thick. Make the white sauce and stir in the cayenne pepper, salt, egg yolks, and cheese. Stir over medium heat until the cheese melts. Spoon a film of sauce over the bottom of the casserole and place a layer of potatoes over it. Continue alternating sauce and potatoes, finishing with sauce. Sprinkle the buttered crumbs on top and place in the oven. Bake for 20–25 minutes or until the sauce is bubbling.

Baked Sweet Potatoes or Yams
(allow one medium potato per serving)

Preheat the oven to 375°F (190°C). Scrub the potatoes and cut a small piece off one end so the potato won't burst during baking. Place the potatoes, slightly apart, on the oven rack. Bake for about 1 hour or until tender when pierced with a knife. Fork open and put a pat of butter inside to serve.

Sweet Potato and Apple Scallop (serves four)

2 cups (½ L) thinly sliced boiled sweet potatoes
   or yams (about 2 medium potatoes)

1½ cups (3½ dL) peeled, thinly sliced tart apples
½ cup (1 dL) brown sugar
4 tablespoons butter
Salt

Preheat the oven to 350°F (180°C). Butter a 1½-quart baking dish. Put half the potatoes in the baking dish. Cover with half the apples, sprinkle with half the sugar, dot with half the butter, and sprinkle with salt. Repeat. Cover and bake for 30 minutes. Uncover and bake about 30 minutes more or until the apples are soft.

Candied Sweet Potatoes or

Yams (serves four)

4 medium sweet potatoes or yams
4 tablespoons butter
⅓ cup (¾ dL) brown sugar

Boil the potatoes until tender; drain. Peel and cut in half lengthwise. Put the butter and sugar in a heavy skillet and heat, stirring occasionally, until melted. Add the potatoes and turn until lightly browned. Add ¼ cup water, cover, and simmer over low heat for about 10–15 minutes.

Baked Candied Sweet Potatoes or Yams. After the butter and sugar have melted, put the potatoes in a buttered baking dish, pour the butter-sugar mixture on top, cover, and bake in a preheated 350°F (180°C) oven for 45 minutes to 1 hour.

Basic Method for Cooking
Spinach (serves two to three)

1 pound (450 g) spinach
Melted butter
Salt
Freshly ground pepper

Wash the spinach leaves well in several changes of water and remove tougher stems. Bring a large pot of water to a fast boil, plunge the spinach into the boiling water, cook for 3–6 minutes, depending on how young it is, and drain it in a colander. Leave the cooked spinach whole or chop it, toss it with melted butter, season with salt and pepper, and serve at once.

Puréed Spinach. Purée the cooked spinach in a blender or food processor. Reheat it with some butter, season with salt and freshly ground pepper, and add a little *heavy cream,* if you wish.

Basic Method for Cooking Summer
Squash (serves four)

1 pound (450 g) summer squash, in ½-inch slices
3 tablespoons butter
Salt
Freshly ground pepper

Bring 1½ cups water to a boil, add the squash, and simmer over medium heat, covered, 3–5 minutes or until just tender; drain. Add the butter, season to taste, and toss to coat. Serve hot.

Summer Squash and Onion. Add *1 coarsely chopped onion* and cook with the squash.

Summer Squash and Tomatoes. Two minutes before the squash is done, add *2 tomatoes, peeled, seeded, and chopped with some of the liquid gently squeezed out.*

Summer Squash with Horseradish Cream. Mix *½ cup sour cream* with *1 tablespoon prepared horseradish,* add to the cooked squash, and reheat for a few minutes before serving.

Sautéed Zucchini (serves four)

2 tablespoons olive or other oil
2 cloves garlic, minced
1 pound (450 g) zucchini, in ½-inch slices
Salt
Freshly ground pepper

Heat the oil in a skillet, add the minced garlic, and cook for a few minutes without letting the garlic brown. Add the zucchini and cook over low heat, stirring occasionally, until the squash is tender, about 10 minutes. Season to taste.

Stuffed Zucchini (serves four)

These are also good served cold.

4 medium zucchini
4 tablespoons olive oil
½ cup (1 dL) finely chopped onion
1 clove garlic, minced
¼ pound (115 g) ground beef, or 1 cup (¼ L)
    leftover cooked beef or pork, ground
2 tomatoes, peeled, seeded, and chopped
½ cup (1 dL) freshly made dry bread crumbs
1 tablespoon minced parsley
Salt
Freshly ground pepper
¼ teaspoon basil, crumbled

Preheat the oven to 350°F (180°C). Oil a shallow
baking dish large enough to hold the eight halves of
zucchini in one layer. Trim the ends off the zucchini and cook in a large pot of boiling salted water
for 3 minutes. Drain, cut in half lengthwise. Scoop
out the pulp, leaving a sturdy shell; chop and reserve the pulp. Sauté the onion slowly in the oil for
5 minutes, then add the garlic and meat. Cook, stirring constantly, until the meat loses its color. Remove from the skillet and set aside. Pour off all but
2 tablespoons of oil from the skillet, heat again, and
add the chopped zucchini pulp and tomatoes. Sauté
for 1 minute and add to the meat mixture. Add the
bread crumbs, parsley, salt, pepper, and basil. Toss
together lightly until mixed. Fill the zucchini shells,
without packing down, and place on baking dish.
Bake for 30 minutes.

Baked Winter Squash   (serves four)

2 small acorn or butternut squash
Salt
2 tablespoons butter
3 tablespoons maple syrup

Preheat the oven to 400°F (205°C). Split the squash
and remove the seeds. Sprinkle the cut sides with
salt. Place cut side down in a baking dish and bake
for about 40–50 minutes or until the squash is easily
pierced with a fork. Turn and make indentations
with a fork across the cut side of the squash.
Spread with the butter, drizzle with the maple syrup, and return to the oven for a minute or two.
Serve hot.

Sautéed Tomatoes   (serves six)

The secret of this recipe is to cook the tomatoes
only slightly, browning them quickly in hot butter. They are firm and flavorful with the basil and
cream.

6 large tomatoes
½ cup (70 g) flour
½ teaspoon freshly ground pepper
¼ pound (115 g) butter
2 tablespoons chopped fresh basil, or 1
    tablespoon dried, crumbled
¾ cup (1¾ dL) heavy cream
Salt

Slice the tomatoes ½ inch thick. Mix the flour and pepper together. Heat the butter over medium high heat. Dip the tomato slices into the flour mixture and coat on each side; shake free of excess flour. Put the slices into the hot butter and cook just a minute on each side or until lightly golden. Remove and keep in warm oven. Pour off all but 1 tablespoon of the butter, then stir in the basil, cream, and salt to taste. Bring to a boil and boil rapidly about 3 or 4 minutes. Pour over the tomato slices and serve.

Braised Herb Tomatoes (serves four)

4 tablespoons butter
4 scallions, chopped
1 tablespoon finely chopped parsley
4 teaspoons chopped fresh basil, or 2 teaspoons
  dried, crumbled
2 teaspoons chopped fresh thyme, or 1 teaspoon
  dried, crumbled
8 medium tomatoes, peeled
Salt
Freshly ground pepper

Melt the butter in a skillet. Stir in the scallions, parsley, basil, and thyme. Cook over low heat, stirring often, for 5 minutes. Add the tomatoes, cover, and cook over low heat for 5 more minutes. Season to taste. Place the tomatoes on a platter and spoon the herb juices over them.

Stewed Tomatoes (serves six)

This is the old-fashioned way of stewing tomatoes. If it seems too sweet for your taste, use less sugar.

6 large tomatoes, peeled or 2½ cups (6 dL) canned tomatoes
1 tablespoon butter
2 tablespoons finely chopped onion
2 teaspoons sugar
⅛ teaspoon cloves
Salt
Freshly ground pepper
1 slice fresh bread, torn in pieces (optional)

Cut the tomatoes into eighths. Melt the butter in a pan, add the onion and sugar, and cook for 3 or 4 minutes, stirring, over medium heat. Add the tomatoes and cloves. Cover and simmer for 15 minutes. Season to taste. If a thicker stew is desired, add the bread and cook another 10 minutes.

Baked Stuffed Tomatoes (serves four)

About 2 cups of stuffing will fill four large tomatoes nicely.

4 firm large tomatoes
Salt
1¼ cups (3 dL) dried homemade bread crumbs
1 teaspoon chopped fresh basil, or ½ teaspoon dried, crumbled
2 tablespoons finely chopped onion

2 tablespoons finely chopped green pepper
1½ tablespoons olive oil
Coarsely ground pepper

Preheat the oven to 400°F (205°C). Film a shallow baking pan with oil, using a pan large enough so that 8 tomato halves will not be crowded. Carefully cut a slice from the top of each tomato and scoop out most of the pulp, leaving a thick shell so that the tomato will hold its shape. Sprinkle the insides of the tomatoes with salt, invert them on paper towels, and let them drain for about 15 minutes. Squeeze the juice out of the pulp and chop pulp fine. In a bowl, *lightly* toss the bread crumbs, basil, onion, green pepper, and tomato pulp, then add the olive oil and season to taste with salt and pepper. Lightly fill each tomato, without packing. Place on the baking pan and bake for 15–20 minutes.

Baked Tomatoes with Mushroom Stuffing. Omit the basil, green pepper, and olive oil and reduce the amount of bread crumbs to ½ cup. Clean and chop *½ pound mushrooms* and sauté them with the onion in *4 tablespoons butter* over moderate heat for about 5 minutes: cool. Lightly toss the bread crumbs, tomato pulp, mushroom and onion mixture, salt, and pepper together and proceed as for Baked Stuffed Tomatoes.

Baked Tomatoes with Tuna Stuffing. Omit the basil and reduce the amount of bread crumbs to ½ cup and the onion and green pepper to 1 tablespoon each. Add *½ teaspoon chopped fresh tarragon or ¼ teaspoon dried tarragon, crumbled,* and *a 6½-ounce can tuna,* well drained and broken into small pieces. Lightly mix the bread crumbs, tomato pulp, tarragon, tuna, onion, and green pepper, then add the olive oil, salt, and pepper. Proceed as for Baked Stuffed Tomatoes.

Baked Tomatoes with Meat, Fish, or Chicken Stuffing. Omit the basil, green pepper, and olive oil and reduce the amount of bread crumbs to ½ cup. Add *1 teaspoon chopped fresh thyme or ½ teaspoon dried thyme, crumbled, 2 tablespoons melted butter,* and *1 cup minced cooked meat, fish,* or *chicken.* Proceed as for Baked Stuffed Tomatoes.

Baked Tomatoes with Spinach and Water Chestnut Stuffing. Omit the green pepper and reduce the amount of bread crumbs to ½ cup. Add *1 cup well-drained chopped cooked spinach* and *¼ cup sliced canned water chestnuts.* Proceed as for Baked Stuffed Tomatoes.

Basic Method for Cooking White Turnips (serves four)

1½ pounds (675 g) white turnips
3 tablespoons butter
Salt to taste
1 tablespoon finely chopped parsley

If the turnips are old, peel them; small young turnips need only be scrubbed. If large, cut them into quarters; if small, cut in half. Drop turnips into a large pot of boiling water and boil for 8–10 minutes or until tender when pierced with a knife or skewer; drain. Add the butter, sprinkle with salt and parsley, and toss until coated.

Whipped Turnips. After boiling, mash with a fork, then add *½ cup heavy cream, heated, 2 table-spoons softened butter, 1 teaspoon grated lemon rind,* and *½ teaspoon salt.* Beat by hand or with an electric mixer until smooth.

Creamed Turnips. After boiling, drain and dice. Melt *2 tablespoons butter* in a skillet, add the turnips, pour *1 cup heavy cream* over them, and stir in *¾ teaspoon ginger* and *salt to taste.* Stir until well blended and hot. If a thicker sauce is desired, boil, drain, and dice the turnips, then toss them in *1 cup White Sauce* (p. 147).

Salad &
Salad Dressings

Chef's Salad   (serves four)

This is a main dish for a summer evening or a lunch.

1 head iceberg lettuce
12 radishes, trimmed, sliced
2 stalks celery, julienned
1½ cups (3½ dL) French Dressing (p. 279), Cream French Dressing (p. 280), or Russian Dressing (p. 283)
4 tomatoes, peeled, cut into 6 wedges each
¾ cup (1¾ dL) Swiss cheese strips, ⅛ inch wide, 1½ inches long
1 cup (¼ L) cooked ham or tongue (or both) strips, ⅛ inch wide, 1½ inches long
1 cup (¼ L) cooked chicken or turkey strips, ⅛ inch wide, 1½ inches long
4 hard-boiled eggs, quartered
Salt
Freshly ground pepper

Core the iceberg lettuce and save four outside leaves for the bed in which to put the salad. Place them around the edges of a large salad bowl. Cut

260

or tear the remaining lettuce into bite-size pieces, place in the bowl, and toss with the radishes, celery, and half of the dressing. Arrange the tomato wedges around the inside edges of the lettuce. Combine the cheese, ham or tongue, and chicken or turkey, toss, and spread it over the lettuce and vegetables. Place the hard-boiled eggs between the tomato wedges. Salt and pepper lightly over the salad. Spoon the rest of the dressing over the salad.

Cucumber Salad (serves six)

This is a sharp cucumber salad, maybe too much so for some tastes—if so add a little sugar.

3 medium cucumbers
Salt
4 tablespoons sour cream or mayonnaise
3 tablespoons minced scallions
1 teaspoon lemon juice
2 tablespoons vinegar
½ teaspoon dry mustard
1 tablespoon minced dill or parsley

Peel the cucumbers and slice thin. Spread them over the bottom of a colander and sprinkle salt on top. Let them drain for 30 minutes, press gently to remove excess liquid, then chill. Blend the sour cream or mayonnaise, scallions, lemon juice, vinegar, and dry mustard together. Add salt to taste. Toss the dressing with the cucumbers. Sprinkle the dill or parsley on top and serve cold.

Caesar Salad (serves four)

Caesar salad can be a tableside performance, made with gusto in front of friends and family, or it can be privately assembled in the kitchen. If you can find young romaine, use just the heart, left whole—one per serving.

2 medium or 4 small heads romaine lettuce
2-ounce (60-g) can anchovy fillets, drained
6 tablespoons olive oil
3 tablespoons lemon juice
2 teaspoons Dijon mustard
1 egg
Salt to taste
½ teaspoon freshly ground pepper
½ cup (1 dL) freshly grated Parmesan cheese
1½ cups (3½ dL) garlic croutons (see below)

Separate the leaves of romaine, discarding outer tough leaves, if any, wash, and *thoroughly* dry. Tear into bite-size pieces. (Or trim small heads to the hearts and leave whole, dipping in and out of cold water and then spinning dry.)

In a small bowl, mash the anchovies; stir in the olive oil and lemon juice, whisking; add the mustard and blend. Put the romaine into the salad bowl, pour the dressing over, add the egg, and toss the salad lightly (using your hands does the best job) until the egg has disappeared. Add remaining ingredients, toss for just a second, and serve.

Garlic Croutons

Cut slices of *bread* in even cubes, removing the

crusts. Sauté in hot *butter,* to which a *minced clove* of *garlic* has been added, turning to brown all sides. Drain on paper towels.

Cole Slaw (serves four)

1 medium head cabbage
1 cup (¼ L) Boiled Dressing (see below)
1 teaspoon celery seed
Salt

Cut the head of cabbage in half, place in a bowl of cold water, and refrigerate for 1 hour. Drain well. Shred finely, and add the dressing and celery seed. Toss to mix well and add salt to taste.

Boiled Dressing   (1¼ cups)

1½ tablespoons flour
1 teaspoon dry mustard
1 tablespoon sugar
2 egg yolks, slightly beaten
Pinch of cayenne pepper
1½ tablespoons butter, melted
¾ cup (1¾ dL) milk
¼ cup (½ dL) vinegar
Salt

Combine the flour, mustard, and sugar in a heavy-bottomed pan. Slowly add the yolks, cayenne pepper, melted butter, milk, and vinegar. Heat, stirring constantly, over low heat until thickened and smooth. Add salt to taste. Remove and store covered in the refrigerator until needed.

Carrot Slaw (serves six)

A great favorite with children.

6 medium carrots
¾ cup (1¾ dL) diced celery
¼ cup (½ dL) diced onion
⅓ cup (¾ dL) raisins
½ cup (1 dL) diced apple
½ cup (1 dL) mayonnaise
Salt
Freshly ground pepper

Grate the carrots by hand or in a food processor. Toss with the celery, onion, raisins, and apple. Mix in the mayonnaise, season well with salt and pepper, and chill thoroughly.

Spinach, Mushroom, and Bacon Salad (serves four)

1 pound (450 g) fresh young spinach
¼ pound (115 g) raw mushrooms, thinly sliced
2 hard-boiled eggs, coarsely chopped
½ cup (1 dL) vegetable oil
½ teaspoon sesame oil (optional)
1 teaspoon sugar
3 tablespoons lemon juice
½ teaspoon Dijon mustard
Freshly ground pepper
Salt to taste
5 strips bacon, fried crisp, crumbled

Wash and dry the spinach and discard the stems. leaves are small, leave whole; if large, cut or tea into bite-size pieces. Toss the spinach, mushrooms, and eggs together in a salad bowl. Mix in a separate bowl the vegetable oil, sesame oil, if you want to use it, sugar, lemon juice, mustard, pepper, and salt. Beat well, then pour over the salad and toss until all leaves are coated. Serve on individual plates and sprinkle the bacon over each serving.

Watercress, Orange Slices, and Avocado Salad (serves four)

2 bunches watercress, washed, dried, stems
  trimmed
4 large oranges, peeled and sliced
1 large ripe avocado
4 tablespoons vegetable oil
4 tablespoons orange juice
1 tablespoon white vinegar
½ teaspoon celery seed
Salt
4 radishes, grated

Arrange the watercress on a large plate or individual salad plates. Distribute the orange slices over each plate. Peel and dice the avocado and scatter the pieces among the orange slices. Combine the oil, orange juice, vinegar, and celery seed in a jar or small bowl. Shake or whisk to blend the ingredients until smooth and well mixed. Add salt to taste. Pour the dressing over the salad and sprinkle the grated radishes over the top.

# of Palm Salad with

.o (serves four)

4 tablespoons olive oil
1½ tablespoons vinegar
⅛ teaspoon freshly ground pepper
2 teaspoons minced parsley
1 teaspoon finely chopped scallions or chives
   (optional)
Salt
1 head Bibb or butter lettuce
2 ripe avocados
1 can hearts of palm, drained

Combine the oil, vinegar, pepper, and parsley. Add scallions or chives if you wish, and salt to taste. Mix until well blended. Wash and dry the lettuce leaves and arrange on four salad plates. Peel the avocados, cut in half, and remove seed. Place one avocado half on each plate. Slice the hearts of palm in ¼-inch rounds, and divide them evenly over each avocado half. Drizzle the vinaigrette over each salad. Serve.

Zucchini, Potato, and Tomato Salad (serves four)

Cook the vegetables only until tender: about 8 minutes for the zucchini, about 20 minutes for the potatoes (but check—potatoes vary). And remove the salad from the refrigerator half an hour before serving: it tastes better at room temperature.

3 medium zucchini, cooked whole 8 minutes
4 new potatoes, cooked
2 ripe, fresh tomatoes, peeled, chopped
2 tablespoons finely chopped onion
1 recipe French Dressing (p. 279)
Salt to taste
¼ teaspoon freshly ground pepper

Trim away the ends of the zucchini and slice about ¼ inch thick. Peel and dice the potatoes. Combine the zucchini, potatoes, tomatoes, and onion in a bowl. Add the dressing and toss to coat well. Add salt and pepper. Mix well and chill.

Macaroni Salad   (serves six)

One-half pound uncooked macaroni makes 4 cups cooked.

4 cups (1 L) cooked macaroni
1 cup (¼ L) sliced celery
½ cup (1 dL) sliced scallions
4 tablespoons coarsely chopped green pepper
2 tablespoons chopped pimiento
4 tablespoons pitted, chopped black olives
2 tablespoons finely chopped parsley
1 cup (¼ L) mayonnaise
2 tablespoons vinegar
½ teaspoon freshly ground black pepper
Salt

Combine macaroni, celery, scallions, green pepper, pimiento, olives, and parsley in a large bowl; toss to mix. In a small bowl mix the mayonnaise and vinegar together until smooth. Add to the macaroni mixture. Add pepper and salt to taste. Toss and mix well. Refrigerate several hours before serving.

Rice Salad   (serves four)

This is a salad that has so many possibilities for variations that a list of suggestions follows the basic recipe. So use your ingenuity.

3 cups (¾ L) cooked rice
1 cup (¼ L) thin strips cooked ham
1 cup (¼ L) baby frozen peas, defrosted, or fresh young peas, blanched 1 minute
4-ounce (115-g) can whole pimientos, drained, chopped
2 tablespoons finely chopped chives or scallions
1 tablespoon finely chopped parsley
1 recipe French Dressing (p. 279)
1½ teaspoons Dijon mustard
Salt
Freshly ground pepper

Combine the rice, ham, peas, pimientos, chives or scallions, and parsley in a large bowl. In a small bowl mix the dressing and mustard until blended. Combine with the rice mixture, seasoning to taste.

Variations and Additions

1 cup rare roast beef instead of the ham.

1 cup vegetables cut in dice, such as tomatoes, green and red peppers, young raw zucchini, cucumbers in addition to, or in place of, the meat.

½ cup black olives, cut in half.

1 cup cooked shrimp and/or other seafood such as crabmeat, mussels, lobster, baby clams.

Salade Niçoise   (serves four)

Full of the flavors of the Mediterranean.

1 small head lettuce
1 cup (¼ L) lightly cooked green beans
1 can tuna fish
1 recipe French Dressing (p. 279), made with 1
   teaspoon minced garlic
4 anchovy fillets
8 black olives
½ green pepper, cut in thin strips
2 hard-boiled eggs, quartered

Tear up the lettuce and mix with the green beans.
Drain and break up the tuna fish, and add it with
all but a couple of tablespoons of the dressing. Toss
in a salad bowl. Over the top arrange the anchovy
fillets, olives, green pepper strips, and eggs decoratively, and drizzle the remaining dressing over.

Lentil Salad   (serves six)

1 cup (¼ L) lentils
Salt
3 tablespoons oil
1 tablespoon vinegar
1 medium onion, minced
Freshly ground pepper
¼ teaspoon dry mustard
2 tablespoons minced parsley

Simmer the lentils in 3 cups water with 1 teaspoon
salt for 30–40 minutes, until tender. Drain. In a

small bowl, mix the oil, vinegar, onion, pepper, and mustard. Toss with the lentils while they are hot. Refrigerate and, when cool, mix in the parsley and salt to taste.

Potato Salad   (serves six)

8 medium new potatoes
4 tablespoons lemon juice
4 tablespoons vegetable oil
Salt
½ teaspoon freshly ground pepper
2 celery ribs, finely chopped
4 hard-boiled eggs, coarsely chopped
1–1¼ cups (2¼–3 dL) mayonnaise
3 tablespoons cider vinegar
Six large lettuce leaves

Boil the potatoes just until tender when pierced with a fork. Drain, and as soon as you can handle them, peel and dice. Toss with the lemon juice, oil, and salt to taste (the flavor is better when they have this preliminary dressing while very warm, and the potatoes, thus coated, won't absorb as much mayonnaise later). Cool. Add the pepper, celery, and chopped eggs. Blend 1 cup mayonnaise with vinegar, then toss over the potato salad, gently folding until all pieces are coated. If the potatoes seem a little dry, add more mayonnaise. Line a bowl or a platter with lettuce leaves and pile the potato salad in the middle.

Variations and Additions
3 tablespoons finely chopped onion.

2 tablespoons dry mustard mixed into the mayonnaise.
3 tablespoons sweet pickle relish.
2 tablespoons minced parsley.

Hot or German Potato Salad
(serves six)

8 medium new potatoes
6 slices bacon
2½ tablespoons flour
6 tablespoons cider vinegar
1½ tablespoons sugar
1 teaspoon dry mustard
Salt to taste
½ teaspoon freshly ground pepper
10 romaine lettuce leaves
3 large ripe tomatoes

Boil the potatoes in their jackets until just tender. Meanwhile, fry the bacon until crisp. Reserving 4 tablespoons bacon fat, drain the bacon well and crumble; set aside. Heat the bacon fat and stir in the flour. Cook slowly, continuing to stir for a minute. Off heat add 1½ cups hot water and the vinegar, mix well, return to low heat, and cook, stirring, until smooth and thickened. Add sugar, mustard, salt, and pepper, and cook 2 minutes. Drain the potatoes, peel and slice them warm. Toss with the dressing until well coated. Arrange lettuce leaves in a large bowl and mound the hot salad in the center. Cut the tomatoes in wedges and arrange around edge. Sprinkle the crumbled bacon on top and serve warm.

Avocado with Chicken Stuffing (serves four)

½ cup (1 dL) mayonnaise
2 tablespoons lemon juice
1½ cups (3½ dL) diced cooked chicken
¼ cup (½ dL) finely chopped celery
Salt
⅓ cup (¾ dL) coarsely chopped blanched
   almonds
2 ripe, firm avocados
8 leaves of Bibb lettuce

Blend the mayonnaise and lemon juice together. Mix with the diced chicken and celery. Salt to taste and stir in the almonds. Peel the avocados and cut in half lengthwise. On each salad plate, place two lettuce leaves with one avocado half on top. Spoon one-fourth of the chicken salad into the hollow of each avocado half, letting some spill over onto the lettuce.

Avocado with Seafood Stuffing: Substitute *1¾ cups cooked shellfish* or *fish,* or a combination thereof, for the chicken. Eliminate the almonds and sprinkle *½ dozen or so capers* on top of each serving.

Egg Salad (serves four)

Have all the ingredients chilled.

⅔ cup (1½ dL) mayonnaise
2 tablespoons lemon juice

272

2 teaspoons vinegar
1 tablespoon finely chopped chives
1 tablespoon chopped fresh dill, or 1½ teaspoons dried, crumbled
⅛ teaspoon freshly ground pepper
Salt
⅓ cup (¾ dL) finely chopped green pepper
8 hard-boiled eggs, diced
4 crisp outer leaves of iceberg lettuce and 2 cups (½ L) shredded iceberg lettuce, or 1 head Boston or Bibb lettuce and several sprigs watercress

Combine the mayonnaise, lemon juice, vinegar, chives, dill, and pepper. Mix until well blended, and add salt to taste. Add the green pepper and eggs; gently toss to mix. Arrange one lettuce leaf on each salad plate and put ½ cup shredded lettuce on top. Or make a bed of lettuce leaves and watercress (reserving a few leaves for the top). Put a portion of egg salad on each lettuce bed. Serve.

Tuna Salad (serves four)

Canned salmon or crab may be used instead of tuna, but omit the sweet pickle relish (some may not like it even with tuna). Add a teaspoon of capers to the salmon or crab. Chill all the ingredients.

1½ cups (3½ dL) canned tuna, well drained, flaked
½ cup (1 dL) finely chopped celery
2 tablespoons sweet pickle relish (optional)

3 tablespoons lemon juice
½ cup (1 dL) mayonnaise
4 outer crisp leaves of iceberg lettuce and 2 cups
   (½ L) shredded iceberg lettuce, or 1 head
   Boston lettuce
1 tablespoon minced parsley

Combine the tuna, celery, pickle relish (if you wish), lemon juice, and mayonnaise. Toss until well mixed. Put the lettuce leaves on four salad plates with ½ cup shredded lettuce on top of each, or make a bed of loose lettuce leaves. Put a fourth of the tuna salad on each lettuce bed. Sprinkle with parsley and serve.

Chicken Salad (serves four)

4 cups (1 L) bite-size pieces cooked chicken
2 teaspoons grated onion or chopped scallions
   (optional)
1 cup (¼ L) sliced celery
⅔ cup (1½ dL) mayonnaise
4 tablespoons heavy cream
2 tablespoons vinegar
⅛ teaspoon freshly ground pepper
Salt to taste
1 head Bibb lettuce, washed, dried

Put chicken in a bowl and add the onion or scallions (if you like) and celery. Combine the mayonnaise, cream, and vinegar and blend well. Add pepper and salt, and toss with chicken, until well mixed. Make a bed of the lettuce leaves and spoon the chicken salad over.

Variations and Additions

Sprinkle *1 cup chopped almonds* over salad.

Instead of the celery add *1 cup seedless grapes* to chicken mixture.

Add *2 teaspoons curry powder* to the mayonnaise.

Omit the celery and add *½ cup peeled, seeded, diced cucumber* and *½ cup pineapple bits*.

Add *1 cup diced, unpeeled red apple* and *½ cup chopped walnuts*.

Shrimp and Artichoke Salad
(serves four)

1½ pounds (675 g) medium-size raw shrimp
10-ounce (285-g) package frozen artichoke hearts
1 tablespoon minced parsley
1 recipe Handmade Basic Mayonnaise (p. 282)
Salt
1 head Bibb lettuce

Bring a pot with enough water to cover the shrimp to boil. Add the shrimp and cook only until pink (about 5 minutes). Drain, rinse with cold water, peel, shell, and remove any black vein, then chill in the refrigerator. Cook the artichoke hearts as directed. Drain and chill. Mix the parsley into the mayonnaise. Toss the shrimp and artichoke hearts in the mayonnaise until well coated. Add salt to taste. Arrange the shrimp mixture on lettuce leaves.

Crab Louis (serves four)

½ large head iceberg lettuce, shredded
3 cups (¾ L) cooked crabmeat
1 cup (¼ L) mayonnaise
⅓ cup (¾ dL) whipped cream
4 tablespoons chili sauce
2 teaspoons grated onion
Pinch of cayenne pepper

Arrange the lettuce on four salad plates. Divide crabmeat and place on top. Combine remaining ingredients and mix until well blended. Spoon over each serving of crabmeat.

Lobster Salad (serves four)

Lobster salad is at its best when made very simply with lobster meat, a little crunchy celery, and adequately dressed with a creamy, mild homemade mayonnaise. Have all the ingredients chilled.

3 cups (¾ L) cooked lobster meat
½ cup (1 dL) finely chopped celery
½ cup (1 dL) mayonnaise
1½ tablespoons heavy cream
Salt to taste
1 head Bibb lettuce

Cut the lobster meat into large bite-size pieces, place them in a bowl, and add the celery. Blend the mayonnaise and cream in a small bowl, then gently combine with the lobster, toss to mix, and add salt.

276

Arrange a bed of lettuce leaves and put the lobster salad on top.

Waldorf Salad (serves four)

Sometimes it's pleasing to have two different kinds of apples in a Waldorf salad, if the season is right and you can get different varieties like a sweet Delicious and a tart Greening. In any case, be sure the apples you use are crisp.

2 firm ripe green apples
1 firm ripe red apple
1 tablespoon lemon juice
1 cup (¼ L) sliced celery
½ cup (1 dL) coarsely chopped walnuts
½ cup (1 dL) mayonnaise
1½ teaspoons honey (optional)
Iceberg or Bibb lettuce leaves

Core and quarter the apples (leave the skin on unless it is tough) and slice thin. Put in a bowl and toss with the lemon juice to coat. Add the celery and walnuts. Cover and chill. Mix the mayonnaise and honey (if you like a little sweetness in the dressing) together until smooth, add to the apple mixture, and toss. Serve on a bed of lettuce.

Fish Mousse (serves six)

If you have a fish-shaped mold, this delicate mousse will look very pretty when it is turned out on a platter garnished with black olives, sprigs of parsley, and lemon slices.

1 pound (450 g) lean fillets of turbot or flounder, fresh or frozen
2 cups (½ L) fish stock (p. 23), chilled
2 egg yolks, lightly beaten
2 envelopes gelatin
⅓ cup (¾ dL) dry white wine
¾ pound (340 g) cooked shrimp, or 1¼ cups small, canned
2 tablespoons chopped parsley
1 tablespoon chopped scallion greens or chives
1 tablespoon chopped fresh basil, or ½ teaspoon dried, crumbled
Few drops of fresh lemon juice
Salt
Freshly ground pepper
Several dashes of cayenne pepper
¾ cup (1¾ dL) heavy cream, whipped

Cover the fish fillets with cold fish stock and bring slowly to a boil. Simmer about 8 minutes, until fish is opaque through. Remove the fish and purée in a blender or in a food processor with a little of the stock. Temper the egg yolks by gradually adding the hot stock, then return to the pan and cook gently, stirring, until the liquid thickens enough to just coat the spoon. Remove from the heat. Soften the gelatin in the wine and mix into the hot stock until completely dissolved. Reserving 6 shrimp for garnish, cut the remaining into ½-inch pieces and toss with the chopped herbs and lemon juice. Combine the puréed fish, the shrimp mixture, and the stock, and season liberally with salt, pepper, and a little cayenne pepper. Refrigerate until the mixture is somewhat thickened—about the consistency of egg whites. Then fold in the whipped cream and pour into a lightly oiled 3-cup mold. Refrigerate until set. Turn out and decorate the platter with the remaining shrimp and other suggested garnishes.

French Dressing or Basic Vinaigrette (serves four)

2 tablespoons vinegar
½ teaspoon salt
¼ teaspoon freshly ground pepper
½ cup (1 dL) olive oil or salad oil

In a small bowl mix the vinegar and salt and let stand a few minutes. Add the pepper and slowly stir or whisk in the oil. Taste for acid and salt and add more if too bland. Stir to blend before using, or store in a jar with a tight lid and shake well before using.

Mustardy French Dressing. Add an additional *1–1½ tablespoons Dijon mustard.* Blend well. Include onion and garlic, if desired.

Onion or Garlic French Dressing. Add *1–2 tablespoons minced onion, scallions, or shallots* or *½–1 teaspoon minced garlic.*

French Dressing with Fresh Herbs. Add *2 teaspoons fresh chopped herbs,* such as basil, chervil, or tarragon.

Curried French Dressing. Add *1 teaspoon curry powder* and blend well.

Cream French Dressing. Add *3 tablespoons heavy cream* or *sour cream* and blend well.

Fruit Salad French Dressing. Use *lemon juice* instead of vinegar and add *⅓ cup honey*. Blend well.

Blue Cheese Dressing. Add *3 tablespoons crumbled blue cheese*. Blend well.

Cumberland Dressing. Add *1 teaspoon heavy cream, 1 tablespoon currant jelly,* and *¼ teaspoon grated lemon rind*. Mix until well blended.

Chiffonade Dressing. Add *1 tablespoon minced parsley, 2 tablespoons minced sweet red pepper, 1 tablespoon minced onion,* and *2 hard-boiled eggs, finely chopped*. Blend all ingredients well.

Pineapple Honey Dressing (¾ cup)

For fruit salads.

½ cup (1 dL) honey
3 tablespoons crushed pineapple
¼ cup (½ dL) lemon juice
Salt

Combine honey, pineapple, and lemon juice in a jar, cover with a snug-fitting lid, and shake until well blended. Add salt to taste.

Lime Dressing (⅓ cup)

For fruit salads.

¼ cup (½ dL) salad oil
2 tablespoons lime juice
¼ teaspoon Tabasco
2 teaspoons sugar
¼ teaspoon freshly ground pepper
Salt to taste

Combine all ingredients in a jar with a snug-fitting lid. Shake until blended.

Thousand-Island Dressing (½ cup)

For green salads.

⅓ cup (¾ dL) salad oil
2 tablespoons orange juice
1 tablespoon lemon juice
½ teaspoon paprika
2 teaspoons minced onion
2 teaspoons Worcestershire sauce
½ teaspoon dry mustard
2 teaspoons minced parsley
Salt to taste

Combine all ingredients in a pint jar, place lid on securely, and shake until well blended.

Handmade Basic Mayonnaise (1 cup)

Have your eggs at room temperature. Always add the oil drop by drop when first incorporating it with the egg and seasonings. After emulsion has begun, the oil may be added in a slow thin stream. Be patient! If you follow these rules, you should have no trouble.

1 egg yolk
½ teaspoon Dijon mustard or dry mustard
½ teaspoon salt
Pinch of cayenne pepper
1 tablespoon vinegar
¾ cup (1¾ dL) olive oil or salad oil

Put the yolk, mustard, salt, cayenne pepper, and vinegar in a clean bowl, put the bowl on a towel so it will remain stationary, and whisk until blended. Beat in the oil, drop by drop. As the sauce thickens, increase the flow of oil, but be slow and patient. The sauce, when finished, should be very thick. Taste critically and adjust the seasoning, adding a little more vinegar or salt, if necessary.

Cream Mayonnaise. Fold into the finished mayonnaise *½ cup heavy cream, whipped.* Serve with fruit salads, cold fish.

Mustard Mayonnaise. Blend *2 additional tablespoons Dijon mustard* thoroughly into the finished mayonnaise.

Green Mayonnaise. Cover *10 sprigs watercress, 10 leaves spinach,* and *4 sprigs parsley* with boiling water. Let stand for 3 minutes. Drain, put in cold

282

water, and drain again. Chop into a purée. Add to the finished mayonnaise and mix well.

Applesauce Mayonnaise. Add *1 cup unsweetened applesauce* and *1 tablespoon prepared horseradish* to the finished mayonnaise and mix well. Serve with cold ham or pork.

Russian Dressing. Add to the finished mayonnaise *1 cup chili sauce, 2 tablespoons minced celery, 2 tablespoons minced green pepper,* and add more *salt to taste.* Blend well.

Blender Mayonnaise (1½ cups)

A whole egg is needed when making mayonnaise in a blender. For a food processor 1 whole egg plus 1 yolk will give you the right consistency.

1 egg
¼ teaspoon salt
½ teaspoon dry mustard, or 1 teaspoon Dijon mustard
1 cup (¼ L) olive, peanut, or vegetable oil (or a combination)
1½ tablespoons vinegar or lemon juice
Salt to taste

Place the egg, salt, mustard, and ¼ cup of the oil in the electric blender. Turn on the motor and add the remaining ¾ cup oil in a slow, thin stream. Add the vinegar or lemon juice, and 1 tablespoon boiling water. Taste, correct the seasoning, and refrigerate until needed.

Food Processor Mayonnaise. Use 1 egg *plus 1 egg yolk* and mix in the food processor. Add up to ½ *cup more oil* and adjust the amount of vinegar or lemon juice. Omit the tablespoon of boiling water.

Green Mayonnaise (Machine-made) (1¾ cups)

This must be used within a few days; after that the greens tend to turn sour. If you plan to keep it longer, blanch the greens for a minute in boiling water, then squeeze dry before using.

¾ cup (1¾ dL) fresh greens: parsley, watercress, young spinach leaves
¼ cup (½ dL) fresh herbs: basil, tarragon, chervil, or 2 tablespoons dill, or 1 tablespoon dried herbs (1 teaspoon if using dried dill)
1 egg
1 egg yolk
Freshly ground pepper to taste
1 cup (¼ L) olive, peanut, or vegetable oil (or a combination)
1½ tablespoons mild vinegar or lemon juice or a combination
Salt to taste

Place the greens and the herbs with the egg, egg yolk, and pepper in an electric blender or food processor and blend until the greens are puréed. Start adding the oil in a slow, thin stream until the mixture becomes too thick, then add the vinegar and/or lemon juice and continue until all the oil is used up. If too thick, add a small amount of boiling water. Taste, add salt, and refrigerate in a covered jar or bowl until needed.

Yogurt Dressing (1¼ cups)

1 cup (¼ L) yogurt
2 tablespoons white vinegar
1½ tablespoons lemon juice
⅛ teaspoon freshly ground pepper
2 tablespoons finely chopped chives
2 tablespoons finely chopped parsley
Salt to taste

Combine all ingredients in a bowl and blend until well mixed. Refrigerate and use as needed.

Honey Yogurt Dressing. Add *2 tablespoons honey* and omit the chives and parsley.

Yogurt, Garlic, and Blue Cheese Dressing. Add *4 tablespoons crumbled blue cheese* and *2 cloves garlic, finely chopped.*

Yogurt and Mayonnaise Dressing. Add up to *1 cup mayonnaise* and mix well.

Sour-Cream Dressing (1¼ cups)

For fruit salads and vegetable salads.

1 cup (¼ L) sour cream
4 tablespoons vinegar
2 teaspoons sugar (for fruit salad), or 1 teaspoon

sugar (for vegetable salad)
1 teaspoon dry mustard
⅛ teaspoon cayenne pepper
Salt to taste

Combine all ingredients in a bowl and whisk until well blended.

Bacon Dressing (1¼ cups)

Very good on bitter or robust greens, such as spinach.

3 tablespoons bacon fat
2 tablespoons flour
2 teaspoons grated onion
½ teaspoon freshly ground pepper
¼ teaspoon sugar
2 teaspoons prepared mustard
1 tablespoon vinegar
Salt

Melt the bacon fat in a skillet, slowly stir in the flour and onion, and cook, stirring constantly, for 2 minutes. Add the pepper, sugar, mustard, and vinegar. Blend and stir, then slowly add 1 cup water. Continue to stir and cook over medium heat until thickened. Add salt to taste. Can be served hot or cold.

Breads

White Bread (2 loaves)

A pure, tender loaf, exactly what a basic white bread should be.

2 tablespoons shortening
2½ teaspoons salt
2 tablespoons sugar
1 cup (¼ L) hot milk
1 package dry yeast
6 cups (840 g) white flour

Mix the shortening, salt, and sugar in a large bowl, add the hot milk and 1 cup hot water, and let cool to lukewarm. In a small bowl or cup mix the yeast with ¼ cup warm water and let it stand for 5 minutes to dissolve. Add the dissolved yeast and 3 cups of the flour to the first mixture and beat until well blended. Add 2 more cups of flour, mix, and turn out onto a lightly floured board. Knead for a minute or two and then let rest for 10 minutes. Adding just enough of the remaining flour so that the dough is not sticky, resume kneading until the dough is smooth and elastic. Put the dough in a large, greased bowl, cover, and let rise in a warm spot until double in bulk. Punch down and shape into two loaves. Place in greased loaf pans, cover, and let double in bulk again. Preheat oven to 425°F (220°C). Bake bread for 15 minutes, reduce heat to 375°F (190°C), and bake for 30 minutes more. Remove from pans and cool on racks.

Cheese Bread. Mix *1½ cups grated Cheddar or other sharp cheese* with the last flour added.

Whole-Wheat Bread (2 loaves)

You'll get fine-textured wheat slices with a whole-grain flavor from these loaves.

1 cup (¼ L) milk
¼ cup (50 g) sugar
2 teaspoons salt
1 package dry yeast
2 cups (280 g) whole-wheat flour
4 cups (560 g) white flour

Bring ½ cup water to a boil, mix it with the milk, sugar, and salt in a large bowl, and let cool to lukewarm. In a separate container, measure ½ cup warm water, stir in the yeast, and let it stand for 5 minutes to dissolve. Add the dissolved yeast, the whole-wheat flour, and 2 cups of the white flour to the first mixture. Beat thoroughly, then turn out onto a lightly floured board, adding enough flour so that the dough handles easily. Knead for a few minutes and let rest for 10 minutes. Add as much of the remaining flour as necessary to keep the dough from being sticky. Resume kneading for 10 minutes or until the dough is smooth and elastic. Place in a greased bowl, cover, and let rise in a warm spot until double in bulk. Punch down and shape into two loaves. Place in greased loaf pans, cover, and let rise again until almost double in bulk. Preheat oven to 375°F (190°C). Bake bread for about 45 minutes. Remove from pans and cool on racks.

Whole-Wheat Bread with Wheat Berries. Simmer *½–¾ cup dry wheat berries* in water to cover for several hours or until soft. Drain and knead them into the Whole-Wheat Bread dough after the first rising.

Whole-Wheat Bread with Wheat Germ. Mix *½ cup wheat germ* in with the flour.

Whole-Wheat Oatmeal Bread. Knead in *1 cup uncooked rolled oats* with the whole-wheat flour. You will need ½–1 cup less of the white flour if you add the oats.

Oatmeal Bread   (2 loaves)

Honey-colored, chewy, and moist with a distinct molasses flavor.

1 cup (¼ L) instant oats
1 package dry yeast
½ cup (1 dL) molasses
2 teaspoons salt
1 tablespoon butter
5½ cups (770 g) white flour

Put the oats in a large bowl. Bring 2 cups water to a boil, pour it over oats, and let stand for at least 15 minutes. Stir the yeast into ¼ cup warm water and let it stand for 5 minutes to dissolve. Feel the oats at the bottom of the bowl to be sure they're lukewarm, then add the molasses, salt, butter, and dissolved yeast. Work in enough of the flour so that the dough is easy to handle. Turn out onto a lightly floured board, knead for a minute or two, and let rest for 10 minutes. Resume kneading until the dough is smooth and elastic, adding more flour as necessary. Place in a buttered bowl, cover, and let rise in a warm spot until double in bulk. Punch down and shape into two loaves. Place in buttered loaf pans, cover, and let rise again until double in bulk. Preheat oven to 375°F (190°C). Bake bread for 45 minutes. Remove from pans and cool on racks.

Oatmeal Bread with Honey. Use *⅓ cup honey* instead of molasses.

Rye Bread (2 loaves)

Rye flour will remain a bit sticky, even when it has been thoroughly kneaded. This recipe makes a light, moist loaf.

1 cup (¼ L) milk
2 tablespoons shortening
2 tablespoons dark-brown sugar
1 tablespoon salt
2 packages dry yeast
3 cups (420 g) rye flour
3 cups (420 g) white flour

Bring 1 cup water to a boil, mix it with the milk, shortening, sugar, and salt in a large bowl, and let cool to lukewarm. Measure ½ cup warm water in a separate container, stir in yeast, and let it stand for 5 minutes to dissolve. Add the dissolved yeast and the rye flour to the first mixture and combine thoroughly. Add enough of the white flour so that you can handle the dough. Turn out onto a lightly floured board, knead for a minute or two, then let rest for 10 minutes. Resume kneading for about 10 minutes, adding the remaining flour as necessary. Put the dough in a greased bowl, cover, and let rise in a warm place until almost double in bulk. Punch down and shape into two loaves. Place in greased loaf pans, cover, and let rise again until double in bulk. Preheat oven to 375°F (190°C). Bake bread for 45–50 minutes. Remove from pans and cool on racks.

French Bread (two 15-inch loaves)

This is French bread, American style. Its soft, fine texture and light-brown crust make it a pleasing dinner bread.

2 packages dry yeast
2 tablespoons sugar
4 tablespoons melted shortening
Salt
6 cups (840 g) white flour
Cornmeal
1 egg white

Stir the yeast into 2 cups warm water in a large bowl and let it stand for 5 minutes to dissolve. Add the sugar, the shortening, and 1 tablespoon salt, and stir well. Add 2 cups of the flour and beat thoroughly. Add 3 more cups of the flour and mix well. Turn out onto a lightly floured board, knead for a few minutes, and let rest for 10 minutes. Resume kneading, adding some of the remaining flour until the dough is no longer sticky but very smooth and elastic. Place in a greased bowl, cover, and let rise in a warm spot until double in bulk. Punch down and knead for a few seconds. Shape by rolling and stretching into two long, cylindrical 15-inch loaves and place on a greased cookie sheet lightly sprinkled with cornmeal. Cover and let rise again until double in bulk. Preheat oven to 375°F (190°C). Lightly beat egg white with 1 tablespoon water and 1 teaspoon salt. Brush tops of loaves with this glaze before baking. Bake for 35–45 minutes. Remove from pan and cool on racks.

Hot Buttered Bread. Soften *4 tablespoons unsalted butter.* After baking and cooling, cut French Bread in diagonal slices without cutting all the way through. Spread the butter between the slices, wrap the bread in foil, and heat in a 400°F (205°C) oven until very hot.

Garlic Bread. Mash *1 minced garlic clove* into *4 tablespoons softened butter* and proceed as for Hot Buttered Bread.

Herb Bread. Mix some *finely chopped chives, watercress, or fresh herbs* and a few drops of *lemon juice* into the butter and proceed as for Hot Buttered Bread.

Cheesed Bread. Follow the directions for Hot Buttered Bread, spreading the slices with *soft cheese* or *butter mixed with grated Cheddar cheese*.

Pizza (two 12-inch pizzas)

1 package dry yeast
4 cups (560 g) flour
Olive oil
2 teaspoons salt
2 cups (½ L) Tomato Sauce (p. 154)
2 cups (½ L) grated mozzarella cheese
2 teaspoons oregano, crumbled

Dissolve the yeast in ⅓ cup warm water. Add the flour, 2 tablespoons oil, 1 cup warm water, and the salt, and knead for 10 minutes. Put in an oiled bowl to rise, covered with plastic wrap. When the dough has doubled in bulk, about 2 hours, punch it down and divide in two. Let rest 5 minutes. Preheat the oven to 400°F (205°C). Roll the dough with a rolling pin or stretch it over your fists until you have two 12-inch circles. Place on pizza pans or cookie sheets and prick all over. On each circle, spoon 1 cup tomato sauce; sprinkle with 1 cup mozzarella and 1 teaspoon oregano. Drizzle with about 1 tablespoon olive oil. Let rest another 10 minutes and then bake for 25 minutes, until lightly brown. Cut into wedges and serve hot.

Pizza with Tomato-Mushroom Filling. Add to the filling *2 cups sliced mushrooms* sautéed 3 minutes in *2 tablespoons olive oil* and sprinkle *2 tablespoons capers* on top.

Pizza with Anchovy Filling. Arrange over the tomato filling *16 anchovy fillets* like the spokes of a wheel and decorate each pizza with *½ cup black olives.*

Pizza with Sausage. Distribute over the tomato filling *¾ pound pepperoni* cut in thin slices, or *1 pound other cooked sausage* sliced.

Brioche Bread and Rolls
(1 loaf and 6 rolls)

Bread and rolls with a mildly sweet, pale yellow crumb and the gentle flavor of lemons and butter.

2 packages dry yeast
1 cup (¼ L) warm milk
⅔ cup (1½ dL) butter
1 egg
4 egg yolks
½ cup (100 g) sugar
1½ teaspoons salt
Grated rind of 1 lemon
5½ cups (770 g) white flour

Stir the yeast into the milk in a large mixing bowl and let it stand for 5 minutes to dissolve. Add the butter, egg, egg yolks, sugar, salt, lemon rind, and about 2½ cups of the flour. Beat thoroughly, then add as much of the remaining flour as is necessary for a dough that handles easily. Turn out onto a lightly floured board. Knead for a minute or two and let rest for 10 minutes. Continue to knead until smooth and elastic. Put the dough in a large, buttered bowl, cover, and let rise in a warm spot until double in bulk. Punch down and let it rise again until slightly less than double in bulk, for at least 4 hours or in a covered bowl in the refrigerator overnight. Butter a loaf pan and a 6-cup muffin pan and fill them one-third full. Cover and let double once again. Preheat oven to 375°F (190°C). Bake bread, allowing about 20 minutes for the muffins and 45 minutes for the bread. Remove from pans and cool on racks.

Bran and Honey Bread (2 loaves)

Sweet, light, and wholesome.

1 tablespoon butter
4 tablespoons honey
2½ teaspoons salt
1 cup (¼ L) milk
1 package dry yeast
1 cup (¼ L) bran
5 cups (700 g) white flour

Bring 1 cup water to a boil, mix it with the butter, honey, salt, and milk in a large bowl, and let cool to lukewarm. In a separate container, stir the yeast into ¼ cup warm water and let it stand for 5 minutes to dissolve. Add the dissolved yeast, the bran, and 2 cups of the white flour to the first mixture and stir vigorously. Add 2 more cups of the white flour and mix well. Turn out onto a lightly floured board and let rest for 10 minutes. Adding as much of the remaining flour as necessary to keep the dough from sticking, knead until smooth and elastic—about 10 minutes. Put the dough in a greased bowl, cover, and let rise in a warm place until double in bulk. Punch down and shape into two loaves. Place in greased loaf pans, cover, and let rise again until double in bulk. Preheat oven to 425°F (220°C). Bake bread for 10 minutes, reduce heat to 375°F (190°C), and continue to bake for 30–35 minutes more. Remove from pans and cool on racks.

Raisin and Nut Bread (2 loaves)

A soft-crumbed, tender loaf. It's good toasted, too—with honey.

1 cup (¼ L) milk
4 tablespoons butter
4 tablespoons sugar
1 tablespoon salt
1 package dry yeast
6 cups (840 g) white flour
¾ cup (1¾ dL) raisins
¾ cup (1¾ dL) chopped nuts

Bring 1 cup water to a boil, mix it with the milk, butter, sugar, and salt in a large bowl, and let cool to lukewarm. In a separate container, measure ½ cup warm water, stir in the yeast, and let it stand for 5 minutes to dissolve. Add the dissolved yeast and 3 cups of the flour to the first mixture and combine thoroughly. Add the raisins and nuts. Work in enough of the remaining flour so that the dough is easy to handle. Turn out onto a lightly floured board, knead for a few minutes, and let rest for 10 minutes. Resume kneading until the dough is smooth and elastic. Put the dough in a buttered bowl, cover, and let rise in a warm spot until double in bulk. Punch down and shape into two loaves. Place in buttered loaf pans, cover, and let rise again until almost double in bulk. Preheat oven to 375°F (190°C). Bake bread for 45–55 minutes. Remove from pans and cool on racks.

Anadama Bread (2 loaves)

Brown and crusty with a chewy, springy texture, this old-fashioned batter bread, quick and easy to make, is an American classic.

½ cup (1 dL) yellow cornmeal
1 package dry yeast
½ cup (1 dL) molasses
2 teaspoons salt
1 tablespoon butter
4½ cups (630 g) white flour

Put the cornmeal in a large mixing bowl. Bring 2 cups water to a boil and pour it over the cornmeal. Stir until smooth, making sure that the cornmeal does not lump. Let stand for 30 minutes. Stir the yeast into ½ cup warm water and let it stand for 5 minutes to dissolve. Add the molasses, salt, butter, and dissolved yeast to the cornmeal mixture. Stir in the flour and beat thoroughly. Spoon into 2 buttered loaf pans, cover, and let rise in a warm spot until double in bulk. Preheat oven to 350°F (180°C). Bake bread for 45–50 minutes. Remove from pans and cool on racks.

Cincinnati Coffee Bread (1 loaf)

1 cup (¼ L) hot milk
⅓ cup (65 g) sugar
5 tablespoons butter
1 teaspoon salt
1 package dry yeast
2 eggs, well beaten
4 cups (560 g) white flour

Topping

½ cup (1 dL) bread crumbs
2 tablespoons sugar
1 tablespoon cinnamon
2 tablespoons melted butter

Mix the milk, sugar, butter, and salt in a large bowl and let cool to lukewarm. Stir the yeast into ¼ cup warm water and let stand for 5 minutes to dissolve. Add the dissolved yeast, eggs, and flour to the first mixture and beat very well. Cover and let rise until double in bulk. Stir down with a spoon and beat thoroughly. Spoon into a buttered loaf pan. Mix the topping ingredients together and sprinkle them on the batter, cover the pan, and let rise again until double in bulk. Preheat oven to 350°F (180°C). Bake loaf for about 40–50 minutes.

Standard Rolls (2½–3 dozen rolls)

With this basic recipe you can make fine, light rolls and biscuits in a variety of shapes.

4 tablespoons butter
2 tablespoons sugar
2 teaspoons salt
2 cups (½ L) warm milk
1 package dry yeast
6 cups (840 g) white flour
Melted butter

Mix the butter, sugar, salt, and milk in a large bowl and let cool to lukewarm. Stir the yeast into ¼ cup warm water and let it stand for 5 minutes to dissolve. Add 3 cups of the flour and the dissolved yeast to the first mixture and beat vigorously for 2 minutes. Cover and let rise in a warm place until double in bulk. Stir the dough vigorously and add as much of the remaining flour as necessary in order to knead the dough. Turn out onto a lightly floured board, knead for a minute or two, and let rest for 10 minutes. Resume kneading until smooth. Shape (see following suggestions). Arrange the shaped dough in buttered muffin tins or close together on buttered cookie sheets, brushing between them with melted butter so that they separate easily after baking. Cover and let rise again until double in bulk. Preheat oven to 425°F (220°C). Bake rolls for about 12–15 minutes.

Shaping Rolls

Biscuits. Using a rolling pin, roll out the dough for Standard Rolls on a lightly floured board until it is ⅓ inch thick; cut with a small, round biscuit cutter. Or shape the dough into a long, thin cylinder and with a floured knife cut off pieces about ⅓ inch thick.

299

Finger Rolls. Cut the dough for Standard Rolls as you would for Biscuits, then roll each piece with one hand on an unfloured board into a long, thin oval.

Clover Leaf Rolls. Shape the dough for Standard Rolls into 1-inch balls, brush with *melted butter,* and place three balls in each section of a buttered muffin tin.

Parker House Rolls. Using a rolling pin, roll out the dough for Standard Rolls until it is ⅓ inch thick and cut with a round biscuit cutter or with an oval Parker House roll cutter. Using the dull edge of a knife, make a crease through the center of each piece of dough, brush with *melted butter,* fold in half along the crease, and press edges lightly together. Place 1 inch apart on a buttered cookie sheet.

Bowknots or Twists. Using your hands, roll thin strips of the dough for Standard Rolls into sticks 8–10 inches long. Twist them or tie them loosely in knots.

Butter Rolls. Using a rolling pin, roll the dough for Standard Rolls into a rectangle about 12 × 16 inches. Spread with *softened butter.* Cut lengthwise into four strips and stack them evenly in a pile. Cut into 1-inch pieces and arrange them on their sides in a buttered muffin tin.

Pinwheel Biscuits. Using a rolling pin, roll out the dough for Standard Rolls until it is ¼ inch thick and spread it with *softened butter.* Roll from the long side like a jelly roll. Cut in ¾-inch pieces and place close together on a buttered cookie sheet, cut side down.

Feather Rolls (12 rolls)

Feather rolls, as their name indicates, are high and very light.

1 package dry yeast
4 tablespoons soft butter
1 tablespoon sugar
¾ teaspoon salt
1 egg
¾ cup (1¾ dL) warm milk
2 cups (280 g) white flour

Stir the yeast into ¼ cup warm water and let it stand for 5 minutes to dissolve. Mix the butter, sugar, salt, egg, milk, and dissolved yeast in a large bowl and beat until smooth. Add the flour and beat vigorously until well blended. Cover and let rise in a warm spot for about 1 hour. Stir down and fill buttered muffin tins half full. Cover and let rise for about 30 minutes. Preheat oven to 400°F (205°C). Bake rolls for 15–20 minutes.

Potato Biscuits (about 15 biscuits)

Old-fashioned potato biscuits are light, moist, and golden. And they do taste good!

½ cup (1 dL) hot milk
2 tablespoons shortening
2 tablespoons sugar
½ cup (1 dL) warm mashed potatoes
1 teaspoon salt

301

3¼ cups (450 g) white flour
1 package dry yeast

Mix the hot milk, shortening, sugar, potatoes, salt, and ¼ cup of the flour in a large bowl and let cool to lukewarm. Stir the yeast into ¼ cup warm water and let it stand for 5 minutes to dissolve. Add the dissolved yeast to the first mixture and beat vigorously. Cover and let rise in a warm place until light. Stir, add the remaining 3 cups of flour, and mix well. Cover and let rise again to double in bulk. Turn out onto a lightly floured board. Pat the dough until it is ¼ inch thick and cut into 2-inch rounds. Place the rounds about 1 inch apart on a greased baking sheet, cover, and let rise until amost double. Preheat oven to 425°F (220°C). Bake biscuits for about 15 minutes.

Sweet Rolls (about 18 rolls)

These rolls are made from a dependable, basic sweet dough, good for buns and coffee cakes. The texture is fine, rather dense, and rich. Doughs like this, enriched with eggs, milk, butter, and more sugar than usual, do not rise as rapidly as plainer doughs.

¾ cup (1¾ dL) warm milk
¼ cup (50 g) sugar
1 teaspoon salt
4 tablespoons soft butter
2 eggs
1 package dry yeast
2½ cups (350 g) white flour

Mix the milk, sugar, salt, butter, and eggs in a large bowl and let cool to lukewarm. Stir the yeast into ¼ cup warm water and let it stand for 5 minutes to dissolve. Add the dissolved yeast to the first mixture, beat thoroughly, and add 1½ cups of the flour, beating well. Cover and let rise in a warm place for about 1 hour. Add the remaining cup of flour and blend in well, adding more flour if necessary to make the dough firm enough to handle. Knead until smooth and elastic. Put the dough in a buttered bowl, cover, and let rise until almost double in bulk. Punch down, shape into rolls (see p. 299 for directions), and let rise for about 1 hour. Preheat oven to 400°F (205°C). Bake rolls for 15–20 minutes.

Cinnamon Buns. Add *1 tablespoon cinnamon* to the dough in the first step.

Orange Rolls. Use *¾ cup orange juice* instead of milk and add *1 tablespoon grated orange peel.* Shape like Parker House Rolls (p. 300). Dip *orange sections* in sugar and put one in the center of each roll before folding and baking.

Cinnamon Rolls (about 16 rolls)

These rolls rise very high and are mildly sweet with a soft cinnamon flavor.

1 package dry yeast
4½ cups (630 g) white flour
1 cup (¼ L) lukewarm milk
¾ cup (145 g) granulated sugar

1 teaspoon salt
1 tablespoon cinnamon
2 eggs
2 tablespoons butter
½ cup (1 dL) raisins
Milk
¾ cup (1¾ dL) confectioners' sugar
1 teaspoon vanilla

Stir the yeast into ¼ cup warm water and let it stand for 5 minutes to dissolve. Add the dissolved yeast and 3 cups of the flour to the milk and blend well. Cover and let rise in a warm place until light. Add the granulated sugar, salt, cinnamon, eggs, butter, and ¾ cup of the flour and blend. Turn out onto a lightly floured board and knead gently, slowly adding the remaining ¾ cup of flour until the dough can be easily handled. Knead in the raisins. Pull off pieces of dough the size of medium lemons, roll each about 8 inches long, and wind it into a coil. Arrange on two buttered 9-inch cake pans, cover, and let rise until double in bulk, then brush tops with milk. Preheat oven to 375°F (190°C). Bake rolls for 25 minutes. Mix the confectioners' sugar and vanilla with 4 teaspoons warm water to make a glaze, and spread a thin layer on rolls immediately after removing from the oven.

Sally Lunn Tea Cakes
(24 tea cakes or one 10-inch tube cake)

They say that Sally Lunn lived in Bath, England, and sold this kind of tender, semisweet tea cake—almost weightless with a light yellow crumb, they can also be made as one large cake.

1 cup (¼ L) hot milk
¼ pound (115 g) butter
⅓ cup (65 g) sugar
1 teaspoon salt
1 package dry yeast
3 eggs
3½ cups (490 g) white flour

Mix the hot milk, butter, sugar, and salt in a large bowl and let cool to lukewarm. Stir the yeast into ¼ cup warm water and let it stand for 5 minutes to dissolve. Add the dissolved yeast and the eggs to the first mixture and beat vigorously. Gradually add the flour. Cover and let rise in a warm place until about double in bulk. Spoon the dough into buttered muffin tins, filling each section about half full, or put it all in a buttered 10-inch tube pan. Preheat oven to 425°F (220°C) for muffins, 350°F (180°C) for cake. Bake muffins for 20 minutes, tube cake for about 50 minutes.

Nut Bread (1 loaf)

2 cups (280 g) flour
½ cup (1 dL) dark-brown sugar
2 teaspoons baking powder
1 teaspoon salt
1 egg
1 cup (¼ L) milk
2 tablespoons melted butter
½ cup (1 dL) chopped nuts

Preheat the oven to 350°F (180°C). Butter a loaf pan. Mix the flour, brown sugar, baking powder, and salt in a large bowl, add the egg, milk, and butter, and stir until well blended. Add the nuts. Spoon into the pan and bake for 45 minutes. Remove from the pan and cool on a rack.

Date Nut Bread (1 loaf)

Date nut bread is moist and sweet, and it keeps very well.

1 cup (¼ L) chopped dates
½ cup (100 g) sugar
4 tablespoons butter
1 egg, well beaten
1 teaspoon baking soda
1¾ cups (245 g) flour
½ teaspoon salt
½ cup (1 dL) walnuts, chopped

Preheat the oven to 350°F (180°C). Butter a loaf pan. Bring ¾ cup water to a boil, mix it with the dates, sugar, and butter in a large bowl, and let cool to lukewarm. Stir in the egg, baking soda, flour, salt, and nuts, and blend well. Spoon into the pan and bake for about 50 minutes. Remove from the pan and cool on a rack.

Apricot Almond Bread (1 loaf)

Brown and crusty on the outside, with bits of tart apricot and white almonds scattered throughout.

1½ cups (3½ dL) coarsely chopped dried apricots
2 tablespoons butter
1 cup (200 g) sugar
1 teaspoon salt
1½ cups (210 g) white flour
1 cup (140 g) whole-wheat flour
1 teaspoon baking soda
1 cup (¼ L) almonds, chopped
1 egg, well beaten
1 teaspoon orange extract

Preheat the oven to 350°F (180°C). Butter a loaf pan. Put the apricots in a bowl and pour 1½ cups boiling water over them. Add the butter, sugar, and salt and let cool to lukewarm. Stir in remaining ingredients and mix very well. Spoon into the pan and bake for 1¼ hours. Remove from the pan and cool on a rack.

Pumpkin Bread (1 loaf)

1½ cups (210 g) flour
½ teaspoon salt
1 cup (200 g) sugar
1 teaspoon baking soda
1 cup (¼ L) pumpkin purée
½ cup (1 dL) vegetable oil
2 eggs, beaten
¼ teaspoon nutmeg
¼ teaspoon cinnamon
¼ teaspoon allspice
½ cup (1 dL) chopped nuts

Preheat the oven to 350°F (180°C). Sift together the flour, salt, sugar, and baking soda. Mix the pumpkin, oil, eggs, ¼ cup water, and spices together, then combine with the dry ingredients, but do not mix too thoroughly. Stir in the nuts. Pour into a well-buttered 9 × 5 × 3-inch loaf pan. Bake 50–60 minutes until a straw comes out clean. Turn out of the pan and cool on a rack.

Cranberry Nut Bread (1 loaf)

1 orange
2 tablespoons butter
1 egg
1 cup (200 g) sugar
1 cup (¼ L) cranberries, chopped
½ cup (1 dL) chopped walnuts
2 cups (280 g) white flour
½ teaspoon salt
1½ teaspoons baking powder
½ teaspoon baking soda

Preheat the oven to 325°F (165°C). Butter a loaf pan. Grate the rind of the orange, and squeeze out all the juice into a measuring cup and add enough boiling water to make ¾ cup. Add the orange rind and the butter and stir to melt the butter. Beat the egg in another bowl and gradually add the sugar, beating well. Add remaining ingredients and orange mixture, and blend well. Spoon into the pan and bake for 1 hour. Remove from the pan and cool on a rack.

Banana Nut Bread (1 loaf)

This is pure and simple banana bread, heavy, moist, and dark.

3 ripe bananas, well mashed
2 eggs, well beaten
2 cups (280 g) flour
¾ cup (145 g) sugar
1 teaspoon salt
1 teaspoon baking soda
½ cup (1 dL) coarsely chopped walnuts

Preheat the oven to 350°F (180°C). Grease a loaf pan. Mix the bananas and eggs together in a large bowl. Stir in the flour, sugar, salt, and baking soda. Add the walnuts and blend. Put the batter in the pan and bake for 1 hour. Remove from the pan to a rack. Serve still warm or cooled, as you like it.

Basic Muffins (12 muffins)

What could be nicer than warm muffins wrapped in a napkin on the morning breakfast table? And they are so quick and easy to make, particularly since the ingredients are only lightly mixed, not beaten smooth.

2 cups (280 g) white flour
3 teaspoons baking powder
½ teaspoon salt
2 tablespoons sugar
1 egg, slightly beaten

1 cup (¼ L) milk
¼ cup (60 g) melted butter

Preheat the oven to 375°F (190°C). Butter muffin pans. Mix the flour, baking powder, salt, and sugar in a large bowl. Add the egg, milk, and butter, stirring only enough to dampen the flour; the batter should *not* be smooth. Spoon into the muffin pans, filling each cup about two-thirds full. Bake for about 20–25 minutes.

Blueberry Muffins. Use *½ cup sugar.* Reserve *¼ cup of the flour*, sprinkle it over *1 cup blueberries*, and stir them into the batter last.

Pecan Muffins. Use *¼ cup sugar.* Add *½ cup chopped pecans* to the batter. After filling the cups, sprinkle with *sugar, cinnamon,* and more *chopped nuts.*

Whole-Wheat Muffins. Use *¾ cup whole-wheat flour* and *1 cup white flour.*

Date or Raisin Muffins. Add *½ cup chopped pitted dates* or *⅓ cup raisins* to the batter.

Bacon Muffins. Add *3 strips bacon, fried crisp and crumbled,* to the batter.

Bran Muffins (12 muffins)

Split, toasted, and lightly spread with butter, these are earthy and good.

1 egg, slightly beaten
1 cup (¼ L) milk

2 tablespoons melted butter
1 cup (¼ L) bran
1 cup (140 g) white flour
3 teaspoons baking powder
¼ cup (50 g) sugar
½ teaspoon salt

Preheat the oven to 375°F (190°C). Butter muffin pans. Put the egg, milk, butter, and bran in a mixing bowl and let stand for 10 minutes. Add the flour, baking powder, sugar, and salt and stir just enough to dampen. Spoon into the muffin pans, filling each cup about two-thirds full. Bake for about 20 minutes.

Baking Powder Biscuits (16 biscuits)

Light-gold and crusty outside, moist and fine-textured inside.

2 cups (280 g) flour
½ teaspoon salt
4 teaspoons baking powder
½ teaspoon cream of tartar
1 tablespoon sugar
½ cup (1 dL) vegetable shortening
⅔ cup (1½ dL) milk

Preheat the oven to 425°F (220°C). Grease two 8-inch cake pans. Put the flour, salt, baking powder, cream of tartar, and sugar in a bowl. Cut the shortening into the flour with two knives or a pastry blender until the mixture resembles coarse meal. Add the milk all at once and stir just until the dough

311

forms a ball around the fork. Turn the dough onto a lightly floured board and knead 14 times. Pat until ½ inch thick. Cut into rounds with a 2-inch cookie cutter. Place touching each other in the cake pans and bake for 15–20 minutes.

Crusty Baking Powder Biscuits. Roll biscuits to ¼ inch thick and place 1 inch apart. Bake in a 450°F (230°C) oven for 12 minutes. This will yield almost twice as many biscuits.

Buttermilk Biscuits. Use *⅔ cup buttermilk* instead of sweet milk and *½ teaspoon baking soda,* cutting the amount of baking powder in half—i.e., 2 teaspoons.

Cheese Biscuits. Add *½ cup grated sharp Cheddar cheese* to the dry ingredients.

Drop Biscuits. Add an additional *⅓ cup milk* and drop by teaspoonfuls onto a buttered baking sheet.

Popovers   (about 10 popovers)

Forget what you've read elsewhere. The secret in making good popovers is to start them in a cold oven.

2 eggs
1 cup (¼ L) milk
1 tablespoon melted butter
1 cup (140 g) white flour
¼ teaspoon salt

Put all ingredients in a large bowl and mix thoroughly, without overbeating. Half-fill buttered muffin tins or custard cups. Put them in a cold oven and set the heat for 450°F (230°C). Bake for 15 minutes, then reduce heat to 350°F (180°C) and bake for another 15 to 20 minutes. Test one to be sure it's done by removing it from the pan: it should be crisp outside and moist and tender inside.

Whole-Wheat Popovers. Use *⅔ cup whole-wheat flour* and *⅓ cup white flour* instead of all white flour. (Whole-wheat popovers will not rise as high as regular popovers.)

Corn Bread (sixteen 2-inch squares)

Sturdy, solid, slightly dry—a direct legacy from our American past.

¾ cup (1¾ dL) yellow cornmeal
1 cup (140 g) flour
⅓ cup (65 g) sugar
3 teaspoons baking powder
½ teaspoon salt
1 cup (¼ L) milk
1 egg, well beaten
2 tablespoons melted shortening or bacon fat

Preheat the oven to 425°F (220°C). Grease an 8-inch square cake pan. Mix the cornmeal, flour, sugar, baking powder, and salt in a large bowl. Add the milk, egg, and shortening or bacon fat, and blend well. Spoon into the pan and bake for about 20 minutes. Cool and cut in squares.

Corn Muffins. Thoroughly grease a muffin pan and pour the batter into the cups about three-quarters full. You should have 12 muffins.

Irish Bread (9-inch round loaf)

A large round biscuit with a brown, flaky crust and the flavor of raisins and caraway seeds. Serve with lots of butter.

2 cups (280 g) white flour
4 teaspoons baking powder
½ teaspoon salt
1 tablespoon sugar
3 tablespoons vegetable shortening
⅔ cup (1½ dL) milk
½ cup (1 dL) raisins
1 tablespoon caraway seeds

Preheat the oven to 375°F (190°C). Grease a 9-inch round cake pan. Put the flour, baking powder, salt, and sugar in a large bowl. Work in the shortening with a pastry blender, then quickly stir the milk into the dough. Add the raisins and caraway seeds, stirring just enough to distribute them evenly. Turn out onto a lightly floured board and knead about 20 times. Put the dough in the pan and bake for 20–30 minutes. Cut into wedges to serve.

Boston Brown Bread (10 or more slices)

This bread is traditionally served with baked beans. Use a 1-pound coffee tin if you do not have a pudding mold, and cover it with aluminum foil tied tight with string.

½ cup (70 g) rye flour
½ cup (1 dL) cornmeal

½ cup (70 g) whole-wheat flour
1 teaspoon baking soda
½ teaspoon salt
⅓ cup (¾ dL) molasses
1 cup (¼ L) buttermilk

Mix the rye flour, cornmeal, whole-wheat flour, baking soda, and salt in a large bowl. Stir in the molasses and milk and blend well. Butter a 1-quart pudding mold or a 1-pound coffee tin and fill no more than two-thirds full. Cover tightly and place in a deep kettle. Add boiling water halfway up the mold. Cover the kettle and steam over moderate heat for 2 hours, replacing the water if necessary. Remove from mold. Cut slices with a string while hot by drawing the string around the bread, crossing, and pulling the ends. Or reheat, if necessary, in a 300°F (150°C) oven.

Raisin Brown Bread. Add *½ cup seedless raisins* to the batter.

Cream Scones (12 wedges)

Wedge-shaped with lightly browned sides and tops, cream scones and English tea are traditional partners. Serve with a plump mound of butter and some marmalade or jam.

2 cups (280 g) flour
2 teaspoons baking powder
1 tablespoon sugar
½ teaspoon salt
4 tablespoons butter

2 eggs, well beaten
½ cup (1 dL) cream

Preheat the oven to 425°F (220°C). Lightly butter a cookie sheet. Mix the flour, baking powder, sugar, and salt in a large bowl. Work in the butter with your fingers or a pastry blender until the mixture resembles coarse meal. Add the eggs and cream and stir until blended. Turn out onto a lightly floured board and knead for about a minute. Pat or roll the dough about ¾ inch thick and cut into wedges. Place on the cookie sheet and bake for about 15 minutes.

Quick Coffee Cake   (8-inch square cake)

Simple to make, good to eat.

1 cup (200 g) sugar
1¾ cups (245 g) white flour
2 teaspoons baking powder
4 tablespoons butter
1 egg, slightly beaten
½ cup (1 dL) milk
1 tablespoon sugar mixed with 1½ teaspoons cinnamon

Preheat the oven to 375°F (190°C). Butter an 8-inch square cake pan. Mix the 1 cup sugar, the flour, and the baking powder in a large bowl. Work in the butter with your fingers or a pastry blender until the mixture resembles coarse meal. Add the egg and milk and blend. Spoon into the pan. Sprinkle the sugar-cinnamon mixture evenly over the top. Bake for 20 minutes.

Griddlecakes (16 griddlecakes)

The amount of milk you use will determine how thick these griddlecakes or pancakes are. Start with the smaller amount suggested and add more if the batter seems too thick. Try to have the milk at room temperature before mixing and take care not to overbeat: a few lumps in the batter will do no harm. You can make lighter, fluffier griddlecakes by separating the egg, beating the white, and folding it in last. Serve with maple syrup or honey.

½–¾ cup (1–1¾ dL) milk
2 tablespoons melted butter
1 egg
1 cup (140 g) white flour
2 teaspoons baking powder
2 tablespoons sugar
½ teaspoon salt

Beat the milk, butter, and egg lightly in a mixing bowl. Mix the flour, baking powder, sugar, and salt and add them all at once to the first mixture, stirring just enough to dampen the flour. Lightly butter or grease a griddle or frying pan and set over moderate heat until a few drops of cold water sprinkled on the pan form rapidly moving globules. If you wish small pancakes, drop about 2 tablespoons of the batter onto the pan, or pour about ¼ cup from a measuring cup if larger pancakes are desired. Bake on the griddle until the cakes are full of bubbles on the top and the undersides are lightly browned. Turn with a spatula and brown the other sides. Place finished griddlecakes on a warm plate in a 200°F (95°C) oven until you have enough to begin serving.

Buttermilk Griddlecakes. Use *buttermilk, sour milk, or yogurt* instead of milk and substitute *½ teaspoon baking soda* for the 2 teaspoons baking powder.

Whole-Wheat Griddlecakes. Use *⅓ cup whole-wheat flour* and *⅔ cup white flour*. If you wish, sweeten the batter with *2 tablespoons molasses or honey* instead of sugar.

Oatmeal Griddlecakes. Heat the ½ cup of milk, stir in *½ cup quick-cooking oatmeal*, and let stand for 10 minutes. Add the remaining ingredients, reducing the flour to 2 tablespoons.

Buckwheat Cakes. Use *½ cup buckwheat flour* and *½ cup white flour*.

Apple Griddlecakes. Peel *1 tart, juicy apple*, cut it in thin slices, and stir it in.

Blueberry Griddlecakes. Add *½ cup blueberries*. If you use canned blueberries, strain them before adding.

Crêpes or French Pancakes
(about twelve 7-inch pancakes or sixteen 5-inch pancakes)

This crêpe recipe first appeared in the *Fannie Farmer Cook Book* in 1930, although the thin French pancakes that it produces seem always to have had a place in American cookery. Simple to make and extraordinarily versatile, they are good plain, stuffed and rolled, or sweetened. Like a velvet cape wrapped around a simple dress, they transform good leftovers (see p. 205 for recipes for savory fillings and p. 420 for sweet).

2 eggs
1 cup (¼ L) milk
½ teaspoon salt
1 cup (140 g) flour
2 tablespoons melted butter

Beat the eggs well, then beat in the milk, salt, flour, and butter. (Or mix all the ingredients in a blender until smooth.) Cover and let stand for at least 30 minutes. Heat a 7-inch or 5-inch skillet or crêpe pan until moderately hot, then film it with butter or shortening, using a brush or a folded paper towel. Using a ladle or small cup, pour in several table-spoons of batter, then quickly tilt the pan about so that the batter spreads evenly in the thinnest pos-sible layer. (If there is too much batter in the pan, pour it back into the bowl of batter and use less for the next pancake.) Cook for a few more minutes, until the bottom is lightly browned and the edges lift easily from the pan. The pancake should then slide loosely about in the pan. Turn it with a spatula or by catching an edge with your fingers and flip-ping it over. Cook the second side for a few min-utes; it will brown in spots, not as evenly as the first side, but it doesn't matter because this side should be used inside when the crêpes are rolled. Remove to a plate and film the pan again lightly with butter or shortening before cooking the next pancake. If the batter seems to be getting too thick as you get toward the end of it, add a little milk. Crêpes freeze very well simply stacked and wrapped in foil or plastic with the edges tightly sealed. Defrost at room temperature before separating them.

Cheese Filling   (enough for twelve 7-inch
   pancakes or sixteen 5-inch pancakes)

Make *2 cups White Sauce* (p. 147). Stir in *1½ cups grated Swiss or Cheddar cheese* and heat until melted. Spoon about 4 tablespoons of filling onto the bottom third of each pancake; the mixture will be enough to fill the number of pancakes the preceding recipe yields. Roll up the pancakes and arrange side by side in a shallow, buttered baking dish. Sprinkle with *½ cup grated cheese*. Heat in the upper part of a preheated 350°F (180°C) oven until lightly browned. Or heat thoroughly and then brown quickly under the broiler.

Old-fashioned Doughnuts
(about 18 doughnuts)

Easier to make and more cakelike than yeast-leavened doughnuts, these doughnuts have a fine, creamy crumb. The temperature of the cooking oil is crucial, so use a frying (candy) thermometer.

½ cup (1 dL) milk
½ cup (100 g) sugar
2 teaspoons baking powder
¼ teaspoon nutmeg
½ teaspoon salt
1 egg, beaten
1 tablespoon melted butter
About 1¾ cups (245 g) white flour
Vegetable shortening or oil for frying
Confectioners' or granulated sugar for dusting

Mix the milk, sugar, baking powder, nutmeg, salt, egg, and butter in a large bowl. Add the flour gradually, using just enough so that the dough is firm enough to handle yet as soft as possible. Cover the dough and chill for about 1 hour. Turn out onto a lightly floured board and knead for a few minutes. Roll out about ½ inch thick. Cut with a doughnut cutter or sharp knife into 3-inch rounds, cutting out and saving the centers (which can also be fried). Place on a lightly floured piece of wax paper and let rest for about 5 minutes. Using a heavy pan and a thermometer, heat about 4 inches of shortening or oil to 360°F. Fry three or four doughnuts at a time, turning them with a fork or tongs when one side is browned and continuing to fry until brown all over. Drain on paper towels and dust with sugar.

Crullers (three dozen). Prepare the batter for Doughnuts. Roll it out ⅓ inch thick. Cut it in strips 8 inches long and ¾ inch wide. Let rest for 10 minutes, then twist each strip several times and pinch the ends. Fry, drain, and roll in sugar.

Chocolate Doughnuts. Mix *½ cup unsweetened co-coa* with the flour. Dust the drained doughnuts with sugar or spread with *Creamy Chocolate Frosting* (p. 348).

Waffles (8 waffles)

Many automatic waffle irons have thermostats that indicate when to add the batter. To test one that doesn't, put 1 teaspoon of water inside, close it, and turn it on; when the steaming stops, the iron is ready for the batter. Modern waffle irons do not need greasing. If the first waffle sticks, as it is often inclined to do, bake it a little longer and expect no problem with the others. Remember that a thin batter makes tender waffles. Serve them with melted butter and warmed maple syrup.

2 eggs, well beaten
1 cup (¼ L) milk
3 tablespoons salad oil
1½ cups (215 g) flour
3 teaspoons baking powder
2 teaspoons sugar
½ salt

Mix the eggs, milk, and oil in a large bowl or pitcher. Stir in the flour, baking powder, sugar, and salt and mix until blended. Heat the waffle iron, brush it with melted shortening or oil if necessary, pour in enough batter to just fill. Close and bake until the steaming stops and the waffles are crisp, tender, and brown.

Special Waffles (6 standard-size waffles)

This method makes waffles extra-light.

2 cups (280 g) flour
3 teaspoons baking powder
½ teaspoon salt
3 eggs, separated
1¾ cups (4 dL) milk
4 tablespoons butter, melted
3 tablespoons sugar

Combine the flour, baking powder, and salt in a bowl. In a separate bowl beat the egg yolks well, and add the milk and butter. Combine the flour and yolk mixture and beat until smooth. Beat the egg whites until stiff, but not dry. Slowly add the sugar, beating constantly. Mix a third of the beaten whites gently into the batter, then fold in the remaining whites very carefully. Spread ½ cup of waffle batter in the hot waffle iron. Bake until golden.

Cakes, Frostings & Fillings

Chocolate Cake   (two 8-inch round layers)

A fine-grained, tender cake—ice water is its secret. If you wanted a chocolate cake for a birthday, this would be the one to pick.

2 ounces (60 g) unsweetened chocolate
¼ pound (115 g) butter
1½ cups (300 g) sugar
2 eggs
2 teaspoons vanilla
2 cups (280 g) cake flour
1½ teaspoons baking soda
½ teaspoon salt

Preheat the oven to 350°F (180°C). Butter and lightly flour two 8-inch round cake pans. Melt the chocolate in a small pot or bowl over simmering water; set aside to cool. Cream the butter, slowly beat in the sugar, and beat until light. Add the eggs and the vanilla, mixing well. Add the chocolate and combine thoroughly. Mix the flour, baking soda, and salt together, add to the first mixture, and blend. Add 1 cup ice water and beat until smooth. Pour the batter into the pans and bake for 25–30 minutes, until a toothpick comes out clean. Cool in the pans for 5 minutes before turning out onto racks. Frost with *Portsmouth* (p. 348) or *Creamy Chocolate Frosting* (p. 348).

Chocolate Buttermilk Cake (two 8-inch round layers or one 9 × 13-inch cake)

This eggless cake with its deep chocolate flavor can be made very quickly.

1⅔ cups (235 g) flour
1 cup (200 g) sugar
½ cup (1 dL) cocoa
1 teaspoon baking soda
½ teaspoon salt
1 cup (¼ L) buttermilk
½ cup (1 dL) vegetable oil
2 teaspoons vanilla

Preheat the oven to 350°F (180°C). Butter and lightly flour two 8-inch round cake pans or one 9 × 13-inch pan. Mix the flour, sugar, cocoa, baking soda, and salt in a bowl. Add the buttermilk, vegetable oil, and vanilla, beating until smooth. Spread in the pans or pan and bake, about 20–25 minutes for the small pans, 35–45 minutes for the large one. Test to see if a toothpick comes out clean. Cool for 5 minutes in the pan before turning out onto a rack. Frost with *Creamy Chocolate Frosting* (p. 348) or *Seven-Minute Coconut Frosting* (p. 352).

Fudge Layer Cake   (two 9-inch layers)

A delicious, tender cake, black with chocolate.

4 ounces (115 g) unsweetened chocolate
1½ cups (300 g) sugar
½ cup (1 dL) shortening
1 teasoon vanilla
3 eggs
2 cups (280 g) cake flour
1 teaspoon baking soda
¼ teaspoon salt
⅔ cup (1½ dL) milk

Preheat the oven to 350°F (180°C). Butter and lightly flour two 9-inch cake pans. Put the chocolate, 6
tablespoons water, and ½ cup of the sugar in a
heavy-bottomed small pan over low heat, stirring
often. As the chocolate melts, stir vigorously to
blend. Cook until the chocolate has completely
melted and mixture is smooth. Set aside. Cream the
shortening and remaining 1 cup sugar together until
light. Add the vanilla and beat until well blended.
Add the eggs, one at a time, beating thoroughly after each addition. Sift the flour, baking soda, and
salt together on a piece of wax paper. Add the dry
ingredients alternately with the milk in three parts.
Add the chocolate mixture and beat until well
blended. Pour the batter into the pans. Bake for 35–
40 minutes, or until a straw comes out dry when
inserted in center of cake. Cool in the pans for 10
minutes, then turn cakes out on racks. Frost with
Fudge Frosting (p. 349).

Walnut Mocha Cake (two 8-inch round layers or one 8-inch square cake)

¾ cup (1¾ dL) milk
3 tablespoons instant coffee
2 teaspoons vanilla
¼ pound (115 g) butter
1½ cups (300 g) sugar
3 eggs
2¼ cups (315 g) cake flour
¾ teaspoon salt
3 teaspoons baking powder
1 cup (¼ L) chopped walnuts

Preheat the oven to 350°F (180°C). Butter and lightly flour two 8-inch round cake pans or one 8-inch square pan. Heat the milk and stir in the instant coffee until it dissolves. Add the vanilla and let cool. Cream the butter and gradually add the sugar, beating until light. Add the eggs and beat well. Stir in the coffee mixture. Combine the flour, salt, and baking powder, and add them to the first mixture, mixing well. Stir in the walnuts. Spread batter in the pans and bake, about 30 minutes for the round layers, 40–50 minutes for the square cake. Test to see if a toothpick comes out clean. Cool in the pans for 5 minutes before turning out onto a rack. Frost with *Penuche Frosting* (p. 350).

Velvet Cake (two 8-inch round layers)

This simple cake with its fine flavor and smooth, velvet texture is an old classic. It would be a good simple cake to fill and frost for a child's birthday.

¼ pound (115 g) butter
1 cup (200 g) sugar
4 eggs, separated
1½ cups (210 g) cake flour
½ cup (1 dL) cornstarch
½ teaspoon salt
4 teaspoons baking powder

Preheat the oven to 350°F (180°C). Butter and lightly flour two 8-inch round cake pans. Cream the butter and slowly add the sugar, beating until light. Beat in the egg yolks and ½ cup cold water and combine well. Combine the flour, cornstarch, salt, and baking powder, add to the first mixture, and mix thoroughly. Beat the egg whites separately until stiff but not dry. Gently stir a third of the whites into the first mixture, then fold in the remaining whites. Spread the batter in the pans and bake for about 25 minutes, until a toothpick comes out clean. Cool in the pans for 5 minutes before turning out onto racks. Frost with *Chocolate Butter Frosting* (p. 351) or *Mocha Rum Butter Frosting* (p. 351).

Lady Baltimore Cake
(two 8-inch round layers)

A drift of pure white, Lady Baltimore Cake is fine, soft-textured, and lightly flavored. Fill the layers with its own special filling of nuts and dried fruit or use as a basic white cake with any frosting and filling you prefer.

¼ pound (115 g) butter
1 cup (200 g) sugar
3 cups (420 g) cake flour
2 teaspoons baking powder
¼ teaspoon salt
¾ cup (1¾ dL) milk
1 teaspoon vanilla
4 egg whites

Preheat the oven to 350°F (180°C). Butter and lightly flour two 8-inch round cake pans. Cream the butter until it is smooth, slowly add the sugar, and beat until light and fluffy. Combine the flour, baking powder, and salt, add to the first mixture, add the milk and vanilla, and beat until well blended. Beat the egg whites separately until stiff but not dry. Stir a quarter of the whites into the batter, then gently fold in the remaining whites. Spread in the pans and bake for 25–30 minutes or until a toothpick comes out clean. Cool in the pans for 5 minutes before turning out onto racks. Fill with *Lady Baltimore Filling* (p. 354) and frost with *Seven-Minute Frosting* (p. 351).

Fresh Coconut Cake (two 9-inch layers)

Light, tender, and moist—the fresh coconut adds a good texture.

1 coconut
¾ cup (1¾ dL) shortening

1½ cups (300 g) sugar
3 eggs, separated
½ teaspoon coconut extract
2¼ cups (315 g) cake flour
2 teaspoons baking powder
½ teaspoon salt
1 cup (¼ L) milk

Preheat the oven to 350°F (180°C). Butter and lightly flour two 9-inch cake pans. Remove the meat from the coconut, and grate it in a hand grater or the food processor. You should have about 3 cups. Cream the shortening and slowly add the sugar. Beat until light and smooth. Add the egg yolks, one at a time, beating well after each addition. Stir in the coconut extract. Sift the flour, baking powder, and salt together on a piece of wax paper. Add the dry ingredients alternately in three parts with the milk, beating until well blended. Stir in 1 cup of grated coconut. Beat the egg whites until stiff but not dry, stir a third of the whites into the batter, and gently fold in the remainder. Spoon the batter into the cake pans. Bake for 25 minutes or until a straw inserted in the center of the cake comes out dry. Let the cakes cool for 10 minutes in the pans, then turn onto a cake rack. Cool. Frost with *Seven-Minute Coconut Frosting* (p. 352). Cover the top and sides of the cake with the remaining freshly grated coconut.

Pound Cake   (1 loaf)

½ pound (225 g) butter
1⅔ cups (325 g) sugar

5 eggs
2 cups (280 g) cake flour
½ teaspoon salt
1 teaspoon vanilla, or ½ teaspoon mace

Preheat the oven to 325°F (165°C). Butter and lightly flour a 9 × 5-inch loaf pan. Cream the butter, slowly add the sugar, and beat until light. Add the eggs, one at a time, beating each in well. Stir in the flour, salt, and vanilla or mace and combine well. Spoon into the pan and bake for 1¼–1½ hours, or until a toothpick comes out clean. Cool in the pan for 5 minutes before turning out onto a rack. Serve very thin slices.

Boston Favorite Cake (two 8-inch layers)

This is an excellent basic butter cake. It can also be made as cupcakes or one 7 × 11-inch rectangular.

6 tablespoons butter
1 cup (200 g) sugar
2 eggs, separated
1½ teaspoons vanilla
1¾ cups (245 g) cake flour
2 teaspoons baking powder
½ teaspoon salt
⅔ cup (1 dL) milk

Preheat the oven to 350°F (180°C). Butter and lightly flour two 8-inch round cake pans. Cream the butter until softened and slowly add the sugar, beating until light. Add the egg yolks and vanilla and beat to blend well. Sift the flour, baking powder, and salt onto a piece of wax paper. Alternately blend the dry ingredients and the milk into the butter mixture in three stages. Beat until smooth. In a separate bowl, beat the egg whites until stiff but not dry. Stir a third of the whites into the cake batter and gently fold in the remaining. Spoon into the cake pans. Bake for 30–35 minutes, or until a straw inserted in the center of cake comes out dry. Cool in pans for 5 minutes before turning out onto racks. Fill and frost with *Creamy Chocolate Frosting* (p. 348).

Marble Cake. Divide the batter in half. Melt *1 ounce unsweetened chocolate* over simmering water and add it to half the batter. Fill the pans using large spoonfuls and alternating between the plain and the chocolate batters.

Priscilla Cake. For a richer cake use 1⅓ cups sugar and 3 eggs.

Boston Cream Pie (two-layer round cake)

A simple cake filled with rich cream custard, its top dusted with powdered sugar, this variation of Boston Favorite Cake has become a great American favorite. If you are in a hurry, prepare the custard while the cake is in the oven, but do not fill the cake until it is completely cool.

1 cup (¼ L) milk
½ cup (100 g) granulated sugar
3 tablespoons flour

⅛ teaspoon salt
2 egg yolks
1½ teaspoons vanilla
Two 8-inch layers Boston Favorite Cake
Confectioners' sugar

Heat the milk in a pan until very hot, then briskly stir in the granulated sugar, flour, and salt. Cook over moderate heat, stirring constantly, until very thick. Add the egg yolks and cook, continuing to stir, for another 4–5 minutes. Remove from the heat, add the vanilla, and cool, stirring occasionally. Cover well and refrigerate until ready to use. Spread the custard between the cake layers and dust the top of the cake with confectioners' sugar. Keep refrigerated.

Gingerbread (9-inch square cake)

Moist, spicy, and sweet.

¼ pound (115 g) butter
1 cup (200 g) sugar
2 eggs
¾ cup (1¾ dL) molasses
2½ cups (350 g) flour
2 teaspoons baking soda
½ teaspoon salt
2 teaspoons powdered ginger

Preheat the oven to 350°F (180°C). Butter and lightly flour a 9-inch square cake pan. Cream the butter, add the sugar, and beat until light and fluffy. Add the eggs and beat well. Add ¾ cup boiling water and the molasses and blend. Mix together the flour, baking soda, salt, and ginger, add to the first mixture, and combine thoroughly. Pour into the pan and bake for 35–45 minutes, until a toothpick comes out clean. Cool in the pan for about 5 minutes before turning out onto a plate. Gingerbread is good served warm *with sweetened whipped cream.* You may serve it with *applesauce,* if you wish, or spread it with *Butter Frosting* (p. 351).

Applesauce Cake (two 8-inch round layers or one 9 × 13-inch cake)

This cake keeps well and will stay fresh for picnics or trips. Add a teaspoon of powdered ginger if you want it very spicy.

¼ pound (115 g) butter, or ½ cup (1 dL) shortening
1½ cups (300 g) sugar
1 cup (¼ L) applesauce
2 eggs
2 cups (280 g) flour
1½ teaspoons baking soda
½ teaspoon salt
2 teaspoons cinnamon
½ teaspoon nutmeg
½ cup (1 dL) raisins
½ cup (1 dL) chopped walnuts

Preheat the oven to 350°F (180°C). Butter and lightly flour two 8-inch round cake pans or one 9 × 13-inch cake pan. Cream the butter or shortening, add the sugar gradually, and beat well. Add the applesauce and blend. Beat in the eggs and mix thoroughly. Mix together the flour, baking soda, salt, cinnamon, and nutmeg, add to the first mixture, and beat just until mixed. Stir in the raisins and nuts. Spread in the pans or pan and bake, 25–30 minutes for the layers, 35–40 minutes for the rectangle. Test to see if a toothpick comes out clean. Cool in the pans for 5 minutes before turning out onto racks. Spread with *Cream Cheese Frosting* (p. 350) before serving, if you wish.

Spice Cake (two 8-inch round layers or one 8-inch square cake)

Cinnamon, cloves, nutmeg, and cayenne make this a lively cake.

¼ pound (115 g) butter, or ½ cup (1 dL) shortening
1 cup (200 g) granulated sugar
½ cup (1 dL) dark-brown sugar
4 eggs
½ cup (1 dL) milk
½ cup (1 dL) molasses
2¼ cups (315 g) flour
1 teaspoon salt
½ teaspoon baking soda
2 teaspoons cinnamon
¼ teaspoon cloves
¼ teaspoon nutmeg
⅛ teaspoon cayenne pepper

Preheat the oven to 350°F (180°C). Butter and lightly flour two 8-inch round cake pans or one 8-inch square pan. Cream the butter or shortening and slowly add the two sugars, beating until light and fluffy. Beat in the eggs, then add the milk and molasses, beating thoroughly. Mix together the remaining ingredients and add to the first mixture, beating until well blended. Pour the batter into the pans or pan and bake, about 30 minutes for the round layers, 45–50 minutes for the square cake. Test to see if a toothpick comes out clean. Cool in the pans for 5 minutes before turning out onto racks. Frost with *Quick Caramel Frosting* (p. 349).

Fresh Banana Cake (9-inch square cake)

Moist and banana-sweet, with dark banana flecks throughout.

¼ pound (115 g) butter, or ½ cup (1 dL) shortening
1½ cups (300 g) sugar
1 cup (¼ L) mashed banana (about 2 medium bananas)
2 eggs
1 teaspoon vanilla
2 cups (280 g) cake flour
1 teaspoon baking soda
½ teaspoon salt
½ cup (1 dL) sour cream

Preheat the oven to 350°F (180°C). Butter and lightly flour a 9-inch square cake pan. Cream the butter or shortening, slowly add the sugar, and beat until light. Add the banana, eggs, and vanilla and beat well. Mix the flour, baking soda, and salt, add to

336

the first mixture, and blend. Slowly add the sour cream and beat until well blended. Spread in the pan and bake for about 45 minutes, or until a tooth-pick comes out clean. Cool in the pan for 5 minutes before turning out onto a rack. Split the cake and fill with *Banana Cream Filling* (p. 353) and frost with *Portsmouth Frosting* (p. 348).

Princeton Orange Cake
(two 9-inch round layers)

This orange-flavored velvet cake is fresh and bright with a delicate texture and keen orange taste.

¼ pound (115 g) butter
1 cup (200 g) sugar
4 eggs, separated
½ cup (1 dL) orange juice
Grated rind of 1 large orange
1½ cups (210 g) cake flour
½ cup (1 dL) cornstarch
½ teaspoon salt
4 teaspoons baking powder

Preheat the oven to 350°F (180°C). Butter and light-ly flour two 9-inch round cake pans. Cream the but-ter and slowly add the sugar, beating until light. Add the egg yolks, orange juice, and orange rind and beat well. Mix the flour, cornstarch, salt, and baking powder, stir into the first mixture, and blend until smooth. Beat the egg whites in a separate bowl until stiff but not dry. Gently stir a third of the egg whites into the first mixture, then fold in the remaining whites. Spread the batter in the pans and bake for 30–40 minutes, or until a toothpick comes out clean. Cool in the pans for 5 minutes before turning out onto racks. Frost with *White Mountain Cream* (see below) and sprinkle with *¾ cup grated coconut,* if you wish.

White Mountain Cream (makes about 1½ cups)

1 cup (200 g) sugar
⅛ teaspoon cream of tartar
⅛ teaspoon salt
2 egg whites
1 teaspoon vanilla

Mix the sugar, ⅓ cup water, cream of tartar, and salt in a heavy-bottomed pan. Boil without stirring until the mixture reaches 240°F. Beat the egg whites until stiff, then pour the 240° sugar syrup over them in a slow, thin stream, beating constantly until thick enough to spread. Stir in the vanilla. You will have enough to fill and frost an 8- or 9-inch two-layer cake.

Angel Food Cake (10-inch tube cake)

Save your egg whites and freeze them until you have enough to make this cake.

8 egg whites (1 cup, ¼ L)
¼ teaspoon salt
1 teaspoon cream of tartar
1 teaspoon almond extract

1 teaspoon vanilla
1¼ cups (250 g) sugar
1 cup (140 g) cake flour

Preheat the oven to 325°F (165°C). Beat the egg whites until foamy, add the salt and cream of tartar, and beat until soft peaks form. Add the almond extract and the vanilla, then gradually add the sugar, beating until stiff. Sift the flour over the whites and gently fold it in. Bake in an ungreased 10-inch tube pan for 50–60 minutes, until a straw comes out clean. Invert the pan on a rack and let the cake cool completely before removing from the pan. Frost with *Chocolate Frosting* (p. 351).

Nut Torte   (two 8-inch round cakes)

5 eggs, separated
1 cup (200 g) sugar
2 cups (½ L) ground walnuts
1 cup (¼ L) bread crumbs
1 teaspoon baking powder
1 teaspoon vanilla
⅛ teaspoon salt

Preheat the oven to 325°F (165°C). Butter and lightly flour two 8-inch round cake pans. Beat the egg yolks until pale and thick. Slowly add the sugar and continue to beat until well blended. Stir in the walnuts, crumbs, baking powder, and vanilla, and mix well. Beat the egg whites separately until foamy, add the salt, and continue to beat until stiff but not dry. Gently stir a third of the whites into the batter, then fold in the remaining whites. Spread in the pans and bake for about 30 minutes, or until a toothpick comes out clean. Let cool in the pans for 5 minutes before turning out onto racks. Serve spread with *sweetened whipped cream* between the layers and dust the top with sifted *confectioners' sugar.*

Almond Torte (9-inch round cake)

Moist, delicate, and mildly sweet, just right with sweetened whipped cream.

4 eggs, separated
1½ cups (3½ dL) confectioners' sugar
½ cup (1 dL) fine cracker crumbs
½ cup (1 dL) chopped almonds
2 ounces (60 g) unsweetened chocolate, finely grated
1 teaspoon baking powder

Preheat the oven to 325°F (165°C). Butter and lightly flour a 9-inch springform pan. Beat the egg yolks until thick and pale. Slowly add 1 cup of the sugar and continue to beat until blended. Stir in the crumbs, almonds, chocolate, and baking powder, and mix well. Beat the egg whites separately until they hold soft peaks, then slowly beat in the remaining ½ cup of sugar, continuing to beat until stiff but not dry. Gently stir a third of the whites into the batter, then fold in the remaining whites. Spread lightly in the pan and bake for about 30 minutes, or until a toothpick comes out clean. Run a knife around the edge, remove the rim, and let cool. Serve with *sweetened whipped cream.*

Carrot Torte   (9- or 10-inch round cake)

4 eggs, separated
1 cup (200 g) sugar
1 cup (¼ L) grated raw carrots
Grated rind of 1 lemon
1 tablespoon lemon juice
½ cup (70 g) flour
1 teaspoon baking powder
⅛ teaspoon salt

Preheat the oven to 325°F (165°C). Butter and lightly flour a 9- or 10-inch springform pan. Beat the egg yolks until they are pale and thick. Slowly add the sugar and continue to beat until smooth and blended. Stir in the carrots, lemon rind, lemon juice, flour, and baking powder and mix thoroughly. Beat the egg whites separately until foamy, add the salt, and continue to beat until stiff but not dry. Gently stir a third of the whites into the batter, then fold in the remaining whites. Spread in the pan and bake for 30–40 minutes, or until a toothpick comes out clean. Run a knife around the edge, remove the rim, and let cool. Sprinkle the top with *confectioners' sugar,* sifted through a strainer.

Nut Roll   (15-inch roll)

This sophisticated version of the classic jelly roll is made with chopped nuts instead of flour.

6 eggs, separated
¾ cup (150 g) sugar
1½ cups (3½ dL) finely chopped walnuts

341

1 teaspoon baking powder
⅛ teaspoon salt
1½ cups (3½ dL) heavy cream
¼ cup (½ dL) confectioners' sugar
2 tablespoons rum

Preheat the oven to 350°F (180°C). Butter a 10½ × 15½-inch jelly-roll pan, line it with wax paper. Beat the egg yolks until they are pale and thick. Slowly add the granulated sugar and continue to beat until blended. Stir in the walnuts and baking powder; set aside. Beat the egg whites until foamy, then add the salt and continue to beat until stiff but not dry. Gently stir a third of the whites into the batter, then fold in the remaining whites. Spread lightly in the pan and bake for 12–15 minutes, until a toothpick comes out clean. Turn out onto a clean kitchen towel. Remove the wax paper and trim off any crisp edges. Roll the cake up in the towel, starting from the long side like a jelly roll, and let it rest for a minute. Unroll the cake, let it rest for a few minutes, then roll it up in the towel again and let it cool completely. Whip the cream, adding the confectioners' sugar and the rum. Spread it over the cake and roll up gently without the towel. Cover and refrigerate until ready to serve.

Chocolate Roll (15-inch roll)

5 eggs, separated
1¼ cups (3 dL) confectioners' sugar
¼ cup (½ dL) cocoa
¼ teaspoon salt

1½ cups (3½ dL) sweetened heavy cream, whipped, or 1 quart (1 L) vanilla ice cream, softened

Preheat the oven to 350°F (180°C). Butter a 10½ × 15½-inch jelly-roll pan and line it with wax paper. Beat the egg yolks until they are pale and thick; set aside. Sift the sugar and cocoa together onto a piece of wax paper. Beat the egg whites until they are foamy, add the salt, and continue to beat until they hold soft peaks. Fold the sugar and cocoa into the whites. Gently fold a third of the egg white mixture into the yolks, then lightly fold in the remaining whites. Spread evenly in the pan and bake for about 20 minutes, until a toothpick comes out clean. Turn the cake out onto a clean kitchen towel. Remove the wax paper and trim off any crisp edges. Roll the cake up with the towel from the long side, and let it rest for a minute. Unroll it and let it rest for a few minutes, then roll it up in the towel again and let it cool completely. Unroll and spread with sweetened whipped cream or softened ice cream. Roll up again without the towel. Dust the top of the roll with more confectioners' sugar sifted through a strainer. Refrigerate the whipped cream roll until ready to serve; keep the ice cream roll in the freezer.

Apple Cobbler (8-inch square cake)

12 tablespoons butter
3 cups (½ L) peeled and sliced tart apples
¾ teaspoon salt

¾ cup (150 g) sugar
½ cup (1 dL) milk
1 egg
1½ cups (215 g) flour
2 teaspoons baking powder

Preheat the oven to 375°F (190°C). Melt 4 table-spoons of the butter and pour it into an 8-inch square cake pan. Spread it evenly and arrange the apples over it. Mix ¼ teaspoon of the salt with ¼ cup of the sugar and sprinkle evenly over the apples; set aside. Melt the remaining 8 tablespoons of the butter in a small pan, remove from the heat, add the milk and egg, and beat well. Mix the flour, baking powder, the remaining ½ cup sugar, and the remaining ½ teaspoon salt in a bowl. Stir in the milk and egg mixture and beat until smooth. Pour over the apples and bake for about 30 minutes, or until a toothpick comes out clean. Serve from the pan in squares, fruit side up. Serve plain or with *whipped cream* or *vanilla ice cream,* if you wish.

Peach Cobbler. Use 3 cups *peeled, sliced peaches* in place of apples.

Berry Cobbler. Use 3 cups *blueberries, blackberries,* or *raspberries.*

Cherry Cobbler. Use 3 cups *pitted cherries* (if sour, increase sugar to 1¼ cups).

Apple Pandowdy (serves six)

3 cups (½ L) peeled and sliced tart apples
½ teaspoon nutmeg
½ teaspoon cinnamon
¾ teaspoon salt
½ cup (1 dL) molasses
1½ cups (215 g) flour
2 teaspoons baking powder
½ cup (100 g) sugar
¼ pound (115 g) butter
½ cup (1 dL) milk
1 egg

Preheat the oven to 350°F (180°C). Butter a 1½-quart baking dish. Arrange the sliced apples in the dish. Sprinkle with the nutmeg, cinnamon, and ¼ teaspoon of the salt, and spoon the molasses evenly over them. Cover the baking dish with foil and bake for 30 minutes. While the apples are baking, combine the flour, baking powder, sugar, and the remaining ½ teaspoon salt in a large bowl. Melt the butter in a small pan, remove from the heat, and stir in the milk and the egg, beating well. Add to the flour mixture and blend. Pour the batter over the apples after they have baked for 30 minutes, and return them to the oven for 30 minutes more, or until a toothpick comes out clean. Serve from the dish or turn out onto a serving plate with the apples on top. Serve with *whipped cream,* if you wish.

Shortcake

(one 8-inch round cake or eight 2-inch round cakes)

Old-fashioned biscuit-dough shortcakes, warm from the oven, should be split, buttered, spread with sugared berries, and graced with lots of heavy cream.

2 cups (280 g) flour
4 teaspoons baking powder
1 teaspoon salt
1½ tablespoons sugar
5 tablespoons butter
⅔ cup (1½ dL) milk
Berries or sliced fresh fruit, sweetened
Heavy cream

Preheat the oven to 425°F (220°C). Butter and lightly flour an 8-inch cake pan or a cookie sheet. Mix the flour, baking powder, salt, and sugar in a bowl. Cut the butter in bits and work it into the flour mixture with a pastry blender or your fingers until it resembles coarse meal. Slowly stir in the milk, using just enough to hold the dough together. Turn out onto a floured board and knead for a minute or two. Pat the dough into the cake pan or roll or pat it ¾ inch thick and cut it into eight 2-inch rounds, using a biscuit cutter. Arrange the rounds on a cookie sheet and bake them for 10–12 minutes or the larger cake for 12–15 minutes. Split with two forks while still warm, butter, fill with sugared fruit or berries, and serve warm with heavy cream.

Cheese Cake (9-inch cake)

1 cup (¼ L) zwieback or graham cracker crumbs
4 tablespoons melted butter
¼ teaspoon cinnamon
¼ teaspoon nutmeg
1¼ cups (250 g) sugar
4 eggs, separated
1 cup (¼ L) sour cream
2 tablespoons flour
¼ teaspoon salt
1 teaspoon vanilla
1 pound (450 g) cream cheese, at room
   temperature

Combine the crumbs, melted butter, cinnamon, nutmeg, and ¼ cup of the sugar in a bowl and mix well. Butter a 9-inch springform pan and pat the crumb mixture over the bottom and 1 inch up the sides. Chill. Preheat the oven to 325°F (165°). Beat the egg yolks with an electric beater until they are thick and pale. Add the sour cream, flour, salt, ¾ cup of the sugar, and the vanilla and beat until well blended. Add the cream cheese and beat until smooth. Beat the egg whites until foamy, then gradually beat in the remaining ¼ cup of sugar, beating until the whites are stiff and shiny. Fold into the cream cheese mixture. Spoon into the crumb crust. Bake about 1 hour, or until the center does not tremble when the cake is gently shaken. Cool, then chill in the refrigerator.

Portsmouth Frosting (makes about 1¾ cups)

This tastes of butter and cream, and what could be nicer?

4 tablespoons melted butter
¼ cup (½ dL) cream
1 teaspoon vanilla or rum
About 3 cups (¾ L) confectioners' sugar

Mix the butter, cream, and vanilla or rum together in a bowl. Slowly beat in the sugar until thick and creamy. This is enough to fill and frost an 8- or 9-inch two-layer cake.

Creamy Chocolate Frosting (makes about 2 cups)

2 ounces (60 g) unsweetened chocolate, grated
1 cup (200 g) sugar
3 tablespoons cornstarch
1 tablespoon butter
1 teaspoon vanilla
⅛ teaspoon salt

Combine the chocolate, sugar, and cornstarch in a heavy-bottomed pan. Stir in 1 cup boiling water, and cook, stirring constantly, until thick and smooth. Remove from the heat and add the butter, vanilla, and salt. Beat well. You will have enough to fill and frost an 8- or 9-inch two-layer cake.

Fudge Frosting (makes about 2 cups)

2 ounces (60 g) unsweetened chocolate, cut in bits
1½ cups (300 g) sugar
½ cup (1 dL) milk
4 tablespoons butter
1 tablespoon corn syrup
¼ teaspoon salt
1 teaspoon vanilla

Stir together all the ingredients except the vanilla in a heavy-bottomed pan. Bring to a rolling boil and cook, stirring vigorously, for just 1 minute; cool. Add the vanilla and beat until thick. This will fill and frost an 8- or 9-inch two-layer cake.

Quick Caramel Frosting
(makes about 1½ cups)

¼ pound (115 g) butter
½ cup (1 dL) dark-brown sugar
¼ cup (½ dL) milk
2 cups (½ L) confectioners' sugar

Melt the butter and brown sugar in a heavy-bottomed pan, stirring over moderate heat until the sugar is dissolved. Add the milk and blend. Cool, then beat in the confectioners' sugar until thick enough to spread. You will have enough to fill and frost an 8- or 9-inch two-layer cake.

Penuche Frosting (makes 1½–2 cups)

Excellent caramel flavor.

1½ cups (3½ dL) dark-brown sugar
¾ cup (150 g) granulated sugar
⅛ teaspoon salt
½ cup (1 dL) milk
3 tablespoons butter
1½ tablespoons corn syrup
1½ teaspoons vanilla

Mix all the ingredients except the vanilla in a heavy-bottomed pan. Bring slowly to the boiling point, stirring constantly, and boil for just 1 minute. Cool to lukewarm, add the vanilla, and beat until thick enough to spread. You will have enough to fill and frost an 8- or 9-inch two-layer cake.

Cream Cheese Frosting
(makes about 1¼ cups)

4 tablespoons cream cheese, softened
1½ cups (3½ dL) confectioners' sugar
1 egg white, slightly beaten
½ teaspoon vanilla
⅛ teaspoon salt

Beat all the ingredients together until light and of spreading consistency. You will have enough to fill and frost an 8-inch two-layer cake.

Butter Frosting (makes about 1 cup)

½ cup (100 g) sugar
1 egg yolk
¼ pound (115 g) chilled butter

Boil the sugar and ¼ cup water without stirring in a heavy-bottomed pan until the mixture reaches 240°F, or the "medium soft-ball stage." While the sugar syrup is cooking, beat the egg yolk well. Slowly pour the 240° syrup over the beaten yolk, beating constantly. Beat in bits of the cold butter until it is all incorporated. Continue to beat until the frosting is of spreading consistency. You will have enough to frost a 9-inch two-layer cake.

Chocolate Butter Frosting. Melt *4 ounces semisweet chocolate* and add to the frosting after the butter has been incorporated.

Coffee Butter Frosting. Add *2 teaspoons instant coffee* to the frosting after the butter has been incorporated.

Mocha Rum Butter Frosting. Add *1½ tablespoons rum* and *2 teaspoons instant coffee* after the butter has been incorporated.

Seven-Minute Frosting
(makes about 2 cups)

A light, billowy frosting with a sheen, very much like a "boiled" frosting. Seven-minute frosting dries out quickly, so keep it refrigerated if you're not using it within a few hours.

1½ cups (300 g) sugar
¼ teaspoon cream of tartar
⅛ teaspoon salt
2 egg whites
2 teaspoons vanilla

Mix sugar, cream of tartar, salt, egg whites, and ¼ cup water in a pot or bowl over simmering water. Beat steadily over low heat with a rotary or electric hand beater until the frosting stands in peaks, about 5–7 minutes, no more. Remove from the heat and continue to beat until thick enough to spread. Add the vanilla before spreading. You will have enough to fill and frost an 8- or 9-inch two-layer cake.

Caramel Frosting. Omit the vanilla and substitute *1 cup dark-brown sugar* for 1 cup of the white sugar.

Coconut Frosting. Omit the vanilla and stir in *½ cup shredded coconut* before spreading.

Coffee Frosting. Omit the vanilla and add *1 tablespoon instant coffee* before spreading.

Lemon or Orange Frosting. Omit the vanilla and substitute *¼ cup lemon or orange juice* for the water. Add *1 teaspoon grated lemon or orange rind* before spreading.

Peppermint Frosting. Omit the vanilla. Add *½ teaspoon oil of peppermint* and a few drops of *green food coloring* before spreading.

Basic Cream Filling
(makes about 1¾ cups)

Also known as *crème patissière,* this basic custard is good by itself or used in cream puffs, pies, and other pastries.

1 cup (¼ L) milk
½ cup (100 g) sugar
3 tablespoons flour
⅛ teaspoon salt
2 egg yolks, slightly beaten
2 teaspoons vanilla

Heat the milk in a heavy-bottomed pan until very hot but not boiling. Mix the sugar, flour, and salt together in a bowl, stir in the hot milk, and beat until well blended. Pour back into the pan and continue to stir vigorously over low heat for 4–5 minutes, until very thick and smooth. Add the egg yolks and cook for a few more minutes. Cool, stirring from time to time, then add the vanilla. You will have about enough filling for an 8- or 9-inch three-layer cake.

Banana Cream Filling. Omit the vanilla. Mash *1 large banana* and beat it until smooth, add *2 tablespoons lemon juice,* and stir the mixture into the cooled filling.

Chocolate Cream Filling. Melt *2 ounces unsweetened chocolate* in the milk and use *1 cup sugar* instead of ½ cup.

Lady Baltimore Filling and Frosting   (makes about 3 cups)

Use this with Lady Baltimore Cake (p. 328).

One recipe Seven-Minute Frosting (p. 351)
⅓ cup (¾ dL) chopped pecans
3 dried figs, cut in bits
½ cup (1 dL) raisins
½ teaspoon almond extract

Divide the frosting in half. Fold the pecans, figs, raisins, and almond extract into half the frosting and use it as a filling between two white 8-inch cake layers. Use the remaining plain frosting to cover the sides and the top of the cake.

Lemon Filling   (makes about ½ cup)

Lemon filling also makes a delightful dessert topped with chilled, sliced strawberries, oranges, or bananas.

1 cup (200 g) sugar
2½ tablespoons flour
¼ cup (½ dL) lemon juice
Grated rind of 2 lemons
1 egg
1 tablespoon butter

Mix all the ingredients together in a heavy-bottomed pan. Cook over moderate heat, stirring constantly, until thick and smooth. Cool before spreading between layers. You will have enough filling for an 8- or 9-inch three-layer cake.

Orange Filling (makes about 1¼ cups)

Orange filling can also make a pretty and unusual dessert with cooked prunes or pears spooned over it.

¾ cup (150 g) sugar
¼ cup (35 g) flour
Grated rind of 1 orange
1 tablespoon lemon juice
2 egg yolks, slightly beaten
⅛ teaspoon salt

Mix all the ingredients in a heavy-bottomed pan and cook over moderate heat, stirring constantly, until thickened and smooth. Cool. You will have enough filling for an 8- or 9-inch three-layer cake.

French Cream Filling
(makes about 3 cups)

1 egg white
⅛ teaspoon salt
1 cup (¼ L) heavy cream
¼ cup (½ dL) confectioners' sugar
1 teaspoon vanilla

Beat the egg white until foamy, then add the salt and continue beating until stiff but not dry. Beat the cream separately until it forms soft peaks, then slowly beat in the sugar and the vanilla. Fold the two mixtures together. You will have enough filling for an 8- or 9-inch three-layer cake.

French Coffee Filling. Add *2 teaspoons instant coffee* instead of the vanilla.

French Strawberry Filling. Use *⅓ cup confectioners' sugar* instead of ¼ cup and fold in *½ cup mashed strawberries* at the end.

Chocolate Whipped Cream Filling (makes about 2½ cups)

Try this as a filling for Chocolate Roll (p. 342).

4 ounces (115 g) unsweetened chocolate
2 tablespoons butter
1 cup (¼ L) heavy cream
2 cups (½ L) confectioners' sugar
⅛ teaspoon salt

Melt the chocolate and butter together in a small pan or bowl over simmering water. Combine the cream, 1 cup of the confectioners' sugar, and the salt in a bowl; add the melted chocolate and butter mixture. Beat, slowly adding the remaining cup of sugar, for about 10 minutes, until the filling is light and fluffy. You will have enough filling for an 8- or 9-inch three-layer cake.

Cookies, Cake Squares, Candies & Confections

Sugar Cookies   (about 40 cookies)

Old-fashioned sugar cookies are sweet, rich, and delectable, the essence of what a "plain" cookie should be.

¼ pound (115 g) butter
¾ cup (150 g) sugar
1 egg
½ teaspoon vanilla
1 tablespoon cream or milk
1¼ cups (175 g) flour
⅛ teaspoon salt
¼ teaspoon baking powder

Preheat the oven to 350°F (180°C). Cream the butter, then gradually add the sugar, beating until light. Add the egg, vanilla, and cream or milk, and beat thoroughly. Mix the flour, salt, and baking powder together, add to the first mixture, and blend well. Arrange by teaspoonfuls on cookie sheets, 1 inch apart. Bake for 8–10 minutes or until lightly browned.

Almond Spice Cookies. Fold *1/3 cup finely chopped, blanched almonds, 1/2 teaspoon cinnamon, 1/2 teaspoon ground cloves, 1/2 teaspoon nutmeg,* and the *grated rind of 1/2 lemon* into the cookie dough.

Coconut Cookies. Add *1/2 cup finely chopped coconut* to the dough.

Lemon Sugar Cookies. Omit the vanilla and add *1/2 teaspoon lemon extract* and *2 teaspoons grated lemon rind* to the dough.

Nut Cookies. Add *1/2 cup chopped nuts* to the dough.

Raisin Cookies. Add *1/2 cup chopped raisins* to the dough.

Filled Sugar Cookies. Add *about 1/4 cup flour* to the dough, just enough so that it can be rolled out. Roll 1/4 inch thick and cut into 3-inch circles. Spread half the circles with *jam, jelly, mincemeat,* or the *Fruit and Nut Filling* that follows. Cover with the remaining circles and press the edges together with a fork. Prick well. Bake on buttered cookie sheets in a preheated 325°F (165°C) oven until lightly browned, about 12 minutes.

Fruit and Nut Filling for Filled Sugar Cookies. In a saucepan mix *1/2 cup chopped raisins, 1/2 cup finely cut dates, 1/4 cup chopped walnuts, 1/2 cup water, 1/2 cup sugar,* and *1 teaspoon flour.* Cook slowly until thick. Use as recommended above.

Rich Butter Cookies (about 60 cookies)

½ pound (225 g) butter
1 teaspoon vanilla
⅔ cup (130 g) sugar
2 eggs
1½ cups (215 g) flour
½ teaspoon salt

Preheat the oven to 375°F (190°C). Cream the butter and the vanilla. Gradually add the sugar and the eggs and beat well. Mix the flour and salt together, add to the first mixture, and blend thoroughly. Arrange by half-teaspoonfuls on cookie sheets, leaving 2 inches between the cookies—they will spread during baking. Flatten them with a knife dipped in cold water. Bake for about 8 minutes or until lightly browned.

Sour Cream Cookies (about 60 cookies)

2 eggs
1 cup (200 g) sugar, white or light brown
½ cup (1 dL) sour cream
5 tablespoons melted butter
½ teaspoon vanilla
2 cups (280 g) flour
½ teaspoon baking soda
¼ teaspoon nutmeg

Preheat the oven to 375°F (190°C) and butter some cookie sheets. Beat the eggs well, then add the sugar, sour cream, butter, and vanilla, beating until well incorporated. Mix the flour, baking soda, and nutmeg together and add to the first mixture, beating well. Arrange by teaspoonfuls, 1 inch apart, on the cookie sheets and bake for about 10 minutes or until lightly browned.

Molasses Cookies   (about 40 cookies)

Some like these plain—some spicy.

¼ cup (½ dL) molasses
½ cup (1 dL) shortening
¾ cup (1¾ dL) dark-brown sugar
1 egg
1 cup (140 g) flour
½ teaspoon salt
½ teaspoon baking soda

Preheat the oven to 375°F (190°C). Mix the molasses, shortening, brown sugar, and egg in a bowl, combining well. Mix the flour, salt, and baking soda together, add to the first mixture, and blend thoroughly. Arrange by teaspoonfuls on ungreased cookie sheets, about 1 inch apart, and bake for 7–10 minutes or until crisp and lightly browned.

Spiced Molasses Cookies. Add *¼ teaspoon powdered ginger, ¼ teaspoon ground cloves, ¼ teaspoon cinnamon,* and *¼ teaspoon nutmeg* to the flour mixture.

Cape Cod Oatmeal Cookies
(about 70 cookies)

A fine, chewy oatmeal cookie, wholesome and nourishing.

1½ cups (210 g) flour
½ teaspoon baking soda
1 teaspoon cinnamon
½ teaspoon salt
1 egg, lightly beaten
1 cup (200 g) sugar
½ cup (1 dL) melted shortening, *or*
½ cup (115 g) melted butter
1 tablespoon molasses
¼ cup (½ dL) milk
1¾ cups (4 dL) uncooked oatmeal
½ cup (1 dL) raisins
½ cup (1 dL) chopped nuts

Preheat the oven to 350°F (180°C). Mix the flour, baking soda, cinnamon, and salt together in a large bowl. Stir in the remaining ingredients. Arrange by teaspoonfuls on unbuttered cookie sheets and bake until the edges are brown, about 12 minutes.

Chocolate Chip Cookies
(about 50 cookies)

Is there anyone in America who does not know and love these cookies? They were, incidentally, created by a Massachusetts housewife in 1929.

¼ pound (115 g) butter
½ cup (1 dL) dark-brown sugar
½ cup (100 g) granulated sugar
1 egg
¾ teaspoon vanilla
1⅛ cups (155 g) flour
½ teaspoon salt
½ teaspoon baking soda
½ cup (1 dL) chopped nuts
1 cup (¼ L, 6 ounces) semisweet chocolate chips

Preheat the oven to 375°F (190°C) and grease some cookie sheets. Cream the butter, then gradually add the two sugars, beating until light and smooth. Beat in the egg and the vanilla. Mix the flour, salt, and baking soda together and add it to the first mixture, blending well. Stir in the nuts and the chocolate chips. Drop by teaspoonfuls onto the cookie sheets about 1 inch apart and bake for 8–10 minutes or until lightly browned.

Chocolate Chip Oatmeal Cookies. Use *½ cup uncooked oatmeal* instead of the chopped nuts.

Nut Cookies (about 50 cookies)

2 eggs, separated
1 cup (¼ L) brown sugar
1 cup (¼ L) chopped nuts
Dash of salt
6 tablespoons flour

Preheat the oven to 350°F (180°C). Beat the egg yolks until they are pale and thick. Gradually beat in the sugar, then add the nuts and salt. Beat the egg whites separately until stiff but not dry. Fold them into the first mixture, then stir in the flour. Drop by teaspoonfuls onto ungreased cookie sheets, leaving about 2 inches between cookies for them to spread. Flatten with a knife. Bake for 5–8 minutes or until firm.

Peanut Butter Cookies
(about 50 cookies)

¼ pound (115 g) butter
½ cup (1 dL) chunk-style peanut butter
½ cup (100 g) granulated sugar
½ cup (1 dL) dark-brown sugar
1 egg
½ teaspoon vanilla
½ teaspoon salt
½ teaspoon baking soda
1 cup (140 g) flour

Preheat the oven to 350°F (180°C) and grease some cookie sheets. Cream the butter and peanut butter together. Beat in the two sugars, then add the egg and the vanilla and mix well. Mix together the salt, baking soda, and flour and add to the first mixture, combining thoroughly. Arrange by teaspoonfuls on the cookie sheets, about 1½ inches apart. Press each one flat with the back of a floured spoon. Bake about 7 minutes or until firm.

Chocolate Walnut Wafers

(about 50 cookes)

Take care not to overbake this chewy, brownie-like cookie.

2 ounces (60 g) unsweetened chocolate
¼ pound (115 g) butter
1 cup (200 g) sugar
2 eggs
1 cup (¼ L) chopped walnuts
⅔ cup (100 g) flour
¼ teaspoon salt
¼ teaspoon vanilla

Preheat the oven to 350°F (180°C) and grease some cookie sheets well. Melt the chocolate in a bowl or pot over simmering water; set aside to cool. Cream the butter and gradually beat in the sugar and the eggs, blending well. Add the chocolate and the walnuts and combine thoroughly. Mix the flour and salt together and add to the first mixture, along with the vanilla. Mix well. Arrange by teaspoonfuls on the cookie sheets and bake for 10–12 minutes or until firm but chewy.

Swedish Almond Wafers

(about 50 cookies)

These buttery, lacelike cookies are so delicate they must be handled with extreme care. They are exceptionally easy to prepare, but they really spread in baking, so use scant teaspoonfuls of batter and space them far apart on the cookie sheet.

¾ cup (1¾ dL) finely ground, unblanched almonds
¼ pound (115 g) butter
½ cup (100 g) sugar
1 tablespoon flour
2 tablespoons light cream

Preheat the oven to 350°F (180°C). Mix all the ingredients in a heavy saucepan and cook, stirring, over moderate heat until the butter has melted. Arrange by scant teaspoonfuls, 3 inches apart, on a lightly buttered cookie sheet and bake for 3–5 minutes, watching carefully, until delicately brown at the edges but still bubbling slightly in the center. As soon as the edge is firm enough to lift the cookies with a spatula, remove them to a plate and let them cool. Do not stack the cookies until cool, and handle them with care.

Macaroons (30 cookies)

True macaroons are made of egg whites, sugar, and almond paste.

½ pound (225 g) almond paste
1 cup (200 g) granulated sugar
3 egg whites
⅓ cup (¾ dL) confectioners' sugar
2 tablespoons cake flour
⅛ teaspoon salt

Preheat the oven to 300°F (150°C). Cover cookie sheets with parchment paper or brown paper. Using your hands or the food processor, soften the almond paste. Gradually blend in the granulated sugar and egg whites; then mix in the confectioners' sugar, flour, and salt. Force through a cookie press or drop by teaspoonfuls onto the paper-covered cookie sheets. Cover and let stand 30 minutes. Bake 25 minutes; lay the paper linings on a damp cloth, let cool, and peel off the macaroons.

Cherry Macaroons. Add *2 tablespoons chopped candied cherries* to the dough.

Almond Macaroons. Sprinkle before baking with *2 tablespoons chopped blanched almonds*.

Wasps' Nests (40 cookies)

A traditional Christmas cookie, wonderful all year round.

½ pound (225 g) almonds, blanched and slivered
½ cup (100 g) granulated sugar
6 ounces (180 g) semisweet chocolate
3 egg whites
1¼ cups (3 dL) confectioners' sugar

Preheat the oven to 300°F (150°C). Butter and flour cookie sheets. In a heavy-bottomed pan, cook the granulated sugar in ¼ cup water until the syrup spins a thread or a thermometer registers 240°F. Stir in the almonds and remove from the heat. Grate the chocolate or use the food processor. Beat the egg whites until they are very stiff, adding

366

spoonfuls of confectioners' sugar during the last few minutes of beating. Fold in the almond mixture and the grated chocolate and drop by teaspoonfuls on the cookie sheets. Bake until the cookies are dry, about 20 minutes. Let stand 5 minutes, and remove from the pan.

Old-fashioned Gingersnaps
(about 50 gingersnaps)

½ cup (1 dL) molasses
4 tablespoons shortening
1½ cups (215 g) flour
¼ teaspoon baking soda
1½ teaspoons powdered ginger
¾ teaspoon salt

Preheat the oven to 350°F (180°C). Heat the molasses to the boiling point, pour it over the shortening, and stir to combine well. Mix together the flour, baking soda, ginger, and salt and add to the molasses mixture, blending well. Using a rolling pin, roll the dough out on an unfloured board as thin as possible. Cut into 1½-inch rounds with a small cutter or the edge of a small drinking glass. Bake on ungreased cookie sheets for about 5 minutes or until crisp and dry.

Meringues (about 12 small meringues)

Make these sweet confections, sometimes known as "kisses," anytime you have a few extra egg whites. Be sure the whites are at room temperature before you begin to beat them, and add the sugar very gradually so that the beaten whites do not lose any volume. Meringues are baked in a very slow oven and then left in the turned-off oven for a long time to crisp.

2 egg whites
8 tablespoons sugar, preferably superfine
1 teaspoon vanilla

Preheat the oven to 250°F (120°C). Cover a cookie sheet with brown paper or parchment. Beat the egg whites until stiff but not dry, and add 6 tablespoons of the sugar, a spoonful at a time, beating well between each addition. Add the vanilla, and fold in the remaining 2 tablespoons of sugar. Shape the meringues on the cookie sheet with a pastry bag and tube or a spoon. Bake for 1 hour. Turn off the oven and let the meringues remain in the oven for 6 more hours. Don't open the oven door—they must dry out to be nice and crisp.

Meringue Shells. Using a spoon or a pastry bag, shape the egg-white mixture into 3-inch rings. Bake at 250°F (120°C) until completely dry but not colored. Fill with *whipped cream* or *ice cream* and top with *crushed strawberries, blueberries,* or *chocolate sauce.*

Nut Meringues. Add about *½ cup chopped nuts.*

Chocolate Meringues. Add *4 tablespoons unsweetened cocoa* to the egg whites after you have beaten in the sugar.

Viennese Crescents

(about 50 small cookies)

The meltingly light taste of these rich, buttery confections makes them disappear almost as quickly as you can make them.

½ pound (225 g) butter
¼ cup (50 g) granulated sugar
2 cups (280 g) flour
1 cup (¼ L) ground nuts
1 teaspoon vanilla
Confectioners' sugar

Preheat the oven to 300°F (150°C). Cream the butter, then add the granulated sugar, flour, nuts, and vanilla and mix thoroughly. Shape with your fingers into delicate crescents, about 2 inches long and ½ inch wide and thick. Roll in confectioners' sugar and bake on ungreased cookie sheets for about 30 minutes, until just faintly browned. Cool, then roll in more confectioners' sugar before serving.

Scotch Shortbreads

(about twenty-four 1 × 2-inch bars)

Sandy and crumbly, as the perfect shortbread should be.

½ pound (225 g) butter
½ cup (1 dL) confectioners' sugar
2 cups (280 g) flour
¼ teaspoon salt
¼ teaspoon baking powder

Preheat the oven to 350°F (180°C). Cream the butter, then gradually add the sugar, beating well. Mix the flour, salt, and baking powder together and add to the first mixture, combining thoroughly. Roll out the dough with a rolling pin until it is ¼ inch thick, then cut into rectangles or any other shape desired. Put them on ungreased cookie sheets, prick each cookie with a fork, and bake for 20–25 minutes or until they turn lightly brown around the edges.

Gingerbread Men (about eight 5 × 3½-inch men or twenty-four 2 × 1½-inch men)

½ cup (1 dL) molasses
¼ cup (50 g) sugar
3 tablespoons butter or shortening
1 tablespoon milk
2 cups (280 g) flour
½ teaspoon baking soda
½ teaspoon salt
½ teaspoon nutmeg
½ teaspoon cinnamon
½ teaspoon ground cloves
½ teaspoon powdered ginger

Preheat the oven to 350°F (180°C) and butter some cookie sheets. Heat the molasses to the boiling point, then add the sugar, butter or shortening, and milk. Mix the flour with the baking soda, salt, nutmeg, cinnamon, cloves, and ginger. Add to the first mixture and blend well. Add a few tablespoons of water, enough so that the dough holds together and handles easily. Roll or pat out the dough about ¼ inch thick. Cut into large or small gingerbread men, using special cookie cutters or a very sharp knife. Bake for 5–7 minutes. When cool, frost with *Confectioners' Frosting* (see below) and decorate with *candies, raisins, or bits of citron.*

Confectioners' Frosting (makes 1 cup)

You can give this sweet frosting different flavors by substituting the same amount of hot coffee, lemon juice, or orange juice for the hot water. Or substitute 1 teaspoon of vanilla for the hot water. For a fine creamy consistency, be sure to beat the frosting very well.

About 2½ cups (6 dL) confectioners' sugar

Put 3 tablespoons hot water in a small bowl and beat in the confectioners' sugar until the frosting is thick enough to spread. Continue to beat for several minutes until very creamy.

Norwegian Butter Cookies
(about 30 cookies)

These are excellent cookie-press cookies.

¼ pound (115 g) butter
2 hard-cooked egg yolks
¼ cup (50 g) sugar
1 cup (140 g) flour
½ teaspoon lemon or vanilla extract

Preheat the oven to 375°F (190°C). Cream the butter, then add the egg yolks, and beat well. Beat in

371

the sugar. Add the flour and the lemon or vanilla extract and combine thoroughly. Put through a cookie press or arrange by teaspoonfuls on un-greased cookie sheets. Bake for 10–12 minutes or until lightly browned.

Brownies (16 brownies)

Don't overbake: brownies should be moist and chewy.

3 ounces (85 g) unsweetened chocolate
6 tablespoons butter
1½ cups (300 g) sugar
3 eggs
¼ teaspoon salt
¾ cup (105 g) flour
¾ cup (1¾ dL) chopped walnuts
1½ teaspoons vanilla

Preheat the oven to 350°F (180°C). Butter a 9-inch square cake pan. Melt the chocolate and the butter in a bowl or pot over simmering water, stirring until smooth. Remove from heat, and stir in the sugar, eggs, salt, flour, walnuts, and vanilla. Combine well. Spread in the pan and bake for about 40 minutes, until dry on top and almost firm to the touch. Set the pan on a rack to cool for about 15 minutes, then cut the brownies into squares approximately 2¼ inches.

Butterscotch Brownies (16 brownies)

½ cup (115 g) melted butter
2 cups (½ L) dark-brown sugar
2 eggs
½ teaspoon salt
1½ cups (210 g) flour
2 teaspoons baking powder
1 teaspoon vanilla
1 cup (¼ L) chopped nuts

Preheat the oven to 350°F (180°C). Butter a 9-inch square cake pan. Mix all the ingredients together, combining them well. Spread in the pan and bake for 35–40 minutes or until dry on top and almost firm to the touch. Let cool for 10–15 minutes, then cut in squares approximately 2¼ inches.

Hermits (36 squares or about 60 cookies)

¼ cup (½ dL) raisins or currants
¼ cup (½ dL) chopped nuts
2 cups (280 g) flour
4 tablespoons butter
½ cup (100 g) sugar
½ teaspoon salt
2 eggs
½ cup (1 dL) molasses
1 teaspoon baking soda
½ teaspoon cream of tartar
1 teaspoon cinnamon
½ teaspoon ground cloves
¼ teaspoon mace
¼ teaspoon nutmeg

Preheat the oven to 350°F (180°C). Grease a 9 × 13-inch cake pan or some cookie sheets. Toss the raisins or currants and the chopped nuts in ¼ cup of the flour; set aside. Cream the butter, then add the sugar and blend well. Add the salt, eggs, molasses and beat well. Mix together the remaining 1¾ cups flour, the baking soda, cream of tartar, cinnamon, cloves, mace, and nutmeg, add to the butter-sugar-egg mixture, and beat thoroughly. Stir in the raisins and nuts. Spread in the pan or drop by teaspoonfuls onto the cookie sheets. Bake only until the top is firm and the center chewy, about 15–20 minutes for the squares, 8–10 minutes for the cookies.

Concord Hermits. Substitute *1 cup dark-brown sugar* for the white sugar and molasses and add *½ cup sour cream.* You may also add *3 tablespoons chopped citron or candied orange peel,* if you wish.

Coconut Bars (16 bars)

Rich and sweet as candy, this delicious confection has a pastry base with a chewy coconut topping.

¼ pound (115 g) butter
2 tablespoons confectioners' sugar
1 cup (140 g) plus 2 tablespoons flour
2 eggs
1¼ cups (3 dL) light-brown sugar
1 teaspoon vanilla
¼ teaspoon salt
1 teaspoon baking powder

1 cup (¼ L) coarsely chopped nut meats
1–1½ cups (2 dL–3½ dL) moist shredded
   coconut

Preheat the oven to 350°F (180°C). Line an 8 × 8-inch square pan with wax paper. Cream the butter, then add the confectioners' sugar, and the cup of flour and blend. Pat evenly into the pan and bake for 15 minutes. While the pastry is baking, beat the eggs, then add the brown sugar and vanilla, beating until thick. Mix the remaining 2 tablespoons of flour, salt, and baking powder together and add to the egg mixture, incorporating well. Beat in the nuts and coconut. Spread evenly over the pastry and bake for 25–30 minutes. Cool in the pan, then cut into 1 × 4-inch bars.

Pecan Squares   (36 squares)

These have a good butter and pecan taste, and a nice short texture.

½ pound (225 g) butter
1 cup (200 g) sugar
1 egg, separated
1 teaspoon vanilla
2 cups (280 g) flour
1 cup (¼ L) chopped pecans

Preheat the oven to 375°F (190°C). Grease a jelly-roll pan about 9 × 15 inches. Cream the butter and sugar together until smooth and light. Beat in the egg yolk, vanilla, and flour until well mixed. Pat evenly into pan. Beat the egg white slightly and brush over the dough. Sprinkle the pecans evenly on top and press them in the dough slightly. Bake 16–18 minutes or until golden brown. Cool in the pan and cut into small squares.

Walnut Meringue Bars (24 bars)

¼ pound (115 g) butter
2 cups (½ L) light-brown sugar
½ teaspoon salt
2 teaspoons vanilla
2 eggs, separated
1¼ cups (175 g) flour
1½ teaspoons baking powder
1 cup (¼ L) chopped walnuts

Preheat the oven to 300°F (150°C). Butter a pan about 8 × 12 inches. Cream the butter and 1 cup of the sugar together until light and smooth. Beat in the salt, 1 teaspoon vanilla, and egg yolks. Add the flour and baking powder. Beat well. Spread evenly in the pan. Beat the egg whites until soft peaks are reached, then slowly beat in the remaining 1 cup brown sugar until all is incorporated. Gently stir in the walnuts and remaining teaspoon of vanilla. Spread over the cookie dough. Bake 35 minutes. Cool. Cut in bars 4 × 1 inches.

Chocolate Fudge (1½ pounds)

Old-fashioned basic fudge, smooth and chocolaty.

2 ounces (60 g) unsweetened chocolate, in small pieces, or 4 tablespoons unsweetened cocoa
2 cups (400 g) sugar
¾ cup (1¾ dL) milk
2 tablespoons light corn syrup
2 tablespoons butter, in small pieces
2 teaspoons vanilla

Oil a jelly-roll pan or an 8 × 8-inch pan. Combine the chocolate or cocoa, sugar, milk, and corn syrup in a 3-quart heavy pot, stirring to blend all the ingredients. Set over low heat and, stirring slowly, bring to a boil. Cover the pot and let boil for 2–3 minutes. Uncover and wash down the sides of the pot with a pastry brush dipped in cold water, then continue to boil slowly, without stirring, until the syrup reaches the soft-ball stage (234°F). Remove from the heat, add the butter without stirring, and set the pot on a cooling surface or rack. Do not stir until the syrup is lukewarm (110°F), then add the vanilla and stir without stopping until the mixture loses its gloss and thickens. Pour it into the oiled pan and mark into squares. When firm, cut into pieces and store airtight.

Chocolate Sour-Cream Fudge. Substitute *¾ cup plus 2 tablespoons sour cream* for the milk and butter.

Chocolate Nut Fudge. Stir in *1 cup chopped nuts* before turning the candy out of the pot.

Chocolate Marshmallow Fudge. Add *1½ cups small marshmallows* before turning the candy out of the pot.

Million-Dollar Fudge (2 pounds)

A very fast, very easy method, resulting in a fine, creamy fudge.

12 ounces (340 g) semisweet chocolate bits, or
  squares, in small pieces
1 cup (¼ L) marshmallow cream
2 cups (400 g) sugar
2 tablespoons butter
¾ cup (1¾ dL) evaporated milk
⅛ teaspoon salt
1 teaspoon vanilla
1 cup (¼ L) chopped nuts

Oil a jelly-roll pan or a 9 × 9-inch pan. Combine the chocolate and the marshmallow cream in a large bowl and set aside. Mix the sugar, butter, and milk in a 3-quart heavy pot, stirring to combine well. Gradually bring to a boil over low heat, stirring until the sugar dissolves. Dip a pastry brush in cold water and wash down the sides of the pot. Continue to boil, stirring constantly without touching the sides of the pot, for 5 minutes, then pour the mixture over the chocolate mixture and add the salt and vanilla. Stir until the chocolate melts and the mixture is smooth, then stir in the nuts. Spread on the cookie sheet or pan and let stand until firm. Cut into squares and store airtight.

Opera Fudge (1 pound)

A cream-colored, vanilla-flavored fudge. For the best flavor, let it mellow overnight.

2 cups (400 g) sugar
1 cup (¼ L) heavy cream
⅛ teaspoon salt
1 teaspoon vanilla

Oil a jelly-roll pan or 8 × 8-inch pan. Combine the sugar, cream, and salt in a 3-quart heavy pot, stirring to blend well. Place over medium heat and, stirring, bring to a boil. Cover and let boil for 2–3 minutes. Uncover and wash down the sides of the pot with a pastry brush dipped in cold water. Continue to boil over medium heat, without stirring, until the syrup reaches the soft-ball stage (234°F). Remove the pot to a cooling surface or rack and, without stirring, let cool to lukewarm (110°F). Add the vanilla, stir until creamy, then spread in the oiled pan. To keep it creamy, cover the top of the candy with a damp cloth or paper towels for 30 minutes. Uncover, let it set until firm, then cut into squares and store airtight.

Peanut Butter Fudge (1 pound)

A firm fudge, rich in peanut butter flavor.

2 cups (400 g) sugar
⅛ teaspoon salt
¾ cup (1¾ dL) milk or cream
2 tablespoons light corn syrup
¼ cup (½ dL) peanut butter
1 teaspoon vanilla

Oil a jelly-roll pan or 8 × 8-inch pan. Combine the sugar, salt, milk or cream, and corn syrup in a heavy 3-quart pot, stirring to mix well. Stir over medium heat until it boils, then cover and let boil for 2–3 minutes. Uncover and wash down the sides of the pot with a pastry brush dipped in cold water. Continue to boil over medium heat, without stirring, to the soft-ball stage (234°F). Put the pot on a cooling surface or rack and, without stirring, let the syrup cool to lukewarm (110°F). Mix in the peanut butter and vanilla, stirring until thickened. Spread in the oiled pan. Cut into squares when firm, and store airtight.

Pecan Penuche (1½ pounds)

Penuche is firmer than classic fudge, but because of its deep sweet flavor, it's often called "brown sugar fudge."

2 cups (½ L) firmly packed dark-brown sugar
¾ cup (1¾ dL) milk
⅛ teaspoon salt
2½ tablespoons butter, in small pieces
1 teaspoon vanilla
¾ cup (1¾ dL) chopped pecans

Oil a jelly-roll pan or an 8 × 8-inch pan. Combine the sugar, milk, and salt in a 3-quart heavy pot, stirring to mix well. Place over medium heat and bring to a boil, stirring constantly until the sugar dissolves. Cover and let boil for 2–3 minutes. Uncover, and wash down the sides of the pot with a pastry brush dipped in cold water. Continue to boil over medium heat to the firm-ball stage (244°F), stirring only if it starts to burn. Remove from the heat and immediately place the pot into a larger pan filled with cold water; this will stop the cooking process and bring the temperature down. Drop in the butter and let cool slightly, without stirring. Beat until it starts to thicken, add the vanilla and the pecans, and continue to beat until the candy loses some of its gloss. Spread evenly in the pan and mark into squares. When firm, cut into pieces and store airtight.

Maple Pralines (1½ pounds)

Pecans are especially good in this candy.

2 cups (½ L) confectioners' sugar
1 cup (¼ L) maple sugar or maple syrup
½ cup (1 dL) heavy cream
2 cups (½ L) large pieces of nuts

Combine the confectioners' sugar, maple sugar or syrup, and cream in a 3-quart heavy pot, stirring to blend well. Bring to a boil over medium heat, stirring constantly until the sugar dissolves. Cover and let boil for 2–3 minutes, then uncover and wash down the sides of the pot with a pastry brush dipped in cold water. Without stirring, boil to the soft-ball stage (234°F). Remove from the heat to a cooling surface and let stand, without stirring, until lukewarm (110°F). Beat with a wooden spoon until it starts to thicken and becomes cloudy, then beat in the nuts. Using two metal tablespoons, scoop up the mixture and drop small patties onto a sheet of wax paper. Let stand until firm, then store airtight.

Caramels (1 pound)

Lovely, classic, chewy caramels. Take care that the easily scorched syrup doesn't burn or become granular: stir it continuously over medium-low heat, without touching the sides of the pan. Light cream is called for but you can as easily use half-and-half or ¾ cup milk mixed with ¾ cup heavy cream.

1 cup (200 g) sugar
⅔ cup (1½ dL) corn syrup
1½ cups (3½ dL) light cream
1 teaspoon vanilla

Oil a jelly-roll pan or an 8 × 8-inch pan. Put the sugar, corn syrup, and ½ cup of light cream or milk-and-cream combination in a 3-quart heavy pot. Stir until well mixed, then bring to a boil, stirring over medium-low heat until the sugar dissolves. Cover and let boil for 2–3 minutes. Uncover and wash down the sides of the pot with a pastry brush dipped in cold water. Continue to boil over medium-low heat, stirring gently without touching the sides of the pot with the spoon. When the syrup reaches the soft-ball stage (234°F), slowly, without breaking the boil, stir in another ½ cup of light cream. Continue to boil, stirring constantly until the soft-ball stage (234°F) is again reached, then slowly add, without breaking the boil, the remaining ½ cup light cream. Keep it boiling gently, stirring constantly, to the firm-ball stage (244°F). Remove from the heat and stir in the vanilla. Turn into the oiled pan, spreading a layer about ¾ inch deep. Mark into squares and let stand until cool. When firm, cut with a sharp knife into pieces and wrap each piece in plastic wrap or wax paper. Store airtight in a cool place.

Toffee (1 pound)

A smooth dark brittle with a deep butterscotch taste.

2 cups (½ L) firmly packed dark-brown sugar
¼ cup (60 g) butter
1 tablespoon vinegar
Pinch of salt

Oil a jelly-roll pan or an 8 × 8-inch pan. Combine all the ingredients with 2 tablespoons boiling water in a 3-quart heavy pot, stirring to blend well. Place over moderate heat, stirring as the sugar dissolves and the mixture comes to a boil. Cover and let boil for 2–3 minutes, then uncover and wash down the sides of the pot with a pastry brush dipped in cold water. Boil slowly over moderate heat until it reaches the hard-crack stage (290°F), stirring gently, without touching the sides of the pot, only if it starts to scorch. Pour it out into the oiled pan and let cool partially, then cut into squares. When completely cool and hard, cut or break into pieces and transfer to an airtight tin.

Old-fashioned Peanut Brittle
(1½ pounds)

A thick, opaque, golden brittle.

1½ cups (3½ dL) skinned salted peanuts
2 cups (400 g) sugar
1 cup (¼ L) light corn syrup
2 tablespoons butter, cut in pieces
2 teaspoons baking soda

Oil two jelly-roll pans and divide the nuts evenly between them, spreading them close together in one layer. Combine the sugar, corn syrup, and ¼ cup water in a heavy 3- or 4-quart pot, stirring to blend well. Stir over moderate heat until the sugar dissolves and comes to a boil. Cover and let boil for 2–3 minutes, then uncover and wash down the sides of the pot with a pastry brush dipped in cold water. Without stirring, continue to boil over moderate heat to the soft-crack stage (280°F). Remove from the heat and drop the butter in, swirling the pan gently so the butter melts; the syrup will turn golden. Return to the heat and cook to the hard-crack stage (295°F). Remove from the heat, thoroughly stir in the baking soda (the syrup will foam up), and pour it evenly over the nuts. When the brittle is cool enough to handle, in just a few minutes, pick it up and pull and stretch it as thin as possible. When cold, blot it with paper towels and break into irregular pieces. Store in an airtight tin.

Butterscotch Nut Brittle (1 pound)

A dark-brown glossy brittle with a distinct toffee taste.

1 cup (¼ L) chopped salted mixed nuts
¼ cup (½ dL) unsulfured molasses
1 cup (200 g) sugar
¼ pound (115 g) butter
1 tablespoon cider vinegar

Oil a jelly-roll pan and sprinkle the nuts close together in one layer over the bottom. Grease a sturdy wooden spoon or metal spatula and set aside. Combine the molasses, sugar, butter, vinegar, and 2 tablespoons water in a 3-quart heavy pot, stirring to mix well. Stir over moderate heat until the sugar dissolves and it comes to a boil. Cover and boil for 2–3 minutes, then uncover and wash down the sides of the pot with a pastry brush dipped in cold water. Continue to cook at a slow boil over moderate heat; stir, without touching the sides of the pan, only if the syrup starts to scorch. Cook to the hard-crack stage (290°F), then pour out over the nuts, using the greased spoon or spatula to spread it evenly. Cool, blot with paper towels, and break into irregular pieces. Store in an airtight tin.

Spiced Nuts (about 4 cups)

Sweet, spicy, and delicious.

1 cup (200 g) sugar
1 teaspoon cinnamon

Pinch of salt
6 tablespoons milk
1 teaspoon vanilla
3 cups (¾ L) walnut halves

Lightly oil a cookie sheet. Mix the sugar, cinnamon, salt, and milk together in a 3-quart heavy pot and stir over low heat until the sugar dissolves. Bring to a boil, cover, and let boil for 2–3 minutes. Uncover, wash down the sides of the pot with a pastry brush dipped in cold water, and continue to cook, without stirring, to the soft-ball stage (236°F). Remove from the heat, stir in the vanilla and walnuts, and stir vigorously until creamy. Spread out on the cookie sheet and separate the nuts with two forks. Let cool. Keep them in a tin at room temperature.

Popcorn Balls (fifteen 3-inch balls)

An authentic old-fashioned version.

3 quarts (3 L) popped corn, unsalted, unbuttered
2 cups (½ L) light corn syrup
1 tablespoon cider vinegar
½ teaspoon salt
2 teaspoons vanilla

Put the popped corn into a large greased bowl and keep warm in a 250°F (120°C) oven. Oil a large fork and set aside. Combine the corn syrup, vinegar, and salt in a 3-quart heavy pot. Cook over medium heat, stirring occasionally, until the syrup reaches the hard-ball stage (250°F). Remove from the heat and add the vanilla. Slowly pour the syrup over the popcorn, tossing with the fork until it is well distributed. As soon as the mixture is cool enough to handle, quickly and gently shape it into 3-inch balls. Let them stand on wax paper until they are cool and no longer sticky, then wrap each in plastic wrap, a tied plastic bag, or tissue paper, and store at room temperature.

Coconut Cakes (20 small balls)

These are chewy, toasted, and just sweet enough. A fine complement to fresh fruit desserts.

2 cups (½ L) coarsely grated fresh coconut
2 tablespoons light corn syrup
½ cup (100 g) sugar
Pinch of salt
1 egg white
¼ teaspoon coconut or almond extract

Mix the coconut, corn syrup, sugar, and salt together in a 3-quart heavy pot. Stir over medium heat until the mixture thickens a little, about 5–6 minutes. Stir in the egg white and cook, stirring, for another 5–6 minutes, until the mixture feels sticky; cool a little and feel it with your fingers. Stir in the coconut or almond extract. Remove from the heat. Rinse a shallow pan with cold water, shake out the excess, and spread the mixture over the bottom. Rinse paper towels in cold water, wring them out, and place them over the mixture. Refrigerate until chilled. Preheat oven to 300°F (150°C).

Lightly grease a cookie sheet. Dip your hands in cold water, then shape the coconut mixture into small balls. Heat the cookie sheet slightly and place the balls on it. Bake for 20 minutes or until golden on top. Store in an airtight container at room temperature.

Walnut Balls (½ pound)

Nut bonbons, with a dusting of confectioners' sugar.

¼ cup (½ dL) light corn syrup
1 teaspoon vanilla
⅛ teaspoon salt
½ cup (1 dL) instant nonfat dry milk
¼ cup (½ dL) finely chopped walnuts, or other nuts
¼ cup (½ dL) confectioners' sugar

Mix the syrup, vanilla, salt, dry milk, and walnuts together in a bowl, using your hands to blend well. Sprinkle a board with a little of the confectioners' sugar and knead the candy on the board until it becomes creamy. Shape into 1-inch balls and dust with the remaining confectioners' sugar. These keep best in the refrigerator.

Pies

Basic Pastry

Don't handle this pastry dough any more than necessary or it will be tough: treat it firmly, not timidly, but don't fuss with it. The flour and shortening should not be blended too well: it is the bits of shortening left in the dough that puff and expand during baking and give the pastry its flaky identity. For that reason, the dough cannot be mixed as successfully in a food processor.

(8-inch pie shell)

1 cup (140 g) plus 2 tablespoons flour
¼ teaspoon salt
⅓ cup (¾ dL) shortening
2–3 tablespoons cold water

(8-inch two-crust pie)

2 cups (280 g) flour
½ teaspoon salt
⅔ cup (1½ dL) shortening
⅓ cup (¾ dL) cold water

(9-inch pie shell)

1½ cups (215 g) flour
¼ teaspoon salt
½ cup (1 dL) shortening
3–4 tablespoons cold water

2½ cups (350 g) flour
½ teaspoon salt
¾ cup (1¾ dL) shortening
6–7 tablespoons cold water

Mix the flour and salt. Cut in the shortening with a pastry blender or two knives. Combine lightly only until the mixture resembles coarse meal or very tiny peas: its texture will not be uniform but will contain crumbs and small bits and pieces. Sprinkle water over the flour mixture, a tablespoon at a time, and mix lightly with a fork, using only enough water so that the pastry will hold together when pressed gently into a ball.

Pie Shell

Roll the dough out 2 inches larger than the pie pan, then fit it loosely but firmly into the pan. Crimp or flute the edges. For a *baked pie shell* (sometimes known, incidentally, as baking blind) prick the bottom dough all over with a fork and bake the shell for 16–18 minutes in a preheated 425°F (220°C) oven (for a partially baked shell, bake 10 minutes). Open the oven door once or twice during the baking and see if the shell again has begun to swell up in spots; if it has, push it down gently. Or fill the *unbaked pie shell* with pie filling and then bake the pie as directed in the filling recipe.

Two-Crust Pie

Divide the dough into two balls. Roll the bottom crust out 2 inches larger than the pie pan. Ease it into the pan, fitting it loosely but firmly. Roll out the top crust. Fill the pie generously, then put on the top crust and prick in several places with a fork or cut vents in it. Or cover the pie with lattice strips. Crimp or flute the edges. Bake as indicated in the filling recipe.

Tart Pastry (one 9-inch tart)

This well-balanced, basic recipe produces a firm, crisp crust with the taste of butter. You can sweeten it slightly, if you wish, by adding 1½ tablespoons of sugar to the flour. Unlike the preceding basic pastry, tart pastry will not get tough if you handle it a lot and you can mix it in a food processor.

1 cup (140 g) flour
¼ teaspoon salt
6 tablespoons cold butter, in small pieces
1 egg yolk

Mix the flour and salt in a bowl. Cut in the butter with your fingers or a pastry blender until the mixture resembles coarse meal or tiny peas. Whisk the egg yolk and 2 tablespoons water together in another bowl, add to the flour mixture, and blend until the pastry is smooth and holds together in a ball. It can be mixed in a food processor; process first the flour, salt, and butter quickly together, then add the egg yolk and water through the funnel and process until the dough balls up around the blade. Wrap in foil or plastic and refrigerate it for at least 20 minutes. You can roll this dough out with a rolling pin, but you would have to chill it, wrapped in plastic, for at least 20 minutes. We find it easier to pat it into a pie pan or springform with our hands. Pull pieces of dough from the ball and press them over the bottom and sides of the pan, using the heel of your hand. The dough should be thick enough to hold the filling, but be careful that it is not too thick around the bottom edge or the finished tart will seem coarse. If there's time, cover the lined pan snugly with foil and refrigerate it before filling and baking it. Bake as directed in the filling recipe. Or prick the bottom with a fork and bake it unfilled for 12 minutes in a preheated 425°F (220°C) oven. If you use a springform pan, do not remove the sides until you are ready to serve the tart.

Crumb Crust   (8- or 9-inch pie shell)

1½ cups (3½ dL) fine crumbs (graham cracker, gingersnap, rusk, zwieback, or vanilla or chocolate wafers)
⅓ cup (65 g) sugar
⅓ cup (75 g) butter, melted

Mix the crumbs, sugar, and butter together in a bowl. Press and pat the crumb mixture into the pie pan. Bake 8–10 minutes in a preheated 350°F (180°C) oven or fill unbaked as directed in the filling recipe.

Meringue Topping

Meringue toppings for pies often "weep," shrink, or turn rubbery. Follow this somewhat unconventional method and yours will hold up well and stay light for several days. Be sure to refrigerate a meringue pie if it isn't served within a few hours of making it.

(for 8-inch pie)
3 egg whites, at room temperature
⅓ cup (65 g) sugar
⅛ teaspoon salt
½ teaspoon vanilla

(for 9-inch pie)
4 egg whites, at room temperature
6 tablespoons sugar
¼ teaspoon salt
½ teaspoon vanilla

Put the egg whites and sugar in a mixing bowl and place the bowl in a pan of hot water. Stir constantly until the whites feel warm, then add the salt and vanilla. Remove the bowl from the hot water and beat with an electric beater until the meringue is stiff and shiny. Spread the meringue over a filled and baked pie shell. Be sure that the meringue touches the inner edges of the crust; this will keep it from shrinking. Put the pie under the broiler and let the meringue peaks brown a little. Watch carefully, as this will take only a minute or two.

Apple Pie (9-inch pie)

Apple pie is a symbol of the many good things in the American home. You will not be disappointed with this one. It is especially good served warm with a wedge of sharp Cheddar cheese or a spoonful of whipped cream.

Basic Pastry dough for 9-inch two-crust pie (p. 390)
¾–1 cup (150–200 g) sugar
½ teaspoon salt
1 teaspoon cinnamon
½ teaspoon nutmeg
1½ tablespoons flour
6 large, firm, tart apples
2 tablespoons butter

Preheat the oven to 425°F (220°C). Line a 9-inch pie pan with half the pastry dough. Mix the sugar, salt, cinnamon, nutmeg, and flour in a large bowl. Peel, core, and slice the apples and toss them in the sugar mixture, coating them well. Pile them into the lined pan and dot with the butter. Roll out the top crust and drape it over the pie. Crimp the edges and cut several vents in the top. Bake 10 minutes, then lower the heat to 350°F (180°C) and bake 30–40 minutes more or until the apples are tender when pierced with a skewer and the crust is browned.

Fresh Peach Pie (9-inch pie)

If you submerge peaches in boiling water for a minute or two, then plunge them into cold water, their skins will be easier to peel.

Basic Pastry dough for 9-inch two-crust pie
  (p. 390)
1 cup (200 g) sugar
4 tablespoons flour
4 cups (1 L) peeled and sliced fresh peaches
1 tablespoon lemon juice

Preheat the oven to 425°F (220°C). Line a 9-inch pie pan with half the pastry dough. Mix the sugar and flour in a large bowl. Add the peaches and lemon juice and toss well. Pile the fruit into the lined pie pan. Roll out the top crust and drape it over the pie. Crimp or flute the edges and cut several vents in the top. Bake for 10 minutes, then lower the heat to 350°F (180°C) and bake 30–40 minutes more, until the top is browned.

Blueberry Pie (9-inch pie)

Basic Pastry dough for 9-inch two-crust pie
  (p. 390)
4 cups (1 L) fresh or frozen blueberries
3 tablespoons flour
1 cup (200 g) sugar
⅛ teaspoon salt
1 tablespoon lemon juice
1 tablespoon butter

Preheat the oven to 425°F (220°C). Line the pie pan with half the pastry dough. Wash and pick over the blueberries if you are using fresh ones; if you are using frozen berries, it is not necessary to defrost them completely. Mix the flour, sugar, and salt in a large bowl. Add the blueberries and lemon juice and toss well. Pile the mixture into the lined pie pan and dot with the butter. Roll out the top crust and drape it over the pie. Crimp or flute the edges and cut several vents in the top. Bake for 10 minutes, then lower the heat to 350°F (180°C) and bake for 30–40 minutes or until the top is browned.

Sweet Cherry Pie (8-inch pie)

Basic Pastry dough for 8-inch two-crust pie
  (p. 389)
3 cups (¾ L) fresh or canned sweet cherries,
  pitted
¼ cup (50 g) sugar
2½ tablespoons quick-cooking tapioca
2 teaspoons butter

Preheat the oven to 425°F (220°C). Line an 8-inch pie pan with half the pastry dough. Drain the cherries, saving ½ cup of the juice. (If you are using fresh cherries, the natural juices which bubble up during baking are sufficient.) Mix the juice, sugar, and tapioca in a bowl, add the cherries, and toss well. Pile into the lined pan and dot with the butter. Roll out the top crust and drape it over the pie. Crimp the edges and cut several vents in the top. Bake for 10 minutes, reduce the heat to 350°F (180°C), continue to bake for 30–40 minutes more, until the crust is lightly browned.

Glazed Fresh Strawberry Tart
(9-inch tart)

Wait until the spring when strawberries are plump and juicy, then fill a buttery prebaked tart shell with glazed berries topped with clouds of lightly sweetened whipped cream. Other fresh berry tarts can be made the same way—substituting blueberries, raspberries, blackberries for the quart of strawberries.

Tart Pastry dough for 9-inch tart (p. 391)
1 cup (200 g) granulated sugar
3 tablespoons cornstarch
¼ teaspoon salt
¾ cup (1¾ dL) orange juice
1 tablespoon lemon juice
1 quart (1 L) strawberries, hulled and sliced
1 cup (¼ L) heavy cream
Confectioners' sugar

Preheat the oven to 425°F (220°C). Line a 9-inch pie pan or springform with the tart dough, prick the dough all over, and bake for 12 minutes or until lightly browned. Combine the granulated sugar, cornstarch, salt, orange juice, and lemon juice in a saucepan. Cook over low heat, stirring constantly, until thickened, then continue to cook for about 10 minutes. Spoon into a bowl to cool. Fill the baked tart shell with the strawberries and cover them with the cornstarch mixture. Before serving, whip the cream, sweetening it to taste with confectioners' sugar. Spread over the strawberry filling.

Deep-Dish Peach Pie   (serves eight)

1½ recipes Basic Pastry dough for 8-inch pie shell
  (p. 389)
2 tablespoons lemon juice
6 cups (1½ L) peeled, pitted, sliced peaches
1¼ cups (250 g) plus 2 tablespoons sugar
⅛ teaspoon salt
¼ teaspoon nutmeg
¼ teaspoon cinnamon
3 tablespoons flour
4 tablespoons butter
1 cup (¼ L) heavy cream, whipped

Preheat the oven to 450°F (230°C). Prepare the pastry dough and set it aside. Sprinkle the lemon juice over the peaches in a large bowl. Mix 1¼ cups of the sugar with the salt, nutmeg, cinnamon, and flour, then add to the peaches and toss until they are evenly coated. Spread the peaches in a 1½- to 2-quart baking dish and dot all over with the butter. Roll out the pastry dough to cover the top of the dish with a 1½-inch overhang. Press the pastry to the edge of the dish and flute it. Cut two or three vents on top for steam to escape. Sprinkle the top with the remaining 2 tablespoons of sugar. Bake for 10 minutes, then reduce heat to 350°F (180°C) and continue to bake for 30 minutes more. Serve with whipped cream.

Deep-Dish Apple Pie. Substitute *6 cups peeled, cored, sliced apples* for the peaches and use *2 teaspoons cinnamon.*

Deep-Dish Blueberry Pie. Substitute *6 cups blueberries* for the peaches and use *½ teaspoon cinnamon.*

Rhubarb Pie (9-inch lattice pie)

Rhubarb is sometimes called "pie plant." Use only the stalks: the leaves are poisonous. Flatter this pie, if you wish, by adding a cup of crushed, drained strawberries or pineapple to the rhubarb filling.

Basic Pastry dough for 9-inch two-crust pie
  (p. 390)
1¼ cups (250 g) sugar
4 tablespoons flour
⅛ teaspoon salt
4 cups (1 L) ¼-inch pieces rhubarb stalks
2 tablespoons butter

Preheat the oven to 425°F (220°C). Line a 9-inch pie pan with half the pastry dough. Combine the sugar, flour, and salt in a bowl. Add the rhubarb and toss well. Pile the rhubarb filling into the lined pie pan and dot with the butter. Roll out the remaining dough and make a lattice top. Crimp the edges. Bake for 10 minutes, then reduce the heat to 350°F (180°C) and bake for 30–40 minutes more, until the filling is tender when pierced with a skewer and the crust is browned.

Pecan Pie (9-inch open pie)

When you serve this pie, pass around a bowl filled with billows of unsweetened whipped cream.

Tart Pastry dough for 9-inch tart (p. 391)
3 eggs, slightly beaten
¾ cup (150 g) sugar
⅛ teaspoon salt
1 cup (¼ L) dark corn syrup
1 teaspoon vanilla
1 cup (¼ L) pecans, broken in pieces
1 cup (¼ L) heavy cream, whipped

Preheat the oven to 425°F (220°C). Line a 9-inch pie pan with the pastry dough. Combine the eggs, sugar, salt, corn syrup, and vanilla in a bowl and blend well. Stir in the pecans. Pour into the lined pan. Bake for 10 minutes, then reduce the heat to 350°F (180°C) and bake for another 35 minutes. Serve with unsweetened whipped cream.

Apple-Cranberry-Raisin Pie
(9-inch pie)

Basic Pastry dough for 9-inch two-crust pie
    (p. 390)
1 cup (200 g) sugar
½ teaspoon salt
3 tablespoons flour
1 cup (¼ L) cranberries
½ cup (1 dL) raisins
Grated rind of 1 lemon
5 large tart apples
2 tablespoons butter

Preheat the oven to 425°F (220°C). Line a 9-inch pie pan with half the pastry dough. Stir the sugar, salt, and flour together in a large bowl. Add the cranberries, raisins, and lemon rind. Peel, core, and slice the apples and toss them in the sugar mixture. Pile the filling into the lined pie pan and dot with the butter. Roll out the top crust and drape it over the pie. Crimp the edges together and cut several small vents in the top. Bake for 10 minutes, then lower the heat to 350°F (180°C) and continue baking for 30–40 minutes or until the apples are tender when pierced with a skewer and the crust is browned.

Mince Pie (9-inch pie)

In the first edition Fannie Farmer recommended puff paste for special Thanksgiving or Christmas mincemeat pies. Try using puff pastry, if you wish, but basic pastry dough makes a splendid mince pie.

Basic Pastry dough for 9-inch two-crust pie
  (p. 390)
1 pint (½ L) Mincemeat (following recipes)

Preheat the oven to 425°F (220°C). Line a 9-inch pie pan with half the pastry dough. Fill the lined pan with the prepared mincemeat. Roll out the remaining dough and make a top crust or lattice crust. Crimp the edges. Cut vents if a top crust is used. Bake 10 minutes, then lower the heat to 350°F (180°C) and bake about 40 minutes more, until the top is lightly browned. Serve with softly *whipped cream* or *Hard Sauce* (p. 422), if you wish.

Mincemeat I   (20 pints)

Mincemeat developed as a way of preserving meat without salting or smoking it. Traditionally, the minced beef and suet are combined with fruits, spices, and spirits, packed in jars, and sealed with wax. Make it well ahead of time: it keeps indefinitely, mellows with age, and is grand to have on hand as the holiday season approaches.

This is enough mincemeat for ten pies. You can make it in smaller quantities, if you wish, but before you reduce the recipe, consider the fine, old-fashioned holiday gifts that jars of home-made mincemeat make!

4 pounds (1¾ kg) chopped lean beef
2 pounds (900 g) chopped beef suet
3 pounds (1½ kg) dark-brown sugar
2 cups (½ L) molasses
2 quarts (2 L) cider
3 pounds (1½ kg) dried currants
4 pounds (1¾ kg) seeded raisins
½ pound (225 g) citron, chopped
3 pounds (1½ kg) apples, peeled, cored, and sliced
1 quart (1 L) brandy
1 tablespoon cinnamon
1 tablespoon mace
1 tablespoon ground cloves
1 teaspoon nutmeg
1 teaspoon allspice
2 teaspoons salt

Put the beef, suet, brown sugar, molasses, cider, currants, raisins, and citron in a large pot. Cook slowly, stirring occasionally, until the sugar and citron melt. Add the apples and cook until tender. Add the remaining ingredients and cook 15 minutes more, stirring frequently. Spoon into clean, hot jars, leaving 1-inch headspace. Close the jars and process at 10 pounds pressure for 20 minutes. You can then store the mincemeat indefinitely. If you do not want to process it, it is safer to refrigerate.

Mincemeat II   (4 pints)

This recipe for meatless mincemeat will provide enough filling for two 8- or 9-inch pies.

1 pound (450 g) suet, ground
1½ pounds (675 g) apples, peeled, cored, and chopped
1½ cups (3½ dL) dark-brown sugar
1 pound (450 g) dried currants
1 pound (450 g) golden raisins
1 pound (450 g) seedless raisins
4 ounces (115 g) candied lemon peel, diced
4 ounces (115 g) candied orange peel, diced
4 ounces (115 g) citron, diced
Grated rind of 2 lemons
Juice of 3 lemons
1 teaspoon cinnamon
½ teaspoon nutmeg
½ teaspoon mace
1 teaspoon allspice
1 cup (¼ L) brandy

Put all the ingredients in a large bowl and mix with your hands until well blended. Pack into sterilized jars and seal. Store in a cool place. It is not necessary to process this mincemeat because it doesn't contain fresh meat, but if you feel more comfortable about it, follow the directions for processing in the preceding recipe.

Pumpkin Pie   (9-inch open pie)

A really good pumpkin pie that deservedly goes with Thanksgiving.

Basic Pastry dough for 9-inch pie shell (p. 389)
1 cup (200 g) sugar
½ teaspoon salt
1½ teaspoons cinnamon
½ teaspoon powdered ginger
½ teaspoon ground cloves
1½ cups (3½ dL) cooked or canned (unseasoned) pumpkin, mashed or puréed
1½ cups (3½ dL) evaporated milk
½ cup (1 dL) milk
2 eggs, slightly beaten

Preheat the oven to 425°F (220°C). Line a 9-inch pie pan with the pastry dough. Combine the remaining ingredients in a large bowl and beat until smooth. Pour into the lined pie pan. Bake for 10 minutes, then lower the heat to 300°F (150°C) and bake for about 45 minutes or until the filling is firm.

Lemon Meringue Pie   (9-inch open pie)

A classic filling for a prebaked pie shell.

Basic Pastry dough for 9-inch pie shell (p. 389)
4 tablespoons cornstarch
4 tablespoons flour
¼ teaspoon salt
1¼ cups (250 g) sugar
4 eggs yolks, slightly beaten
Grated rind of 1 lemon
½ cup (1 dL) lemon juice
2 tablespoons butter
Meringue Topping for 9-inch pie (p. 393)

Preheat the oven to 425°F (220°C). Line a 9-inch pie pan with the pastry dough, prick the dough all over, and bake for 16–18 minutes, until lightly browned. Mix the cornstarch, flour, salt, sugar, and 1½ cups water in a saucepan. Cook over low heat, stirring constantly, until thickened, then cook 10 minutes more, stirring frequently, until clear. Remove from the heat. Stir ½ cup of the hot mixture into the egg yolks, then stir the yolks into the remaining hot mixture and cook, stirring, for another 3 minutes. Remove from the heat and stir in the lemon rind, lemon juice, and butter. Let cool a bit. Spread the lemon mixture in the baked pie shell and cover with the meringue. Run under the broiler until the meringue peaks are delicately browned, taking care not to burn them. This particular meringue will hold up as long as two days without weeping and shrinking. Refrigerate for storage, but serve at room temperature.

Slipped Custard Pie (9-inch open pie)

This pie is a dandy, sitting smugly on its crisp prebaked crust. An easy, old-fashioned method keeps the piecrust flaky and the custard silken: they meet just before they are served.

Basic Pastry dough for 9-inch pie shell (p. 389)
½ cup (100 g) sugar
¼ teaspoon salt
2½ cups (6 dL) milk, scalded
1½ teaspoons vanilla
4 eggs, slightly beaten

Preheat the oven to 425°F (220°C). Line a 9-inch pie pan with the pastry dough, prick the dough all over, and bake for 16–18 minutes, until lightly browned. Set aside. Reduce the oven heat to 350°F (180°C). Combine the sugar, salt, milk, and vanilla, add the eggs, and mix well. Pour into a buttered 9-inch pie pan the *same size and shape* as the baked pie shell. Set the pan in a larger pan filled with ½ inch hot water. Bake about 35 minutes or until the custard is barely set; overbaking will make it watery. Remove from the oven and cool; refrigerate if the custard is not to be served within a couple of hours. Assemble the pie as close to serving time as possible: loosen the edge of the custard with a sharp knife, shaking gently to free the bottom; hold over the pie shell and ease the filling gently into the shell, shaking it a bit if necessary to make it settle into place.

Coconut Custard Pie. Add *1 cup grated coconut* to the custard before baking.

Chocolate Chiffon Pie (9-inch open pie)

Crumb Crust (p. 392)
1½ cups (3½ dL) cold milk
1 envelope gelatin
½ cup (100 g) sugar
⅛ teaspoon salt
4 eggs, separated
6 tablespoons cocoa

Preheat the oven to 350°F (180°C). Pat the crumb mixture into a 9-inch pie pan and bake for 8–10 minutes; set aside. Put the milk in a saucepan, sprinkle the gelatin over it, and let it soften for about 3 minutes. Stir in the sugar, salt, and egg yolks and beat thoroughly. Cook, stirring, over moderate heat until thickened; do not boil. Add the cocoa and stir until dissolved. Chill just until the mixture mounds when dropped from a spoon. Beat the egg whites until they are stiff but not dry. Fold them into the gelatin mixture. Spoon into the pie shell and chill until ready to serve.

Coffee Chiffon Pie. Substitute *2 tablespoons instant coffee* for the cocoa.

Eggnog Chiffon Pie. Substitute *3 tablespoons rum* for the cocoa. Top the finished pie with a thin layer of *whipped cream* and sprinkle with *nutmeg*.

Strawberry Chiffon Pie
(9-inch open pie)

Crumb Crust for 9-inch pie shell (p. 392)
1 pint (½ L) strawberries

¾ cup (150 g) sugar
1 envelope gelatin
1 tablespoon lemon juice
⅛ teaspoon salt
2 egg whites

Preheat the oven to 350°F (180°C). Pat the crumb mixture into a 9-inch pie pan and bake for 8–10 minutes; set aside. Reserve 6 whole strawberries for a garnish, then slice the rest and toss them in ½ cup of the sugar. Sprinkle the gelatin over ¾ cup cold water and let it soften for about 3 minutes. Add the lemon juice, salt, and remaining ¼ cup sugar. Cook over moderate heat, stirring, until the gelatin dissolves; do not let the mixture boil. Cool a little, then stir in the sliced strawberries. Chill until the mixture mounds when dropped from a spoon. Beat the egg whites until stiff but not dry and fold them into the strawberry mixture. Spoon into the baked pie shell, garnish with the whole strawberries, and chill until ready to serve.

Black-Bottom Pie (9-inch open pie)

Crumb Crust for 9-inch pie shell (p. 392), using
   chocolate wafers
1½ cups (3½ dL) cold milk
1 envelope gelatin
½ cup (100 g) sugar
⅛ teaspoon salt
4 eggs, separated
1½ ounces (45 g) unsweetened chocolate, melted
1 teaspoon vanilla

1 tablespoon rum
½ cup (1 dL) heavy cream

Preheat the oven to 350°F (180°C). Pat the crumb mixture into a 9-inch pie pan and bake for 8–10 minutes; set aside. Put the milk in a saucepan, sprinkle in the gelatin, and let it soften for about 3 minutes. Stir in the sugar, salt, and egg yolks and beat to blend thoroughly. Cook over moderate heat, stirring, until thickened; do not let the mixture boil. Remove from the heat and divide in half. Add the melted chocolate and the vanilla to one half and the rum to the other. Chill until the mixtures mound when dropped from a spoon. Beat the egg whites until stiff but not dry. Divide the beaten whites in half. Fold half into the chocolate mixture and the other half into the rum mixture. Spread the chocolate mixture over the crumb crust, then spread the rum mixture over the chocolate mixture. Whip the cream and spread that over all. Refrigerate until ready to serve.

Fruit or Berry Tarts (6 small tarts)

Tart Pastry dough for 9-inch tart (p. 391)
3 cups (¾ L) drained cooked fruit or fresh
   berries, sugared
1½ cups (3½ dL) currant jelly, or 1 cup (¼ L)
   heavy cream, whipped with some sugar

Preheat the oven to 375°F (190°C). Line six 4-inch tart tins with the pastry dough, prick the bottoms, and bake for about 10 minutes, or until the pastry is golden. Cool and remove from the tins. Just before serving, fill each baked tart shell with ½ cup fruit or berries. Melt the currant jelly in a pan over low heat and pour it over the fruit to glaze. Or top each tart with sweetened whipped cream.

Lemon Tarts (6 small tarts)

Tart Pastry dough for 9-inch tart (p. 391)
¼ pound (115 g) butter
1½ cups (300 g) sugar
Grated rind of 2 lemons
Juice of 3 lemons
6 eggs, slightly beaten
Topping: 1 cup (¼ L) heavy cream, whipped

Preheat the oven to 375°F (190°C). Line six 4-inch tart tins with the pastry dough, prick the bottoms, and bake for about 10 minutes or until the pastry is golden. Cool and remove from the tins. Mix the butter, sugar, lemon rind, lemon juice, and eggs together in a heavy-bottomed pan or double boiler. Cook over moderate heat, stirring constantly, until thick. Cool in the refrigerator. Before serving, fill the tart shells with lemon filling and top with whipped cream.

Pecan Tarts (6 small tarts)

Tart Pastry dough for 9-inch tart (p. 391)
3 eggs
¾ cup (1¾ dL) dark-brown sugar

¼ teaspoon salt
1 cup (¼ L) dark corn syrup
½ teaspoon vanilla
2 tablespoons melted butter
1 cup (¼ L) pecan pieces
Topping: 1 cup (¼ L) heavy cream, whipped;
   sugar

Preheat the oven to 375°F (190°C). Line six 4-inch tart tins with the pastry dough; set aside. Beat the eggs in a bowl for a minute or less, then add the brown sugar, salt, corn syrup, vanilla, and melted butter. Stir vigorously, then add the pecans. Pour filling into tarts. Bake for 25 minutes or until the filling is set. Before serving, top with lightly sweetened whipped cream.

Desserts, Fruit Desserts & Dessert Sauces

Floating Island (serves six)

An ingenious mind conceived this simple, wonderful dessert. All the pieces fit together perfectly, like a puzzle.

2¼ cups (5½ dL) milk
3 egg whites
1 cup (200 g) sugar
5 egg yolks
2 teaspoons vanilla

Put the milk in a skillet and bring to a simmer over moderately low heat. While the milk is heating, beat the egg whites in a large bowl, slowly adding ⅓ cup of the sugar and beating until shiny and stiff. Using two soupspoons, shape the "islands" by scooping the meringue onto one spoon and placing the other spoon gently on top to shape. Slide the meringues into the barely simmering milk, only three or four at a time. Poach them 1 or 2 minutes on each side, just until they feel firm to the touch, then remove them to paper towels to drain. Continue to poach the remaining "islands" until all the meringue is used. You will have about 12 meringues, measuring 1½ × 2½ inches. Put the egg yolks in a bowl and beat them until they are thick and pale, slowly adding the remaining ⅔ cup of sugar. Gradually add the simmering milk in which the meringues were poached, stirring well. Transfer to a heavy-bottomed pan and cook over low heat, stirring constantly, until the mixture thickens; do *not* boil. Pour into a bowl, stir in the vanilla, and let cool. Put the custard in a shallow bowl and arrange the "islands" on top. Chill well before serving.

Baked Custard (serves eight)

This kindly old dessert still nourishes and comforts. Traditionally served in familiar brown custard cups, it can also be made in one large baking dish.

2 egg yolks
3 eggs
½ cup (100 g) sugar
⅛ teaspoon salt
3 cups (¾ L) very hot milk
1½ teaspoons vanilla
Nutmeg

Preheat the oven to 325°F (165°C). Butter a 1-quart baking dish or 8 ramekins. Set a shallow pan large enough to hold the baking dish or ramekins in the oven, and fill it with 1 inch of hot water. Beat the yolks and eggs together just enough to blend. Stir in the sugar and salt and slowly add the hot milk, stirring constantly. Add the vanilla. Strain into the baking dish or dishes and sprinkle with some nutmeg. Put in the pan and bake for about 45 minutes; the custard is set when a knife inserted in the center comes out clean.

Coconut Custard. Add *½ cup flaked coconut* to the custard mixture before putting it into the baking dishes.

Chocolate Custard. Melt *1½ ounces unsweetened chocolate* in the milk while it is being heated to make the custard.

Caramel Custard. Melt *½ cup sugar* in a heavy-bottomed skillet and cook without stirring, swirling the pan so that the sugar moves about as it melts. When the sugar becomes caramel-colored, pour about 1 tablespoon of the caramelized sugar into each custard cup and swirl around to coat the bottom and sides. (Or if you are using a large baking dish, pour all the caramelized sugar into it and swirl quickly to coat the bottom and sides.) The caramel will harden at first, but don't worry, the next step takes care of that. Pour the custard on top of the caramel-lined cups (or dish) and bake as above.

Coffee Custard. Add *2 tablespoons instant coffee* to the milk before it is heated to make the custard.

Crème Brûlée (serves six to eight)

Crème brûlée, or "burnt cream," is a simple and sublime custard dessert. Its brown-sugar topping is melted under the broiler, forming a very thin candied sheet.

2 egg yolks, slightly beaten
2 eggs, slightly beaten
⅓ cup (65 g) granulated sugar
⅛ teaspoon salt
2 cups (½ L) very hot heavy cream
1½ cups (3½ dL) dark-brown sugar, sifted or
    sieved

Mix the egg yolks, eggs, granulated sugar, and salt together in the top of a double boiler. Add the hot cream slowly, beating constantly; cook, stirring constantly, until slightly thickened. Pour into a 10 × 6-inch baking dish about 2 inches deep. Cover and refrigerate. Just before serving, preheat the broiler. Sprinkle the brown sugar *evenly* all over the top of the cream, no more than ¼ inch thick. Run the dish under the broiler and, watching carefully, heat just until the brown sugar melts and turns shiny. Remove and serve immediately.

French Chocolate Mousse
(serves six to eight)

Lighter than many mousses, this has no cream. Serve small portions and you will leave the table feeling almost guiltless.

6-ounce (180-g) package semisweet chocolate
  bits
4 eggs, separated
1 teaspoon vanilla, or 1 tablespoon rum

Melt the chocolate bits in a heavy-bottomed pan over very low heat, stirring often to prevent burning; set aside. Beat the egg yolks until pale and lemon-colored. Slowly stir in the chocolate and blend well. Beat the egg whites until stiff but not dry. Add a third of the whites to the yolks and chocolate, add the vanilla or rum, mix well, then carefully fold in the remaining whites. Spoon into individual serving dishes or a serving bowl. Cover and chill at least 8 hours before serving.

Baked Rice Pudding (serves six to eight)

This bears no resemblance to the standard cafeteria version. Long, slow baking gives the rice a golden color and a thick creamy texture. Some purists don't even like the addition of nutmeg, but it does give the pudding a lovely flavor. Serve warm or cold, with heavy cream.

4 cups (1 L) milk
½ teaspoon salt
⅔ cup (125 g) sugar
½ teaspoon nutmeg (optional)
3 tablespoons rice

Preheat the oven to 300°F (150°C). Put all the ingredients in a buttered baking dish and stir to blend.

Bake for 3½ hours, stirring three times during the first hour of baking so the rice doesn't settle.

Raisin Rice Pudding. Add *½ cup raisins* to the ingredients.

Chocolate Rice Pudding. Add *2 ounces melted unsweetened chocolate* to the ingredients.

Chocolate Bread Pudding
(serves eight)

Soft as a pillow with a full, light, chocolate-pudding taste.

2 ounces (60 g) unsweetened chocolate
1 quart (1 L) scalded milk
2 cups (½ L) homemade bread crumbs
⅓ cup (65 g) sugar
¼ cup (60 g) butter, melted
2 eggs, slightly beaten
¼ teaspoon salt
1 teaspoon vanilla

Preheat the oven to 325°F (165°C). Butter a 1½- or 2-quart baking dish. Break the chocolate into bits and melt in the milk, stirring until smooth. Add the bread crumbs and set aside to cool. When lukewarm, add remaining ingredients. Mix well, pour into the buttered dish, and bake for about 50 minutes or until set. Serve with *whipped cream.*

Lemon Pudding (serves six)

An old favorite, a delicious dessert with its soft lemony custard on the bottom and sponge cake texture on top. Don't let it get too brown.

2 tablespoons butter
⅞ cup (170 g) sugar
3 eggs
1 cup (¼ L) milk
1½ tablespoons flour
⅓ cup (¾ dL) lemon juice
Grated rind of 1 lemon

Preheat oven to 350°F (180°C). Beat the butter until soft, then gradually add the sugar, beating until it is all incorporated. Separate the eggs and beat in the egg yolks one by one. Add the milk, flour, lemon juice, and rind, and beat to mix well, although the mixture will have a curdled look. Beat the egg whites until they form soft peaks, then fold into the batter. Turn into a 1½-quart baking dish and set in a pan of hot water that comes halfway up the sides of the dish. Bake for 50–60 minutes. Let cool and serve either tepid or chilled, with a pitcher of *heavy cream*.

Indian Pudding (serves eight to ten)

Spicy, coarse, and dark brown, an old-fashioned dessert that celebrates the Indians' gift of corn.

4 cups (1 L) milk
½ cup (1 dL) yellow cornmeal

⅓ cup (¾ dL) dark-brown sugar
⅓ cup (65 g) granulated sugar
⅓ cup (¾ dL) molasses
1 teaspoon salt
4 tablespoons butter
½ teaspoon powdered ginger
½ teaspoon cinnamon

Preheat the oven to 275°F (135°C). Heat 2 cups of the milk until very hot and pour it slowly over the cornmeal, stirring constantly. Cook in a double boiler over simmering water for 10–15 minutes, until the cornmeal mixture is creamy. Add the remaining ingredients and mix well. Spoon into a buttered 1½-quart baking dish, pour the remaining 2 cups of milk on top, set into a pan of hot water, and bake for 2½–3 hours or until set. The pudding will become firmer as it cools. Serve with *heavy cream* or *vanilla ice cream*.

Bread-and-Butter Pudding (serves six)

A delectable old-fashioned dessert that emerges puffy from the oven, then falls slowly; golden and slightly crusty on top, it's soft and spoonable inside. Some purists don't even care to flavor this pudding with vanilla and cinnamon, preferring just the good buttery flavor. The important thing is to use a good textured white bread, preferably homemade, which can be a few days old; an equivalent amount of Italian or French bread will do, too, and it's a good way to use up pieces that turn stale so quickly.

Soft butter
7 slices good quality white bread
1 quart (1 L) milk
3 eggs, slightly beaten
½ cup (100 g) sugar
¼ teaspoon salt
½ cup (1 dL) raisins
1 teaspoon vanilla (optional)
½ teaspoon cinnamon (optional)

Preheat the oven to 325°F (165°C). Butter a 2-quart baking dish. Spread a generous amount of butter on one side of each slice of bread and line the bottom and sides of the baking dish. Mix together the milk, eggs, sugar, salt, raisins, and vanilla and cinnamon, if you are using them, and pour over the bread. Place any extra pieces of bread on top and press down so they are submerged. Let stand about 10 minutes, a little longer if the bread is particularly dry. Bake covered for 30 minutes, then uncover and bake for 30 minutes more. If you like a crustier brown top, slip the dish under a hot broiler a few minutes until deep golden. Serve warm with a pitcher of *heavy cream*.

Dessert Crêpes or French Pancakes (sixteen 5-inch pancakes)

Follow the recipe for Crêpes (p. 318), adding *2 tablespoons sugar* to the batter.

Jelly Crêpes. Spread warm crêpes with *jelly, jam,* or *fruit preserves* (*apricot* is particularly good). Roll them and dust them with *confectioners' sugar.*

Whipped-Cream Crêpes. Whip *1 cup heavy cream,* sweetening it with *2 tablespoons confectioners' sugar.* Fold in *1 cup chopped toasted almonds.* Spread on the pancakes and roll them up. Dust with confectioners' sugar and a sprinkling of additional *chopped almonds.*

Crêpes Suzette. Cream *1 cup butter* and add *1 cup confectioners' sugar,* mixing together until light. Add the *grated rind of 3 oranges,* the *juice of 1½ oranges,* and *5 tablespoons Grand Marnier* or *other brandy.* Melt over low heat in a skillet or chafing dish until hot. Fold the pancakes in quarters and add a few at a time to the pan. Heat very slowly, spooning the sauce over them until well saturated. Remove to a heatproof platter and keep warm until all are ready to serve. Pour the sauce in the pan over them and serve. If you wish to flambée, warm ¼ cup brandy, ignite, and pour flaming over the crêpes.

Strawberry (or Other Fresh Berry) Crêpes. Fill each crêpe with about *2 tablespoons crushed strawberries* (or other berries) that have been tossed first with a little sugar and left to stand a short while. Frozen berries, drained of some of the juice, are also good. Roll the crêpe up, top with *confectioners' sugar* and a dollop of *sour cream* or *whipped cream.*

421

English Plum Pudding (serves six)

English plum pudding makes a lovely Christmas gift. Wrapped well in a brandy-dampened towel, it will keep in the refrigerator for several months. Reheat in the top of a double boiler before serving.

10 slices white bread
1 cup (¼ L) scalded milk
½ cup (100 g) sugar
4 eggs, separated
1⅓ cups (3¼ dL) raisins, lightly floured
½ cup (1 dL) finely chopped dried figs
3 tablespoons finely chopped citron
¾ cup (1¾ dL) finely chopped suet
3 tablespoons brandy
1 teaspoon nutmeg
½ teaspoon cinnamon
¼ teaspoon ground cloves
¼ teaspoon mace
1 teaspoon salt

Butter a 2-quart steamed pudding mold. Heat water in a pot large enough to hold the mold. Crumb the bread, and soak it in the hot milk. Cool and add the sugar, the well-beaten egg yolks, raisins, figs, and citron. Break the suet up with a fork and mash until it is creamy or use a food processor. Add to the crumb mixture, then stir in the brandy, nutmeg, cinnamon, cloves, mace, and salt. Beat until well blended. Beat the egg whites until they are stiff but not dry. Stir a third of the whites into the pudding mixture, then gently fold in the remaining whites. Spoon the mixture into the mold and cover. Put in the large pot and steam for 6 hours. Remove and let cool for 10 minutes before unmolding. Serve warm with *Hard Sauce* (see below).

Hard Sauce (1 cup)

5 tablespoons butter
1 cup (¼ L) confectioners' sugar
½ teaspoon vanilla

Cream the butter, then slowly add the sugar, beating well with an electric beater or by hand until creamy and pale yellow. Add the vanilla and blend. Cover and refrigerate until needed. Serve cool, but not chilled.

Chocolate Soufflé (serves six)

This is a first-rate chocolate soufflé, light and yet very chocolaty. Most chocolate soufflés are so dense with flavor that their essential lightness is lost.

1½ ounces (45 g) unsweetened chocolate
5 tablespoons sugar
2 tablespoons butter
2 tablespoons flour
⅛ teaspoon salt
¾ cup (1¾ dL) milk
3 eggs, separated
1 teaspoon vanilla

Preheat the oven to 325°F (165°C). Butter a 1½-quart soufflé dish and sprinkle it with sugar. Put the chocolate, 2 tablespoons of the sugar, and 2 table-spoons hot water in a small pan and heat slowly, stirring occasionally, until the chocolate is melted and smooth; remove from the heat and set aside. Melt the butter in a skillet, then add the flour and salt. Cook over low heat, stirring, for several min-utes, then gradually stir in the milk. Cook to the boiling point, stirring; the sauce will become smooth and thick. Blend in the chocolate mixture. Beat the egg yolks well. Stir a little of the hot sauce into the yolks, then add the yolks to the remaining sauce. Stir well, then set aside to cool. Beat the egg whites until foamy, slowly add the remaining 3 ta-blespoons of sugar, and continue beating until stiff but not dry. Stir a fourth of the whites into the chocolate mixture, then fold in the remaining whites. Stir in the vanilla. Spoon into the soufflé dish and bake for 35–40 minutes. Serve with *whipped cream*.

Fruit Soufflé (serves four to five)

This fruit soufflé, made without a cream-sauce base, is as light as a cloud, a delicate reminder of summer during the long, cold winter months. Use canned applesauce, apricots, sour cherries, or pineapple or fresh berries, apricots, pears, or peaches. None of these fruits need cooking, but they should be well drained. The hot fruit purée will set and stabilize the egg whites.

¾ cup (1¾ dL) fresh or canned fruit purée
1 tablespoon freshly squeezed lemon juice

Pinch of salt
Sugar to taste
3 egg whites

Preheat the oven to 375°F (190°C). Butter a 1-quart soufflé dish and sprinkle it with sugar. Heat the fruit purée in a small pan. Add the lemon juice, salt, and sugar, and stir to blend; remove from the heat. Beat the egg whites until stiff but not dry and stir them into the hot purée until evenly blended. Spoon into the soufflé dish and bake for 20–25 minutes.

Bavarian Cream (serves six)

> Bavarian cream is basically English custard made with beaten egg whites, gelatin, and freshly whipped cream. It should be chilled until firm.

1 envelope gelatin
2 eggs, separated
1¼ cups (3 dL) milk
½ cup (100 g) sugar
Pinch of salt
1½ teaspoons vanilla
1 cup (¼ L) heavy cream

Sprinkle the gelatin over ¼ cup cold water and let it soften for 5 minutes. Beat the egg yolks slightly. Heat the milk in a heavy-bottomed pan until very hot, then stir a little into the beaten yolks. Return the yolks to the remaining milk in the pan and add the sugar, salt, and gelatin. Stir constantly over medium heat until slightly thickened; do not overcook or boil or the egg yolks will curdle. Remove from the heat and refrigerate for about 15 minutes or until cool. Add the vanilla. Beat the egg whites until they are stiff but not dry and fold them into the custard. Beat the cream until it barely holds soft peaks and fold it into the custard. Spoon into a 2-quart mold, cover, and chill until firm. Unmold before serving.

Orange Charlotte (serves eight to ten)

Sections of orange, placed around the mold before the charlotte is spooned in, offer good contrast in taste and texture.

1 envelope gelatin
1 cup (200 g) sugar
4 tablespoons lemon juice
1 cup (¼ L) orange juice
3 egg whites
1 cup (¼ L) heavy cream
Orange sections

Sprinkle the gelatin over ¼ cup cold water and let it soften for 5 minutes. Mix the sugar, ¾ cup water, lemon juice, and orange juice together in a pan, add the gelatin, and heat, stirring, until the gelatin dissolves. Chill until as thick as unbeaten egg white, then beat until frothy. Beat the egg whites stiff but not dry and fold them in. Whip the cream to soft peaks and fold it in. Line a 2-quart mold with orange sections, spoon in the charlotte, and chill. Unmold before serving.

Frozen Vanilla Mousse (serves six)

Light and icy cold, plumped up with rich cream, frozen vanilla mousse provides a gentle end to a hot and spicy meal.

2 egg whites
½ cup (1 dL) confectioners' sugar
2 cups (½ L) heavy cream
2 teaspoons vanilla

Beat the egg whites until foamy, slowly add ¼ cup of the sugar, and continue beating until the whites hold stiff peaks. Whip the cream, slowly adding the remaining ¼ cup sugar, until the cream barely holds soft peaks. Stir in the vanilla, then fold in the egg whites. Spoon into a mold and freeze. Unmold before serving.

Frozen Apricot Mousse. Gently add *1 cup apricot purée* after the egg whites and cream have been folded together.

Frozen Coffee Mousse. Dissolve *3 tablespoons instant coffee* in *¼ cup hot water*. Follow the recipe for Frozen Vanilla Mousse, gently stirring in the coffee after the egg whites and cream have been folded together.

Frozen Chocolate Mousse (serves six)

1 cup (¼ L) cold milk
1 envelope gelatin
2 ounces (60 g) unsweetened chocolate
¾ cup (150 g) sugar

2 teaspoons vanilla
2 cups (½ L) heavy cream

Put the milk in a heavy-bottomed pan, sprinkle the gelatin over it, and let soften for 5 minutes. Add the chocolate and sugar and cook over moderate heat, stirring constantly, until the chocolate melts and is well blended. Chill until lukewarm. Add the vanilla. Whip the cream until it holds soft peaks, then fold it into the chocolate mixture. Spoon into a mold and freeze. Unmold and serve with *unsweetened whipped cream*.

Angel Parfait (serves six to eight)

This whipped cream dessert has a sugar-syrup foundation. The syrup is poured over stiffly beaten egg whites, and whipped cream and vanilla are folded in. When you taste it you will understand its name: it is truly angelic.

3 egg whites
Pinch of salt
1 cup (200 g) sugar
2 teaspoons vanilla
2 cups (½ L) heavy cream

Combine the egg whites and salt in a bowl and beat until stiff but not dry; set aside. Combine the sugar and ½ cup water in a small, heavy-bottomed pan. Heat *without stirring* until the syrup boils. Cover with a lid to steam the sugar crystals down the sides and continue to boil for 3 minutes. Remove the lid and boil without stirring for 10–15 minutes more until the syrup registers 230°–232°F on a candy thermometer. Slowly pour the syrup over the beaten egg whites and beat constantly until the meringue is almost at room temperature. Add the vanilla and blend. Whip the cream to soft peaks and fold it in. Spoon into a mold, bowl, or parfait glasses, cover, and freeze until ready to serve. You will have about 5 cups.

Frozen Raspberry Soufflé (serves eight)

By freezing this in a straight-sided dish with a collar around it, the final presentation will look like a soufflé rising above the dish. Pipe extra whipped cream on top and decorate with a few extra raspberries, if you want it to look particularly elegant.

5 egg whites
¾ cup (150 g) sugar
3 cups (¾ L) raspberries
2 cups (½ L) heavy cream, whipped

Combine the egg whites and sugar in a metal bowl and place over hot water until the mixture is tepid (warm to the touch). Remove from the heat and beat with an electric beater until stiff. Set aside. Purée the raspberries and remove the seeds by forcing the purée through a strainer. Fold the raspberry purée into the egg-white mixture and fold in the whipped cream. Make a collar around a 1½-quart soufflé dish. Spoon the raspberry mousse into the dish and freeze at least six hours. Remove the collar to serve.

Frozen Strawberry Soufflé. Use *3 cups strawberries* instead of the raspberries.

Frozen Apricot Soufflé. Use *3 cups mashed apricots* (dried apricots that have been stewed in a little water until soft are fine) instead of the raspberries.

French Vanilla Ice Cream (3 pints)

Excellent, creamy, and smooth, this French ice cream takes a little more trouble to make than the recipe that follows. Use vanilla bean for real French vanilla flavor; vanilla extract is best in the variations. Either this or the Philadelphia Ice Cream that follows lends itself to the many variations in flavor on p. 431.

½ cup (100 g) sugar
⅛ teaspoon salt
4 egg yolks, slightly beaten
2 cups (½ L) very hot milk
1 teaspoon finely grated vanilla bean, or 1
    tablespoon vanilla extract
1 pint (½ L) heavy cream

Mix the sugar, salt, and egg yolks together in a heavy-bottomed pan. Slowly stir in the hot milk and the grated vanilla bean if used. Cook, continuing to stir, until slightly thickened; remove and cool. Strain, then add the cream. Add the vanilla extract, if you are not using vanilla bean. Chill. Freeze in a hand-cranked or electric ice cream freezer.

Philadelphia Ice Cream (3 pints)

Deep in flavor, light in texture, easy to make—
Philadelphia ice cream is richer and creamier
than French vanilla ice cream. If it is too rich for
your taste, use one part light cream to one part
heavy—a better proportion for some of the rich
variations that follow.

1 quart (1 L) heavy cream, or 2 cups (½ L) heavy
   cream and 2 cups (½ L) light cream
¾ cup (150 g) sugar
Pinch of salt
1 teaspoon finely grated vanilla bean, or 2
   teaspoons vanilla extract

Mix everything together and stir until the sugar is
dissolved. Freeze in a hand-cranked or electric ice
cream freezer.

Flavored Ice Creams

Using either one of the preceding recipes for
French Vanilla Ice Cream or Philadelphia Ice
Cream, vary the flavorings as follows:

Butterscotch Ice Cream. First cook the sugar with
2 tablespoons butter until melted and well
browned. Then heat the milk or cream and dissolve
the sugar-butter in it. Add the rest of the ingredients and cool before freezing.

Caramel Ice Cream. First caramelize half the sugar
(see p. 444). Then heat the milk or cream and

431

dissolve the caramelized sugar in it. Proceed with the rest of the recipe and be sure to cool the mixture before freezing.

Burnt Almond Ice Cream. Add, along with the vanilla, *1 cup finely chopped almonds* that have been *blanched and toasted* until golden.

Coffee Ice Cream. Add *2 tablespoons instant coffee* at the same time as you add the vanilla.

Ginger Ice Cream. Add *½ cup finely chopped preserved ginger* and *3 tablespoons ginger syrup* when adding the vanilla.

Maple and Maple Walnut Ice Cream. Use *½ cup maple syrup* instead of the sugar. Add *1 cup chopped walnuts,* if desired.

Mint Ice Cream. Use *1 teaspoon oil of peppermint* instead of vanilla. Color lightly with *green vegetable coloring.*

Pistachio Ice Cream. Omit the vanilla and add *1 teaspoon almond extract* and *½ cup pistachio nuts, chopped fine.* Color lightly with *green vegetable coloring.*

Chocolate Chip Ice Cream. Use only ½ teaspoon vanilla and add *1 cup chocolate chips* to the mixture before freezing.

Chestnut Ice Cream. Add *1 cup chopped preserved chestnuts and their syrup* and use only half the amount of sugar called for.

Peanut Brittle Ice Cream. Omit the sugar. Crush *½ pound peanut brittle* or pulverize in the blender, then sift into the ice cream mixture. Taste and add additional sugar if necessary.

Peppermint Candy Ice Cream. Omit the sugar, Crush *½ pound peppermint-stick candy* and add to heated milk or cream. Cool before freezing.

Praline Ice Cream. Add *1 cup finely chopped almonds* that have been *blanched and toasted* until golden. Caramelize half the sugar, heat the milk or cream, and then add the caramelized sugar slowly. Cool before freezing.

Fresh Fruit Ice Cream
(about 1½ quarts)

Using light cream or milk makes this a fresh fruit sherbet; heavy cream makes a rich ice cream.

2 cups (½ L) milk
2 cups (½ L) heavy cream
1¼ cups (250 g) sugar (depending on how sweet the fruit)
1½ cups (3½ dL) fresh puréed peeled peaches, apricots, strawberries, or raspberries
Pinch of salt

Put the milk and cream in a pan and heat to the boiling point. Remove from the heat and add half the sugar; stir to dissolve. Cool. Sprinkle the remaining half of sugar over the puréed fruit, taste for sweetness and add more sugar, if needed, after adding the sweetened milk and cream. Stir in the salt and blend well. Freeze in a hand-cranked or electric ice cream freezer.

Old-fashioned Chocolate Ice Cream   (1½ quarts)

There is even more richness and depth to this lovely ice cream—a must for chocolate ice cream lovers.

1¼ cups (250 g) sugar
1 tablespoon flour
Dash of salt
2 eggs, slightly beaten
2 cups (½ L) milk
2 squares bitter chocolate
2 cups (½ L) cream
1 tablespoon vanilla

Mix the sugar, flour, and salt together, and add the eggs. Heat the milk and melt the chocolate in it. Combine the mixtures and cook over medium heat in a heavy-bottomed saucepan, stirring constantly, until lightly thickened. Cool, then add the cream and the vanilla. Strain and freeze in a hand-cranked or electric ice cream freezer.

Lemon Milk Sherbet   (3 pints)

Pleasingly acid, light, and creamy. The unchilled mixture may look curdled, but it will be smooth after freezing.

1 cup (¼ L) freshly squeezed lemon juice
1½ cups (300 g) sugar
Pinch of salt
1 quart (1 L) milk

Mix all the ingredients together in a bowl. Freeze in metal bowls or three ice cube trays in the refrigerator freezer.

Lemon Ice (3 pints)

Lovely, fresh, and sharp.

1¾ cups (350 g) sugar
1 tablespoon grated lemon rind
¾ cup (1¾ dL) lemon juice

Bring 3 cups water to a boil, and stir in the sugar until dissolved. Cool, then add the lemon rind and juice. Freeze in a hand-cranked or electric ice cream freezer or in the refrigerator freezer, using three ice cube trays or a metal bowl.

Orange Ice. Omit the lemon rind and juice and substitute *3 cups orange juice, ½ cup lemon juice,* and the *grated rind of 2 oranges.*

Grape Ice. Omit the lemon rind and juice and substitute *2 cups grape juice, ⅔ cups orange juice,* and *¼ cup lemon juice.*

Raspberry Ice. Omit the lemon rind and juice and substitute *2 cups raspberry juice.*

Hot Fruit Compote (serves eight)

1 can pears
1 can Bing cherries
1 can whole apricots, pitted

1 tablespoon slivered orange peel
1 tablespoon brandy or rum, or 1 teaspoon vanilla

Drain the juice from the cans. Add to the juice the slivered orange peel, and simmer gently for 30 minutes. Add the fruit and the brandy, rum, or vanilla, and heat through. Serve with *whipped cream* flavored with the same flavoring you have used in the fruit.

Other combinations:

Peaches, plums, raisins (added to the juice for the last 10 minutes of simmering), and slivered toasted almonds scattered over the cream.

Peaches, pears, apricots, and chestnuts.

Plums, apricots, and cherries.

Pineapple, mandarin orange sections, and black cherries.

Prunes, apricots, and greengage plums.

Cooked apple slices, raisins (simmered as above), and walnut halves on top of the cream.

Baked Fruit Compote   (serves four)

2 cups (½ L) canned fruit: peaches, apricots, pears, greengage plums, cherries
2 tablespoons brown sugar
Grated rind and juice of ½ lemon
½ cup (1 dL) macaroon or other cookie crumbs

Preheat the oven to 350°F (180°C). Arrange layers of fruit in a deep baking dish, sprinkling each layer with brown sugar, lemon rind, and lemon juice. Then pour the reserved juice from the can(s) on top, sprinkle on the crumbs, and bake 35 minutes. Serve warm or cold with *cream*.

Applesauce (serves four)

Use a food mill for this, if you have one: you won't have to peel or core the apples if you do, and cooking them with their skins adds taste and color. Late summer and fall apples are so flavorful that they don't need spices, but apples that are kept long into winter will need some tarting up and the added smoothness of butter.

8 tart apples
Sugar
½-inch cinnamon stick (optional)
2 cloves (optional)
2 tablespoons butter (optional)
Few gratings of nutmeg (optional)

Cut the apples in large chunks; pare and core them if you do not have a food mill. Put them in a pan, add a very small amount of water, about 2 tablespoons sugar, and the cinnamon and cloves, if you wish. Cover and cook slowly until tender, about 15–20 minutes. Put the apples through a food mill to remove the skins, seeds, and spices, or simply remove the spices if you have peeled and cored the apples before cooking them. Stir in the butter, if you like, and add more sugar to taste and nutmeg if desired.

Apple Crisp (serves six)

Sweet soft apples, mildly spiced, with cinnamony crisp brown crumbs on top.

5 cups (1¼ L) peeled and sliced apples
¾ cup (105 g) flour
1 cup (200 g) sugar
½ teaspoon cinnamon
¼ teaspoon salt
¼ pound (115 g) butter, in small pieces

Preheat the oven to 350°F (180°C). Butter a 1½-quart baking dish, spread the apples in it, and sprinkle ⅓ cup water on top. Combine the flour, sugar, cinnamon, and salt in a bowl, and rub in the butter with your fingers until it resembles coarse crumbs. Spread evenly over the apples. Bake for about 30 minutes or until the crust is browned. Serve with *heavy cream.*

Apple Brown Betty (serves six)

If your apples are full of flavor, you won't need the lemon.

5 tablespoons melted butter
2 cups (½ L) homemade dry bread crumbs
5 cups (1¼ L) (about 1½ pounds, 675 g) peeled, sliced tart apples
½ cup (1 dL) brown sugar
½ teaspoon cinnamon
Grated rind and juice of ½ lemon (optional)

438

Preheat the oven to 350°F (180°C). Butter a 1½-quart casserole or baking dish, preferably one with a lid. Toss the melted butter and crumbs together lightly in a bowl. Spread about a third of the crumbs in the baking dish. Toss the apples, sugar, cinnamon, lemon rind, and lemon juice together in a bowl. Spread half the apple mixture over the crumbs, add another layer of crumbs, a layer of the remaining apples, and a final layer of crumbs on top. Add ⅓ cup hot water. Cover with a lid or with foil and bake for 25 minutes. Uncover and bake 20 minutes more. Serve with *heavy cream*.

Peach Brown Betty. Omit the cinnamon, and optional lemon juice and rind, and substitute *5 cups sliced peaches* for the apples.

Apricot Brown Betty. Substitute *3 cups fresh apricots* or *stewed and drained dried apricots* for the apples and use *⅓ cup stewing liquid* instead of the water.

Glazed Baked Apples (4 apples)

Use firm apples that will hold their shape, such as Delicious, Rome Beauty, Cortland, greening, or other hard fall apples.

4 firm apples
½ cup (100 g) sugar

Preheat the oven to 375°F (190°C). Core the apples and pare them one-third of the way down from the stem end. Put them close together in a baking dish, peeled side up. Add ½ inch of water and bake, basting every 10 minutes or so with the pan juices, until the apples can be pierced easily with a fork but still hold their shape. Turn up the oven heat to 425°F (220°C). Sprinkle the apples with the sugar and bake until the sugar dissolves and the tops are crisp and lightly browned, about 5–10 minutes. Serve with some of the juices.

Sautéed Bananas (4 bananas)

This lovely dessert is also a fine accompaniment to curry or chicken dishes.

4 tablespoons butter
4 firm ripe bananas
4 tablespoons confectioners' sugar

Melt the butter in a skillet. Peel the bananas and cut them in half lengthwise. Cook over moderate heat for 5 minutes, turning once. Remove to a dish and spoon the butter from the pan over them. Sift the confectioners' sugar on top.

Blackberry Rolypoly (serves six)

You may substitute any other berry for the blackberries.

6 cups (1½ L) blackberries
1 cup (200 g) sugar

½ teaspoon salt
1 recipe Shortcake dough (p. 346)
2 tablespoons butter, melted
1½ cups (3½ dL) heavy cream, whipped

Preheat the oven to 425°F (220°C). Butter an 8 × 10-inch pan. Combine the berries, sugar, and salt in a bowl. Toss very gently to mix. Set aside. Roll the shortcake dough into a rectangle ½ inch thick. Brush with the melted butter. Spread half the berries over the dough. Roll up like a jelly roll and put into the pan, fold side down. Put the rest of the berries around the roll. Bake for 30 minutes. Slice and serve warm or cold with whipped cream.

Cherries Jubilee (serves six)

2 cups (½ L) fresh Bing cherries, or 1 large can
  black cherries
Sugar
1 tablespoon cornstarch
¼ cup (½ dL) brandy
1 quart (1 L) vanilla ice cream

If using fresh cherries, stem and pit them, then cook them about 5 minutes in 1 cup water and 3 tablespoons sugar. If using canned cherries, add only 1 tablespoon sugar. Dissolve the cornstarch in 1 tablespoon water, then add 1 cup of the cherry cooking juice or of the canned juice, bring to a boil, and simmer with the cherries for 2 minutes. Heat the brandy, add to the cherries, then light and pour them flaming over the ice cream.

Stewed or Baked Pears (serves four)

4 firm pears
½ cup (100 g) sugar
Lemon rind or cinnamon stick
Heavy cream

Peel the pears, cut them in quarters lengthwise, and remove the cores. Combine the sugar with ½ cup water and some lemon rind or cinnamon stick; cook rapidly for 5 minutes. Add the pears, cover, and cook slowly until tender but still firm; or bake in a 300°F (150°C) oven. Serve warm or cold with cream.

Pears with Cointreau. When pears are cooked, remove them from the syrup and cook the syrup until it is as thick as honey. Add *1 tablespoon Cointreau,* pour over the pears, and chill. Serve with cream.

Pears in Port Wine. Pour *Port wine* over the cooked pears, cover, and let sit for at least 1 hour.

Pears Helene. When pears are cooked, add *vanilla or brandy* to taste and let cool in the syrup. Serve with *vanilla ice cream* and top with *Creamy Chocolate Sauce* (see below).

Creamy Chocolate Sauce (1½ cups)

1½ cups (3½ dL) milk
2 ounces (60 g) unsweetened chocolate
½ cup (100 g) sugar
1 tablespoon flour
Pinch of salt

2 tablespoons butter
1 teaspoon vanilla

Heat the milk and chocolate in a heavy-bottomed pan until the chocolate melts; beat until smooth. Mix the sugar, flour, and salt together and stir slowly into the chocolate mixture. Cook, stirring constantly, for 5 minutes. Remove from the heat and blend in the butter and vanilla.

Strawberries Romanoff (serves eight)

1 pint (½ L) vanilla ice cream
1 cup (¼ L) heavy cream
Juice of 1 lemon
4 tablespoons Cointreau
2 quarts (2 L) strawberries, washed and hulled

Put the ice cream in a 2-quart bowl and beat lightly to soften. Whip the cream until soft peaks form. Fold the cream, lemon juice, and Cointreau into the ice cream. Add the strawberries and stir gently. Serve immediately.

Rich Butterscotch Sauce (2 cups)

Creamy and not very thick, this is good over mousses, custards, and the like.

¼ pound (115 g) butter
2⅔ cups (6½ dL) light-brown sugar (1 pound, 450g)
½ teaspoon vinegar

½ cup (1 dL) heavy cream
Pinch of salt

Mix all the ingredients together in a heavy-bottomed pan. Cook over low heat, stirring occasionally, for 30 minutes.

Caramel Sauce (1 cup)

A thin caramel syrup, clear and deep gold, this is just right over egg custards or vanilla pudding. It will keep indefinitely.

1 cup (200 g) sugar

Put the sugar in a small, heavy-bottomed pan and swirl it over very low heat *without stirring;* it will slowly melt and turn golden. When completely melted, stir in 1 cup boiling water. Cook for 3–4 minutes.

Fudge Sauce (2 cups)

A medium-thick, silky sauce with deep chocolate taste. It is just right over vanilla ice cream.

2 ounces (60 g) unsweetened chocolate
¾ cup (150 g) sugar
¼ teaspoon salt
½ cup (1 dL) light corn syrup
½ cup (1 dL) milk
2 tablespoons butter
1 tablespoon vanilla

Mix the chocolate, sugar, salt, corn syrup, and milk together in a heavy-bottomed pan. Cook over low heat, stirring often, for 20–25 minutes or until thickened. Add the butter. Cool a little, then add the vanilla.

English Custard (Crème Anglaise) (serves five)

A pale-yellow softly flavored vanilla sauce, one of the best of all the dessert sauces and basic to many Bavarian creams and mousses.

2 cups (½ L) milk
4 egg yolks
½ cup (100 g) sugar
1½ teaspoons vanilla

Heat the milk in a heavy-bottomed pan until it is very hot. Beat the egg yolks for about 3 minutes while slowly adding the sugar until mixture is a pale lemon color and thick. Very slowly pour in the hot milk, stirring constantly, until blended. Return the mixture to the pan and cook over medium-low heat to just below the boiling point, stirring constantly, until slightly thickened and the froth has disappeared. Do not boil or the sauce will "curdle." Remove from the heat, quickly pour into a bowl, and stir for a minute or two to cool. When completely cool add the vanilla and blend. Cover and chill until needed. You will have about 2½ cups of custard.

Sea-Foam Sauce (1½ cups)

Creamy, but not heavy; beaten egg white is added just before serving. Try this over Chocolate Bread Pudding (p. 417).

2 tablespoons butter
2 tablespoons flour
½ cup (100 g) sugar
1 egg, separated
1 teaspoon vanilla

Cream the butter, flour, and sugar together in a small saucepan. Beat the egg yolk with ½ cup water, then add to the creamed mixture. Cook over low heat, stirring constantly, until thickened. Cool. Just before serving, add the vanilla. Beat the egg white until stiff but not dry and fold it in.

Sabayon Sauce (1½ cups)

This sauce is especially good over fruit. It is also sometimes served by itself in small glasses as a very light whipped-custard dessert. It must be served at once or it will slowly fall.

Grated rind of ½ lemon
Juice of ½ lemon
¼ cup (½ dL) sherry or Madeira wine
⅓ cup (65 g) sugar
2 eggs, separated

Put the lemon rind, lemon juice, wine, sugar, and egg yolks into the top of a double boiler. Beat with a whisk over simmering water until thick; remove

446

from the heat. Beat the egg whites until stiff but not dry and fold them in. Serve at once.

Melba Sauce (1 cup)

Nothing more than sweetened raspberry juice, but very good over peaches, ice cream, or vanilla mousse.

1 cup (¼ L) fresh or frozen raspberries
¼ cup (50 g) sugar

Purée the raspberries in a blender or food processor. Strain the purée to remove the seeds, put it in a small pan, and stir in the sugar. Cook over medium heat, stirring frequently, until the sugar dissolves; remove and cool. Cover and refrigerate.

Beverages

Irish Coffee (serves one)

1 jigger Irish whiskey
1 teaspoon sugar
1 cup (¼ L) very hot after-dinner coffee
2 tablespoons whipped cream

Put the Irish whiskey in the bottom of a glass or mug. Stir in the sugar and add piping hot strong coffee. Top with the whipped cream and serve immediately.

Café Brûlot (serves six)

Café Brûlot, which has long been a specialty of New Orleans, can provide a dramatic climax to a fine meal. In New Orleans, it is usually prepared in and served from a special silver brûlot bowl that is warmed over an alcohol flame. A chafing dish will do the job effectively.

1½-inch stick cinnamon
5 cloves
3 tablespoons slivered orange peel
3 tablespoons slivered lemon peel
2 lumps sugar

⅓ cup (¾ dL) brandy
2 tablespoons curaçao
3 cups (¾ L) hot after-dinner coffee

Put the cinnamon, cloves, orange and lemon peels, and sugar in a chafing dish or brûlot bowl with a flame under and mash together with the back of a spoon or a pestle. Add the brandy and curaçao, and when hot, ignite. Stir to dissolve the sugar, then gradually add the coffee. Serve in demitasses.

Rum Punch (about 5 quarts)

1 cup (¼ L) sugar
1½ cups (3½ dL) lemon juice
1½ cups (3½ dL) grapefruit juice
5 cups (1¼ L) orange juice
6 cups (1½ L) unsweetened pineapple juice
1 fifth (¾ L) dark Jamaica rum
2 fifths (1½ L) light West Indian rum

Make a sugar syrup by boiling the sugar with 1 cup of water for 5 minutes. Let cool. Mix together with all the other ingredients and let mellow for at least 1 hour. Pour over a large block of ice in a punch bowl and serve when thoroughly chilled.

Champagne Punch (6 quarts)

2 cups (½ L) sugar
1¼ cups (3 dL) lemon juice
2 cups (½ L) apricot nectar

One 6-ounce (1¾ dL) can frozen orange juice
  concentrate
3 cups (½ L) unsweetened apple juice
2 cups s(½ L) unsweetened pineapple juice
2 quarts (2 L) ginger ale
2 fifths (1½ L) champagne

Make a sugar syrup by boiling the sugar with 2 cups of water for 1 minute. Cool. Add the lemon juice, apricot nectar, orange, apple, and pineapple juices to the sugar syrup. Chill. Pour over a large block of ice in a punch bowl and just before serving add the ginger ale and champagne.

Fish House Punch   (4 quarts)

Fish House is the informal name of The State in Schuylkill, the oldest men's club in America, and this is the authentic recipe for its much-esteemed and highly potent punch. For a milder version, more suitable for a wedding reception or holiday bowl, try the variation, but if you want the real thing, this is it.

2 cups (½ L) sugar
1 quart (1 L) lemon or lime juice, or a
  combination
2 fifths (1½ L) dark rum
1 fifth (¾ L) cognac
2–3 ounces peach brandy

Dissolve the sugar in the citrus juice and 2 cups water. Mix in the rest of the ingredients and "brew" by letting it sit 2 hours to exchange flavors. Pour over a block of ice in a punch bowl and serve.

Milder Fish House Punch. Dissolve the sugar in 2 cups water and 2 cups citrus juice. Use only 1 fifth rum and add *3½ cups tea* and *3 quarts ginger ale* to the mixture.

Basic Fruit Punch (nonalcoholic) (3½ quarts)

1½ cups (3½ dL) sugar
1 quart (1 L) strong hot tea
1 quart (1 L) orange juice
1 cup (¼ L) lemon juice
1 quart (1 L) ginger ale
Fresh mint leaves

Dissolve the sugar in the hot tea. Mix together with the citrus juices. Pour over a large block of ice and just before serving add the ginger ale and scatter fresh mint leaves on top.

Variations. Use *½ cup fruit syrup* such as raspberry or strawberry instead of the sugar. You may need some additional sugar; taste and add what is needed. Add *fresh fruits,* such as shredded pineapple, strawberries, sliced peaches or mangoes, to the bowl.

Sangria   (about 4½ quarts)

1 quart (1 L) orange juice
3 quarts (2¾ L) dry red wine
2 oranges, washed and sliced
4 fresh peaches, peeled and sliced
1 lemon, washed and sliced
Up to ¼ cup (1¾ dL) confectioners' sugar
  (optional)
Soda water (optional)

Mix together all except the optional ingredients in several large pitchers and let stand for 4–6 hours. Add ice and taste. If you wish it sweeter, stir in confectioners' sugar to taste. If you like it a little lighter, splash in some soda water. Pour into large wine or old-fashioned glasses, letting a little of the fruit fall into each glass.

Eggnog   (about 8 quarts)

1 dozen eggs, separated
½ teaspoon salt
2¼ or more cups (450 g) sugar
2 or more cups (½ L) bourbon
½ cup (1 dL) rum
1 quart (1 L) milk
2 tablespoons vanilla extract
3 pints (1½ L) heavy cream
Nutmeg

Beat together the egg yolks and salt in a large mixing bowl, slowly adding 1½ cups of the sugar. Continue beating until thick and pale. Stir in the bourbon, rum, milk, and vanilla until well mixed. Beat the egg whites until foamy and slowly add the remaining ¾ cup sugar, continuing to beat until stiff and all the sugar has been incorporated. Whip the cream until stiff. Now fold the egg whites into the yolk mixture and then fold in the whipped cream. Taste and add more bourbon and/or sugar if necessary. Pour into a punch bowl and sprinkle the top with nutmeg.

Hot Cocoa (6 cups)

4 tablespoons unsweetened cocoa
2 tablespoons sugar
Pinch of salt
4 cups milk
Few drops of vanilla extract (optional)
Whipped cream (optional)

Mix the cocoa, sugar, and salt with ½ cup water in a medium-sized saucepan and boil gently for 2 minutes. Add the milk and heat slowly just to the boiling point. Beat well with a beater or whisk and, if you wish, flavor with a few drops of vanilla. Pour into cups and top with a dollop of whipped cream, if desired.

Index

455

blue cheese: dressing, 280
  yogurt, garlic, and,
    dressing, 285
bluefish, 49–50
bordelaise sauce, 153
Boston: baked beans, 193
  brown bread, 314–15
  cream pie, 332–33
  favorite cake, 331–32
bouillon: beef, 19–20
  court, 23
bran: and honey bread,
  295–96
  muffins, 310–11
brandied: cherries, 176
  peaches, preserved,
    175–76
breads: anadama, 297
  apricot almond, 306–7
  banana nut, 309
  bran and honey, 295–96
  brioche, 294–95
  brown, Boston, 314–15
  cheese, 288, 293
  Cincinnati coffee bread,
    298
  corn, 313
  cranberry nut, 308
  date nut, 306
  French, 291–93
  garlic, 292
  herb, 292
  Irish, 314
  nut, 305–6
  oatmeal, 289–90
  pumpkin, 308

raisin and nut, 296–97
rye, 290–91
stuffing, 163–64
white, 287–88
whole-wheat, 288–89
bread-and-butter pickles,
  176–77
bread pudding: bread-and-
  butter, 419–20
  chocolate, 417
brioche bread and rolls,
  294–95
broccoli, basic method for
  cooking, 223–24
  in cheese custard, 224–
    25
  puréed, 224
broth: giblet, 120
  Scotch, 39–40
brown Betty, 438–39
brown bread, Boston,
  314–15
brownies, 372
  butterscotch, 373
brown sauce, 152–53
Brussels sprouts, basic
  method for cooking, 225
buckwheat cakes, 318
burnt almond ice cream,
  431
butter: apple, 175
  cookies, 359, 371–72
  frostings, 351
  rolls, 300
butters, flavored: herb,
  152

459

461

462

cranberries: and apple-
  raisin pie, 400–1
  conserve, 173–74
  nut bread, 308
  and orange relish, 168
  sauce, 167–68
cream filling, 353
cream cheese frosting, 350
cream sauce, 148
crème, Anglaise, 445
  brûlée, 415
creole soup, 26–27
crêpes, 318–20
  dessert, 420–21
crêpes, fillings for:
  cheese, 320
  chicken or turkey, 205–6
  mushroom, 207
  seafood, 207–8
croquettes: chicken, 145–
  46
  ham, 115–16
croutons: garlic, herb, 263
  omelet, 210
crullers, 321
crumb crust, 392
cucumbers: salad, 261
  sandwiches, 5
  soup: cold, 31
    yogurt, 41
Cumberland dressing, 280
currant raspberry jam, 171
currant sauce, 153
curries: cream sauce, 148
  rice, 191–92
  sauce, brown, 153

custard, cheese and broc-
  coli in, 224–25
custard, dessert: baked,
  413–14
  caramel, 414
  chocolate, 414
  coconut, 414
  coffee, 414
  crème brûlée, 415
  English, 445
  floating island, 412–13
custard pie, 406
dates: muffins, 310
  nut bread, 306
deep-dish fruit pies, 398
Delmonico potatoes, 248–
  49
Delmonico's deviled
  chicken, 126
dill pickles, 177
dips and spreads, see ap-
  petizers and hors
  d'oeuvre
doughnuts, crullers, 320–
  21
dressings, salad, see salad
  dressings
duck: à l'orange, 138–39
  roast, 138
dumplings, chicken with,
  133–34
duxelles, mushroom, 165
eggs: Benedict, 213
  chasseur, 212–13
  frittatas, 211–12
  omelets, 209–11

fudge (*cont.*)
marshmallow, 377
million-dollar, 378
nut, 377
sour cream, 377
layer cake, 326
opera, 378–79
peanut butter, 379–80
game hens, Rock Cornish,
141
garlic: bread, 292
croutons, 263
French dressing, 279
German potato salad, 271
giblet: broth, 120
stuffing, 164
ginger: apple chutney, 184
ice cream, 432
watermelon pickle, 186
gingerbread, 333–34
men, 370–71
gingersnaps, 367
goose, roast, 140
goulash, Hungarian, 85–86
grapes: conserve, 172–73
ice, 435
gravy: basic, for chicken
or turkey, 119–20
cream, for fried chick-
en, 123–24
red-eye, 115
green mayonnaise, 282,
284
green peppers:
and red peppers, sau-
téed, 244

relish, 179–80
stuffed, 244
green tomato relish, 181
griddlecakes, 317–18
guacamole, 1
gumbo: chicken, 132
soup, chicken, 29–30
halibut: creole, 53
as substitute, 54–55
ham: baked, 113–14
country, boiled, 114–15
croquettes, 115–16
lentils and, 197
with red-eye gravy, 115
spread, 4–5
see also pork
hard sauce, 423
hearts of palm salad with
avocado, 266
herb(s): bread, 292
butter, 152
croutons, 263
on French bread, 292
in green mayonnaise,
284
omelet, 210
souffle, 215
stuffing, 164
hermits, 373–74
hollandaise sauce, 157
blender, 158
mock, 148
honey: and bran bread,
295–96
oatmeal bread with, 290
and pineapple dressing,

469

noodles: Alfredo's, 197
  in beef bouillon, 19
  chicken and, 143
Norwegian butter cookies,
  371–72
nuts: banana nut bread,
  309
  bread, 305–6
  butterscotch nut brittle,
    385
  chocolate nut fudge, 377
  chocolate walnut wa-
    fers, 364
  cookies, 358, 362–63
  cranberry nut bread,
    308
  date nut bread, 306
  maple pralines, 381
  meringues, 368
  roll, 341–42
  spiced, 385–86
  Swedish almond wafers,
    365
  torte, 339–40
oatmeal: bread, 289
  cookies: Cape Cod, 361
    chocolate chip, 362
  griddlecakes, 318
ocean perch fillets, baked,
  54–55
okra, sautéed, 239. *See
  also* gumbo
omelets: bacon, 210
  cheese, 210
  crouton, 210
  French, 209–10

herb, 210
mushroom, 210
other fillings for, 211
onions: baked, 240
  glazed, 240
  in olive oil and season-
    ings, cold, 7
  quiche, 219
  sauce, 151
  scalloped, 241
  soup, 38–39
  stuffing, 164
  white baby, braised, 241
opera fudge, 378–379
orange: cake, Princeton,
  337–38
  charlotte, 426
  duck à l'orange, 138–39
  filling for cakes, 355
  ice, 435
  marmalade, 174
  rolls, 303
  sauce, 160–61
  slices, watercress, and
    avocado salad, 265
oysters: in bacon, 17
  casino, 72
  Rockefeller, 73
  stew, Mildred's, 45
  stuffing, 164
pancakes: French, 318–20
  potato, 247
paprika, chicken, 129–30
parfait, angel, 428–29
Parker Hosue rolls, 300
parsley butter, 151–52

470

A note on the text
Large print edition designed by
Fred Welden
Composed in 16 pt Times Roman
on a Mergenthaler 202
by Compset Inc., Beverly MA